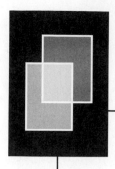

THE WRITER'S SELECTIONS

Shaping Our Lives

Fourth Edition

Kathleen T. McWhorter
Niagara County Community College

HOUGHTON MIFFLIN COMPANY
Boston   New York

Publisher: Patricia Coryell
Senior Sponsoring Editor: Lisa Kimball
Development Editor: Peter Mooney
Associate Project Editor: Rachel Zanders
Senior Project Editor: Kerry Falvey
Editorial Assistant: Sage Anderson
Manufacturing Coordinator: Chuck Dutton
Senior Marketing Manager: Annamarie L. Rice
Marketing Assistant: Andrew Whitacre

COVER IMAGE: © Stavros / Images.com

PHOTO CREDITS: **p. 30:** Brian Fitzgerald / East Valley Tribune / AP-Wide World
Photos; **p. 89:** photo by Chris Curry / © Hedgehog House, N.Z.; map by Parrot Graph-
ics; **p. 194:** Lester Sloan / Getty Images; **p. 209:** © Pace Gregory / Corbis.

TEXT CREDIT: **p. 154:** Excerpts from "The Beautiful Laughing Sisters—An Arrival
Story" in *The Middle of Everywhere,* copyright © 2002 by Mary Pipher, reprinted by
permission of Harcourt, Inc.

Additional acknowledgments for reprinted material appear beginning on page 282.

Printed in the U.S.A.

Library of Congress Control Number: 2004118146

ISBN: 0-618-52872-5

2 3 4 5 6 7 8 9-MP-09 08 07 06 05

Contents

5. Others Who Shape Our Lives   173

6. Media That Shape Our Lives   205

7. Technology That Shapes Our Lives   239

Rhetorical Table of Contents

Illustration

Definition

Comparison and Contrast

Cause and Effect

Process

Argument

Preface

The Writer's Selections: Shaping Our Lives is a thematic reader developed to meet the specific needs of beginning writers. Using readings as springboards for student writing is a well-recognized and established approach to the teaching of writing, but the readings in most anthologies are inappropriate for developing writers in terms of length, difficulty, and subject matter. Furthermore, beginning writers often lack sophisticated reading skills and can find these readings troublesome and frustrating. We have all heard comments such as, "You mean I have to read all this just to write a one-page paper?" or "I got lost just trying to read it, so how could I write about it?" Instructors who use readers often find themselves spending more class time explaining the reading and less time teaching writing skills than they would like. *The Writer's Selections: Shaping Our Lives* addresses these concerns by offering brief, accessible, engaging readings and providing a structured apparatus that focuses and directs students and thus stimulates writing.

Thematic Organization

Reading exposes us to ideas that can, as the book's subtitle suggests, shape or change our lives. The seven chapters in this text explore some major factors that shape our lives: decisions, other people, events, cultures, media, work, and technology. Each is a category relevant to students' daily experience—a category about which they can think and write. As students read about how people's lives have been shaped by these factors, they may become more fully aware of the impact of such factors on their own lives.

The Reading Selections

The 49 reading selections, chosen with the needs, interests, and learning characteristics of beginning writers in mind, offer instructors choices, but do not leave students with the complaint that most of the book was left unassigned. The readings have the following characteristics:

- **Short.** The readings range in length from very brief, three to four paragraphs, to a maximum of two to five pages. Students will regard them as realistic, "do-able" assignments.
- **Readable.** The readings are within the skill range of most beginning writers; they are thought provoking but lack burdensome vocabulary or a complicated writing style. An occasional

longer, more challenging reading is included for instructors to as-
sign to prepare students for readings typically assigned in freshman composition courses.

- **Engaging.** The readings will spark interest and stimulate thought.
Many are personal narratives to which students can relate immediately; others are issue-oriented, about topics such as media
bias, gay marriage, false advertising, the effects of music, media
coverage of the news, and the effects of the September 11, 2001,
terrorist attack. The readings are timely, sometimes humorous,
and within the realm of the students' experience.

- **Representative of a Wide Range of Sources.** There is a wide
sampling of writers, including Asian, Hispanic, Native American, and black writers chosen from a range of periodicals, newspapers, and books. Student writing is well-represented, with one
student essay included in each chapter.

The Apparatus

The Writer's Selections: Shaping Our Lives is a collection of essays, but
it is also an instructional tool. Its apparatus is intended to guide students through the reading, prompt their thinking, and prepare them to
write about the reading.

Reading and Writing Process Introduction

Because beginning writers need instruction in how to read and write
more effectively, the book opens with an overview of the reading and
writing processes. This section guides students through each process,
offering numerous skills and strategies for becoming better writers and
readers. Preceding this introduction are two color inserts that present
the reading and writing processes in a visually appealing format.

Chapter Features

Each chapter opens with an introduction that briefly explores the chapter theme and guides students through preliminary "brainstorming"
that makes the theme real and personal. Each chapter concludes with
a "Making Connections" section containing writing assignments that
link two or more of the readings in the chapter. An "Internet Connections" section guides students in discovering online sources related to
chapter topics. Each of these features encourages students to synthe-
size ideas and to use sources to support their ideas.

Features Accompanying Each Reading

- **Headnote.** A brief introduction precedes the reading; it focuses the students' attention, identifies the source, and establishes a context for the reading.
- **Journal Writing.** A journal writing assignment encourages students to explore their ideas about the topic before reading.
- **Reading Strategy.** This section offers practical advice on how to approach each essay. It suggests a particular reading or review technique that will improve the students' comprehension and recall of each essay.
- **Vocabulary Preview.** A list of challenging words used in the reading together with their meanings is given before the reading. Since students preview the words and their meanings before reading, their comprehension of the essay will be strengthened.
- **Finding Meaning.** These questions guide the students in grasping the literal content of each essay. Answering these questions enables students to assess their understanding. Students either confirm that they understand the key points or realize that they have not read as carefully as necessary, in which case a closer reading is encouraged.
- **Understanding Technique.** This section offers questions designed to guide students in analyzing the writer's methodology. For example, students may be asked to evaluate a writer's thesis statement; assess the effectiveness of a title, introduction, or conclusion; or study how the writer uses topic sentences or transitional words and phrases.
- **Thinking Critically.** These questions engage students by provoking thought, sparking lively discussion, and fostering critical analysis. They may be used as collaborative activities or as brainstorming sessions to generate ideas about the reading.
- **Writing About the Reading.** Paragraph-length assignments offer writers the opportunity to explore a focused topic. Essay-length assignments give students experience in narrowing a topic and developing a short essay. Assignments often provide prompts that offer advice on how to approach the assignment or what to include.
- **A Creative Activity.** This activity is intended to stimulate interest and creativity by offering light, spontaneous writing assignments that, alternatively, may be used as collaborative learning activities.

Changes to the Fourth Edition

- **Fifteen New Readings.** Fifteen new professional readings were added to this edition. New topics include vegetarianism, fast food restaurants, volunteering for the war in Iraq, effects of September 11, 2001, job searching on the Internet, job interviewing strategies, immigrants to the United States, gay marriage, media coverage of the news, online dating, and the effects of cell phones.
- **Revised Writing Process Section.** The introductory section on the Writing Process has been expanded to include sections on Writing a Strong Thesis Statement, Writing an Effective Introduction, Writing a Conclusion, and Choosing a Title. For each, specific guidelines and examples are provided.
- **Revised Internet Connections Section.** Each chapter concludes with an Internet activity that demonstrates the relevance of chapter content, allows the students to explore their own ideas using electronic sources, and culminates in a writing assignment.
- **Journal Writing Activity.** The journal writing activity has been moved to precede the reading, allowing students to explore their own ideas on the topic before reading about it.

Ancillary Materials

Instructor's Resource Manual. This manual provides practical suggestions for teaching writing along with individual discussions of each reading in the book.

Updated! **Expressways 5.0 CD-ROM.** Interactive software guides students as they write and revise paragraphs and essays.

Dictionary Deal. The *American Heritage College Dictionary* may be shrink-wrapped with the text at a substantial savings.

Acknowledgments

I appreciate the excellent ideas, suggestions and advice of my colleagues who served as reviewers:

Greta Buck, *Pima Community College*
Sandy Cohen, *Albany State University*
Mary A. Gervin, *Albany State University*
Andrew M. Knoll, *Bunker Hill Community College*
Jane Lasky-MacPherson, *Middlesex County College*

The entire staff at Houghton Mifflin deserves praise and credit for their assistance. In particular I wish to thank Lisa Kimball for her support of the project and Peter Mooney for his valuable assistance in planning the fourth edition. Finally, I thank my students who have helped me to select appropriate, meaningful readings.

USE PREVIEWING TO GET STARTED

Previewing is a quick way of finding out what a reading will be about *before* you read it. Try previewing the brief reading at the right using the steps listed below.

How to Preview

1. Read the title.

2. Read the introductory note.

3. Check the author's name.

4. Read the introductory paragraph.

5. Read the dark print headings (if any).

6. For readings without headings, read the first sentence of a few paragraphs per page.

7. Glance at any photographs or drawings.

8. Read the last paragraph.

Why Preview?

Previewing has several benefits:

1. It gives you a mental outline of the reading *before* you read it.

2. Reading will be easier because you have a mental outline; your comprehension will improve.

3. You will be able to remember more of what you read.

4. You will find it easier to concentrate.

Friends All of Us
Pablo Neruda

A Nobel Prize–winning poet's backyard lesson in brotherhood

One time, investigating in the backyard of our house in Temuco [Chile] the tiny objects and minuscule beings of my world, I came upon a hole in one of the boards of the fence. I looked through the hole and saw a landscape like that behind our house, uncared for, and wild. I moved back a few steps, because I sensed vaguely that something was about to happen. All of a sudden a hand appeared—a tiny hand of a boy about my own age. By the time I came close again, the hand was gone, and in its place there was a marvelous white sheep.

The sheep's wool was faded. Its wheels had escaped. All of this only made it more authentic. I had never seen such a wonderful sheep. I looked back through the hole but the boy had disappeared. I went into the house and brought out a treasure of my own: a pinecone, opened, full of odor and resin, which I adored. I set it down in the same spot and went off with the sheep.

I never saw either the hand or the boy again. And I have never again seen a sheep like that either. The toy I lost finally in a fire. But even now, in 1954, almost 50 years old, whenever I pass a toy shop, I look furtively into the window, but it's no use. They don't make sheep like that any more.

I have been a lucky man. To feel the intimacy of brothers is a marvelous thing in life. To feel the love of people whom we love is a fire that feeds our life. But to feel the affection that comes from those whom we do not know, from those unknown to us, who are watching over our sleep and solitude, over our dangers and our weaknesses—that is something still greater and more beautiful because it widens out the boundaries of our being, and unites all living things.

That exchange brought home to me for the first time a precious idea: that all of humanity is somehow together. That experience came to me again much later; this time it stood out strikingly against a background of trouble and persecution.

It won't surprise you then that I attempted to give something resiny, earthlike, and fragrant in exchange for human brotherhood. Just as I once left the pinecone by the fence, I have since left my words on the door of so many people who were unknown to me, people in prison, or hunted, or alone.

That is the great lesson I learned in my childhood, in the backyard of a lonely house. Maybe it was nothing but a game two boys played who didn't know each other and wanted to pass to the other some good things of life. Yet maybe this small and mysterious exchange of gifts remained inside me also, deep and indestructible, giving my poetry light.

KNOW WHAT TO LOOK FOR AS YOU READ

If you know what to look for as you read, you'll find reading is easier, goes faster, and requires less rereading. Use the list below to guide you in reading the essays in this book.

What to Look For

1. THE MEANING OF THE TITLE.

In some essays, the title announces the topic of the essay and may reveal the author's viewpoint toward it. In others, the meaning of the title becomes clear only after you have read the essay (as with the sample essay on the right).

2. THE INTRODUCTION.

The opening paragraph of an essay should be interesting, give background information, and announce the subject of the essay.

3. THE AUTHOR'S MAIN POINT.

This is often called the *thesis statement*. It is the one big idea that the entire essay explains. Often it appears in the first paragraph, but in the sample essay at the right, it does not.

4. SUPPORT AND EXPLANATION.

The essay should explain, give reasons, or offer support for the author's main point.

5. THE CONCLUSION.

The last paragraph should bring the essay to a close. Often, it will restate the author's main point. It may also suggest directions for further thought.

Friends All of Us
Pablo Neruda

A Nobel Prize–winning poet's backyard lesson in brotherhood

One time, investigating in the backyard of our house in Temuco [Chile] the tiny objects and minuscule beings of my world, I came upon a hole in one of the boards of the fence. I looked through the hole and saw a landscape like that behind our house, uncared for, and wild. I moved back a few steps, because I sensed vaguely that something was about to happen. All of a sudden a hand appeared—a tiny hand of a boy about my own age. By the time I came close again, the hand was gone, and in its place there was a marvelous white sheep.

The sheep's wool was faded. Its wheels had escaped. All of this only made it more authentic. I had never seen such a wonderful sheep. I looked back through the hole but the boy had disappeared. I went into the house and brought out a treasure of my own: a pinecone, opened, full of odor and resin, which I adored. I set it down in the same spot and went off with the sheep.

I never saw either the hand or the boy again. And I have never again seen a sheep like that either. The toy I lost finally in a fire. But even now, in 1954, almost 50 years old, whenever I pass a toy shop, I look furtively into the window, but it's no use. They don't make sheep like that any more.

I have been a lucky man. To feel the intimacy of brothers is a marvelous thing in life. To feel the love of people whom we love is a fire that feeds our life. But to feel the affection that comes from those whom we do not know, from those unknown to us, who are watching over our sleep and solitude, over our dangers and our weaknesses—that is something still greater and more beautiful because it widens out the boundaries of our being, and unites all living things.

That exchange brought home to me for the first time a precious idea: that all of humanity is somehow together. That experience came to me again much later; this time it stood out strikingly against a background of trouble and persecution.

It won't surprise you then that I attempted to give something resiny, earthlike, and fragrant in exchange for human brotherhood. Just as I once left the pinecone by the fence, I have since left my words on the door of so many people who were unknown to me, people in prison, or hunted, or alone.

That is the great lesson I learned in my childhood, in the backyard of a lonely house. Maybe it was nothing but a game two boys played who didn't know each other and wanted to pass to the other some good things of life. Yet maybe this small and mysterious exchange of gifts remained inside me also, deep and indestructible, giving my poetry light.

What Is Annotation?

Annotating is a way of keeping track of your impressions, ideas, reactions, and questions AS YOU READ. It is also a way of marking key phrases, sentences, or paragraphs to return to. When you are ready to discuss and/or write about the reading, you will find your annotations helpful. Study the sample annotations on this page to see how it is done.

How to Annotate

Here is a partial list of the things you might want to annotate:

1. Questions that come to mind as you read

2. Key events that you may want to refer to again

3. Particularly meaningful expressions or descriptions

4. Important ideas you may want to find again

5. Sections where you need further information

6. Sections where the author reveals his or her feelings or reasons for writing

7. Striking examples

8. Key supporting information— dates, statistics, etc.

9. Your personal reactions (agreement, anger, amazement, shock, surprise, humor)

10. Ideas you disagree with

How did he know?

Why? What has happened in his life?

How can he feel affection for people he doesn't know?

What happened?

Thesis explains why he writes poetry.

<u>Timesaving Tip:</u> Devise a code system. Bracket key ideas, underline key events, circle unusual expressions, etc. Consider using color to distinguish types of annotations.

Friends All of Us
Pablo Neruda

A Nobel Prize–winning poet's backyard lesson in brotherhood

One time, investigating in the backyard of our house in Temuco [Chile] the tiny objects and minuscule beings of my world, I came upon a hole in one of the boards of the fence. I looked through the hole and saw a landscape like that behind our house, uncared for, and wild. I moved back a few steps, because I sensed vaguely that something was about to happen. All of a sudden a hand appeared—a tiny hand of a boy about my own age. By the time I came close again, the hand was gone, and in its place there was a marvelous white sheep.

The sheep's wool was faded. Its wheels had escaped. All of this only made it more authentic. I had never seen such a wonderful sheep. I looked back through the hole but the boy had disappeared. I went into the house and brought out a treasure of my own: a pinecone, opened, full of odor and resin, which I adored. I set it down in the same spot and went off with the sheep.

I never saw either the hand or the boy again. And I have never again seen a sheep like that either. The toy I lost finally in a fire. But even now, in 1954, almost 50 years old, whenever I pass a toy shop, I look furtively into the window, but it's no use. They don't make sheep like that any more.

I have been a lucky man. To feel the intimacy of brothers is a marvelous thing in life. To feel the love of people whom we love is a fire that feeds our life. But to feel the affection that comes from those whom we do not know, from those unknown to us, who are watching over our sleep and solitude, over our dangers and our weaknesses—that is something still greater and more beautiful because it widens out the boundaries of our being, and unites all living things.

That exchange brought home to me for the first time a precious idea: that all of humanity is somehow together. That experience came to me again much later; this time it stood out strikingly against a background of trouble and persecution.

It won't surprise you then that I attempted to give something resiny, earthlike, and fragrant in exchange for human brotherhood. Just as I once left the pinecone by the fence, I have since left my words on the door of so many people who were unknown to me, people in prison, or hunted, or alone.

That is the great lesson I learned in my childhood, in the backyard of a lonely house. Maybe it was nothing but a game two boys played who didn't know each other and wanted to pass to the other some good things of life. Yet maybe this small and mysterious exchange of gifts remained inside me also, deep and indestructible, giving my poetry light.

To get the full meaning out of the essay and to make writing about the reading easier, ask yourself questions during and after reading that will help you think critically and analyze the reading. Here are some useful questions along with sample answers applied to the "Friends All of Us" reading.

Critical Reading Questions and Answers

1. **Q.** What types of evidence or reasons does the author use to explain or support the thesis statement? Was adequate support provided?

   A. Neruda uses an event (the exchange of toys), personal experience, and personal reactions to support his thesis.

2. **Q.** Did the author present a one-sided (biased) view of the topic or were both sides of the issue examined?

   A. Neruda's view was one-sided; he was presenting his personal viewpoint.

3. **Q.** What big issues (big questions about life) does this essay deal with? Do you agree or disagree with the author's viewpoint toward these issues?

   A. The essay deals with human relationships, brotherhood, and the common bond among people.

4. **Q.** Why did the author write the essay?

   A. Neruda wrote to explain how an event helped him understand human relationships and to explain how he sees poetry as a gift to others.

5. **Q.** What key message about "Shaping Our Lives," the theme of this book, does Neruda convey in this essay?

   A. Neruda shows how a simple event —the exchange of toys—can have an impact on one's life.

6. **Q.** What further information, if any, did you need?

   A. More information is needed about the persecution and trouble Neruda experienced.

Friends All of Us
Pablo Neruda

A Nobel Prize–winning poet's backyard lesson in brotherhood

One time, investigating in the backyard of our house in Temuco [Chile] the tiny objects and minuscule beings of my world, I came upon a hole in one of the boards of the fence. I looked through the hole and saw a landscape like that behind our house, uncared for, and wild. I moved back a few steps, because I sensed vaguely that something was about to happen. All of a sudden a hand appeared—a tiny hand of a boy about my own age. By the time I came close again, the hand was gone, and in its place there was a marvelous white sheep.

The sheep's wool was faded. Its wheels had escaped. All of this only made it more authentic. I had never seen such a wonderful sheep. I looked back through the hole but the boy had disappeared. I went into the house and brought out a treasure of my own: a pinecone, opened, full of odor and resin, which I adored. I set it down in the same spot and went off with the sheep.

I never saw either the hand or the boy again. And I have never again seen a sheep like that either. The toy I lost finally in a fire. But even now, in 1954, almost 50 years old, whenever I pass a toy shop, I look furtively into the window, but it's no use. They don't make sheep like that any more.

I have been a lucky man. To feel the intimacy of brothers is a marvelous thing in life. To feel the love of people whom we love is a fire that feeds our life. But to feel the affection that comes from those whom we do not know, from those unknown to us, who are watching over our sleep and solitude, over our dangers and our weaknesses—that is something still greater and more beautiful because it widens out the boundaries of our being, and unites all living things.

That exchange brought home to me for the first time a precious idea: that all of humanity is somehow together. That experience came to me again much later; this time it stood out strikingly against a background of trouble and persecution.

It won't surprise you then that I attempted to give something resiny, earthlike, and fragrant in exchange for human brotherhood. Just as I once left the pinecone by the fence, I have since left my words on the door of so many people who were unknown to me, people in prison, or hunted, or alone.

That is the great lesson I learned in my childhood, in the backyard of a lonely house. Maybe it was nothing but a game two boys played who didn't know each other and wanted to pass to the other some good things of life. Yet maybe this small and mysterious exchange of gifts remained inside me also, deep and indestructible, giving my poetry light.

**WRITING SUCCESS
Strategy
#1**

WORKING THROUGH PROBLEMS IN YOUR WRITING

I HAVE A WRITING ASSIGNMENT.

SELECT A TOPIC.

I have a topic.

- My topic is too broad.
- My topic is too specific.
- My topic is manageable for my assignment.

I need to find a topic.

1. Write about something familiar.
2. Choose a topic that interests you.
3. Think of activities you have done over the past week.
4. Think of upcoming events, holidays, and so on.
5. Think of current news, issues, films, or television programs.
6. Use newspapers or radio talk shows as sources of ideas.

COLLECTING IDEAS ABOUT THE TOPIC

I have ideas.

It worked.

I need ideas.

1. Try brainstorming.
2. Ask questions (Who? What? When? Why? How?).

It didn't work.

1. Try a different technique, such as freewriting, branching, or questioning.
2. Talk into a tape recorder.
3. Talk with a classmate.
4. Refocus your topic.
5. Choose a different topic.

ORGANIZING THE IDEAS

I know how to organize my ideas.

I don't know how to organize my ideas.

1. Develop a possible thesis statement.
2. Draw a diagram (or outline) of how other ideas connect to the thesis.
3. Put ideas on separate index cards so you can rearrange them in different ways.
4. Look for some logical way to connect your ideas (see p. 12).

KEY
- Steps
- Choices
- Instructions

Strategy 5

**WRITING SUCCESS
Strategy
1
(continued)**

WRITING A FIRST DRAFT

I wrote a draft and I like it.

I'm having trouble getting started.

1. Don't try to write the paper in order, from beginning to end; write any part to get started.
2. Just write ideas in sentence form; worry about organizing them later.
3. Write fast and keep writing; don't worry about anything except continuing to write.
4. Dictate into a tape recorder.

I don't like my draft.

1. Let it sit a day; come back when your mind is fresh.
2. Analyze each part; determine which parts are weak.
3. If the draft doesn't seem to say much, collect more ideas about your topic.
4. Refocus your topic; it may be either too broad or too narrow.

REVISING THE DRAFT

I know what to revise.

I don't know what to revise.

1. Let it sit a day; return with a fresh mind.
2. Use a revision checklist (see p. 288).

PROOFREADING

I know how to find my errors.

I'm not sure I will find all my errors.

Spelling Errors

Punctuation Errors

Grammar Errors

1. Use the spelling checker, if you are using a computer.
2. Read your paper backward, from the last sentence to the first.

Read your paper several times, each time checking for a different type of error.

Read your paper aloud, listening for pauses; punctuation is usually needed at the pauses.

KEY
Steps
Choices
Instructions

Strategy 6

FOLLOW AN ORGANIZING PLAN FOR YOUR ESSAY

To make your essay easy to read and understand, you should follow an organizing plan. An essay has specific parts, and each part serves specific purposes for both the reader and the writer.

ESSAY

Note: There is no set number of paragraphs that an essay should contain. This discussion shows six paragraphs, but in actual essays, the number will vary greatly.

PARTS TO INCLUDE

WHAT EACH PART SHOULD DO

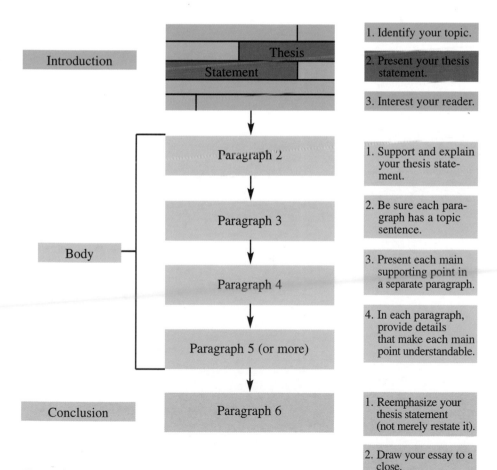

Introduction

Thesis Statement

1. Identify your topic.
2. Present your thesis statement.
3. Interest your reader.

Paragraph 2

1. Support and explain your thesis statement.

Paragraph 3

2. Be sure each paragraph has a topic sentence.

Body

Paragraph 4

3. Present each main supporting point in a separate paragraph.

Paragraph 5 (or more)

4. In each paragraph, provide details that make each main point understandable.

Conclusion

Paragraph 6

1. Reemphasize your thesis statement (not merely restate it).
2. Draw your essay to a close.

Note: Throughout the essay, transitional words, phrases, and sentences work to lead the reader from idea to idea.

SPEND TIME ORGANIZING EACH PARAGRAPH

Before you write each paragraph of your essay, plan what you will say and the order in which you will say it.

PARAGRAPH

PARTS

WHAT EACH PART SHOULD DO

First sentence*	Topic sentence

1. Identify what the paragraph is about.

2. Make a point about the topic.

Supporting detail

Development:
a series of related sentences (sentences 2, 3, 4, 5, or more)

Supporting detail

1. Explain the topic sentence.

2. Make the topic sentence under-standable, using:

- Examples
- Facts
- Statistics
- Personal experience

Supporting detail

Supporting detail

Final sentence*	Concluding or transitional sentence

1. Draw the paragraph to a close.

2. Lead into the next paragraph.

Note: The topic sentence is often placed first, but it may appear elsewhere in the paragraph. For emphasis, writers sometimes even place it last in the paragraph.

Essential Reading and Writing Skills

Many people, events, and ideas influence our lives. This collection of readings explores seven major factors that influence our lives: decisions, events, work, cultures, others, media, and technology. You will read about how other people's lives have been shaped by these factors. By learning how these factors affect others, you will begin to realize more fully how they shape the course of your own life.

As you read these selections about factors that shape our lives, you will be shaping your own reading and writing skills. You will read a variety of articles and essays, some by professional writers and others by student writers from different colleges across the country. You will discover new ideas and new ways of looking at things. As you read, you will encounter a wide range of writing styles, ways of approaching a topic, and methods of organizing ideas. These will give you ideas for your own writing and will also make you a versatile reader who can adapt to a wide range of reading materials.

Following each reading, you will work with different writing tasks that include journal writing as well as paragraph, essay, and creative activity assignments. These assignments will give you an opportunity to explore your ideas about the topic of the reading and to explore how your life is shaped by decisions, events, work, cultures, others, media, and technology. As you complete these writing tasks, you will have the opportunity to plan, organize, write, and revise your ideas. The following section explains and gives examples of each of these steps. This text also contains two useful reference sections, ***Reading Success Strategies 1–4*** and ***Writing Success Strategies 1–3,*** preceding this page. These sections lead you, step-by-step, through reading a selection and writing about it. These sections are perforated so you can remove them easily from the book and refer to them frequently as you work through readings and complete writing assignments. For example, until you are familiar with the steps in previewing, keep ***Reading Success Strategy #1*** handy for quick reference. Refer to *Reading Success Strategies #2–4* as you read, annotate, and evaluate assigned readings. Before you begin a writing assignment, use the flowchart in *Writing Success Strategy #1* to guide you through the process. Refer to *Writing Success Strategy #2* to help you organize your essay and *Writing Success Strategy #3* to help you write effective paragraphs.

THE READING PROCESS

Reading is a means of understanding and responding to an author's message. In this book you will read a wide variety of essays, each written by a different author. As you read each essay, first focus on what the author says and then, once you've understood the message, think about and react to the ideas the essay presents. This introduction will help you to read essays by offering some practical advice on how to get involved, understand the author's message, read and think critically, remember what you have read, and get ready to write.

Getting Involved with the Reading

If you are interested in and involved with an essay, it will be easier to read, as well as easier to react to and write about. Use the following suggestions to get involved with each essay you are assigned.

Choose the right time and place to read.   Be sure to read at a time when you can concentrate—when you are not tired, weary from working on other assignments, hungry, or feeling stressed. Choose a place that is quiet and free of distractions—one in which nothing will compete for your attention.

Preview the essay.   Begin by studying *Reading Success Strategy #1, "Use Previewing to Get Started,"* to become familiar with what the essay is about before you read it. Refer to this color insert frequently until you are familiar with the previewing process. Previewing will enable you to read the essay more easily because you will know what to expect and how the essay is organized.

Connect the topic of the essay with your own experience.   Try to discover what you already know about the topic of the essay. At first, you may think you know little or nothing about it, but for most of the essays in this book, you do have some knowledge of or experience with the topic. For example, suppose an essay is about managing stress. At first, you may not think you know much about it, but all of us have experienced stress and have learned how to deal with it. What do you do when you are under pressure? How do you react? What do you do to

cope with or escape the pressure? These questions are probably bringing ideas to mind. Here are two ways to jump-start your memory on a
given topic:

- Ask as many questions as you can about the topic. Suppose your
  topic is radio talk show hosts. You could ask questions such as
  Why are they popular? What kinds of personalities do they have?
  Who is the most popular? Why do they sometimes insult people?
  Why do people agree to talk with them? Who chooses the topics
  they discuss? Questions such as these will get you interested in the
  reading and help you maintain interest as you read.
- Brainstorm a list of everything you know about the topic. Suppose the topic is the treatment of AIDS. Make a list of the things
  you know. You might list people you know who were treated, information you have read about experimental drugs, and so forth.

**Read the discussion questions or writing assignments before
reading the essay.**   If you know what you will be expected to discuss
and write about after reading, you will find it easier to keep your mind
on the reading.

Getting the Author's Message

Before you can discuss or write about a reading, you have to be sure
you have understood what the author was saying. At times, this is easy.
But sometimes, depending on the author, the style of writing, and the
topic, it is not so easy. Here are some suggestions to use to be sure you
are getting the author's message. (See ***Reading Success Strategy #2.***)

Understand Essay and Paragraph Organization

Begin by studying the chart in ***Writing Success Strategy #2.*** Once you
are familiar with the way essays and paragraphs within essays are organized, you will find them easier to understand. This chart describes
how you should organize essays and paragraphs as you write; however,
it also explains how other writers organize essays and paragraphs as
they write. You are probably beginning to see that as you improve your
skills in writing essays and paragraphs, you will also find that your skill
in reading them increases. As you read, be sure to identify:

- The **thesis statement**
- The **topic sentence** of each paragraph and how it supports the
  thesis statement
- The key supporting **details** that the author provides

Many students find it helpful to underline or highlight these parts as
they find them.

Reading Success Strategy #2, "Know What to Look for As You Read," identifies and illustrates the key parts of the essay. Refer to this color insert often as you read. It will focus your attention on what is important to know and remember.

Use Questions to Guide Your Reading

Be sure you can answer the following questions about each essay you read. These questions together produce a condensed summary of the content of the essay.

- Who (or what) is the essay about?
- What happened? (What action took place?)

- When did the action occur?
- Where did the action occur?
- Why did the action occur?
- How did the action occur?

These questions focus your attention on the literal, or factual, meaning of the essay. You will also want to ask critical questions that help you respond to, react to, and evaluate the essay. Refer to *Reading Success Strategy #4* for a list of useful questions.

Read with a Pen or Highlighter in Hand

Begin by reading through *Reading Success Strategy #3.* To write about a reading, you will need to refer to it frequently; however, you should not have to reread the entire essay each time you want to locate a key point. (Rereading an essay *is* useful at times, and sometimes it is necessary if you are to understand the essay fully, but you should not have to reread to find particular information.) To avoid unnecessary rereading, underline or highlight important parts of the essay, parts you would like to reread, key statements, parts about which you have questions, and parts you think you may want to refer to as you write.

In addition to marking or highlighting key parts, you should also make marginal notes. These are called annotations. Think of annotations as a way of recording your thoughts as you read and as a means of "talking back" to the author. *Reading Success Strategy #3, "Annotate: Read with a Pen in Hand,"* describes and illustrates how to annotate. Refer to this color insert often to remind yourself of the kinds of annotations that are useful to make.

Deal with Difficult Vocabulary

Before each reading, a list of vocabulary words is given, along with a brief definition of each word as it is used in the reading. Be sure to look through this list *before* you read, checking the meaning of each word that is unfamiliar. Highlight or place an asterisk (*) next to each unfamiliar word. While reading, you may need to refer back to the list, since no one expects you to remember a definition after reading it only once.

In addition to the words listed, you may find other unfamiliar words in the essay. If you come across an unfamiliar word while reading, finish reading the sentence it is in. Often, you will be able to figure out enough about the word from the way it is used in the sentence to continue reading without losing meaning. Since you will have a pen in your hand, mark or circle the word so that you can check its exact meaning later. If you cannot figure out what the word means from the way it is used, then you will need to work on it further. First try pronouncing it aloud; often hearing the word will help you find out its meaning. If you still do not know it, take the time to look it up in a dictionary. (Keep one nearby for convenient reference.) Once you find the meaning, circle the word and write its definition or a synonym in the margin—you may want to refer to it again as you discuss or write about the reading.

Reading and Thinking Critically

Begin by studying **Reading Success Strategy #4.** To write about an essay, you must understand the author's message, but you must also react to and evaluate that message. You must be able to do more than summarize what the author said. You must analyze, interpret, judge, and respond to the ideas presented. **Reading Success Strategy #4** lists six useful questions and illustrates how to find clues to their answers in the reading. Refer to this color insert often to get in the habit of reading and thinking critically.

Annotating, as described above, will also help you read and think critically. By "talking back" to the author, you will find yourself adopting a challenging, questioning attitude that promotes critical thinking.

Remembering What You Read

Reading an essay once does not guarantee that you will remember it; in fact, the odds are that you will not remember it in detail unless you take certain steps after you read it. Use the following techniques to increase your recall of material that you have read.

Underline or highlight and annotate as you read.   As noted above, underlining and highlighting are useful ways to locate information without rereading; annotating is an effective way to record your ideas and reactions to the reading. Each of these techniques, however, also will help you remember what you read. To underline or highlight or annotate, you have to *think* about what you are reading. The thinking process aids recall.

Review the reading as soon as you finish.   While it is tempting to close the book and reward yourself for finishing an assignment, doing so is a mistake. Instead, spend three or four minutes reviewing what you have just read. These few minutes will pay high dividends in the amount you will be able to remember later. Review the reading by following the same steps you used to preview the reading (see p. 2). This postreading will fix ideas in your mind, clarify others, and show you how ideas are connected.

Write a summary.   Many students find it helpful to write a summary of an essay right after they finish reading it. Writing the summary is another way to review key points and prevent memory loss. Additionally, your summary will be useful later as a means of refreshing your memory without rereading and as a handy reference during class discussions.

Getting Ready to Write

You can take many steps to make writing about an essay easier. Several of these you have learned already. Underlining, highlighting, annotating, and summarizing prepare you to write about what you have read. Each identifies important ideas that may be used as starting points for writing. Here are a few additional tips.

Write an outline or draw a diagram.   As you write, the organization will become clearer and you will be reviewing the content.

Keep a notebook or journal.   Use it to record your ideas, reactions, feelings, and responses to the reading.

Discuss the reading with classmates.   You may discover new ideas or find that your own ideas become clearer once you express them in conversation.

THE WRITING PROCESS

Writing is a means of expressing your ideas. *Writing Success Strategy #1* describes this process in detail. Study it before continuing with this section. Throughout this book you will be asked to write essays in which you discuss your ideas about a reading or ideas suggested by it. This introduction will help you get started by showing you the steps that most writers follow to produce a well-written essay. The five steps are

1. Generating ideas
2. Organizing ideas
3. Writing a first draft
4. Revising and rewriting
5. Proofreading

If you use each of these steps, writing will become easier for you. You will avoid the frustration of staring at a blank sheet of paper. Instead, you will feel the satisfaction of putting your ideas into words and making headway toward producing a good essay.

As you work through this introduction and complete the questions that follow each reading, note unfamiliar terms about the writing process and check the Glossary on pages 280 to 281.

Generating Ideas

The first step before writing is to generate ideas about your topic. You can use four techniques to do this:

1. Freewriting
2. Brainstorming
3. Branching
4. Questioning

These four techniques can help you overcome the common problem of feeling that you have nothing to say. They can unlock ideas you already have and help you discover new ones. Each of these techniques provides a different way to generate ideas. Feel free to choose from among them, using whichever technique seems most effective for the task at hand.

Freewriting

Freewriting involves writing nonstop for a limited period of time, usually three to five minutes. Write whatever comes into your mind, whether it is about the topic or not. If nothing comes to mind, you can just write, "I'm not thinking of anything." As you write, don't be concerned with grammar, punctuation, or spelling, or with writing in complete sentences. Words and phrases are fine. Focus on recording your thoughts as they come to you. The most important thing is to keep writing without stopping. Write fast; don't think about whether your writing is worthwhile or makes sense. After you finish, reread what you have written. Underline everything that you might be able to use in your paper. On the following page is a sample of freewriting on the topic of playing the lottery.

> Playing the lottery is a get rich quick dream. Many people play it, but hardly anyone wins. Most people think they have a chance to win. They do have a chance, but it is a very small chance. So why do people continue to play? Some people are lucky and they win small amounts often and this keeps them going. My grandfather is like that. He wins a couple of dollars every month—sometimes more. But he has never won anything big. I wonder how much money a state makes from each lottery draw. I think lotteries take advantage of poor people. They really don't have the money to waste on a lottery, but the advertising draws them in. In New York state the slogan "All it takes is a dollar and a dream" is very misleading. Some people are addicted to playing, I don't think they could stop playing if they wanted to. At least the money earned from state-run lotteries should directly help those who play.

Freewriting is a creative way to begin translating ideas and feelings into words, without being concerned about their value or worrying about correctness. You'll be pleasantly surprised by the number of usable ideas this technique uncovers. Of course, some of your ideas will be too broad; others might be too personal; still others may stray from the topic. In the freewriting above, there are several usable sets of ideas: addiction to lotteries, reasons people play, misleading advertising, and use of revenues from lotteries.

Brainstorming

Brainstorming is a way of developing ideas by making a list of everything you can think of about the topic. You might list feelings, ideas, facts, examples, or problems. There is no need to write in sentences; instead, list words and phrases. Don't try to organize your ideas, just list them as you think of them. Give yourself a time limit. You'll find that ideas come faster that way. You can brainstorm alone or with friends. You'll discover many more ideas with your friends because their ideas will help trigger more of your own. When you've finished, reread your list and mark usable ideas. Here is an example of ideas generated during a brainstorming session on the topic of stress.

Sample Brainstorming

pressure
things not under control
feel like you're losing it
little things bother you
how to get rid of or control
daily hassles add up
need to relax
need to learn to manage my time
feeling put upon

headaches, neck aches
feel tired and rushed
can ruin your day
avoid problems
everybody experiences it
stressed-out people are crabby
big problems make it worse
avoid stressful situations
keep a balanced outlook

Stress is too broad a topic for a short essay, but there are several groups of usable ideas here: symptoms of stress, causes of stress, and ways to control stress. Any of these topics would make a good paper.

Branching

Branching is a visual way of generating ideas. To begin, write your topic in the middle of a full sheet of paper. Draw a circle around it. Next, think of related ideas and write them near your center circle. Connect each to the central circle with a line. Call these ideas the primary branches. Your topic is like a tree trunk, and your ideas are like primary limbs that branch out from it. Below is an example of a branching diagram that one student drew on the topic of the value of sports.

BRANCHING DIAGRAM I

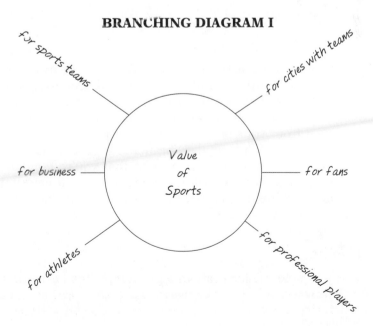

You can connect other related ideas to the main branches with smaller, or secondary, branches. In the next example, the student looked at his first branching diagram and decided to focus on one of the narrower topics (the value of sports for athletes) he had put on a primary branch.

BRANCHING DIAGRAM II

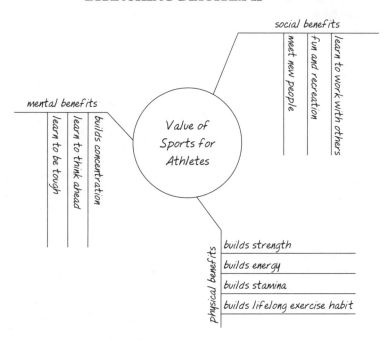

The student used "value of sports for athletes" as the trunk; then he created primary branches: mental benefits, social benefits, and physical benefits. Then he drew secondary branches onto each of the primary ones, and he could have kept going. If you use this technique, you can branch from your branches until you run off the paper. But there's no need to develop secondary branches for every main branch. Choosing one branch that interests you or that you're familiar with and ignoring all the other possibilities is fine. When you have finished branching, use a different color pen to mark those branches that seem usable for your paper.

Questioning

Another way to generate ideas about a given topic is to ask questions. The questions *what? why? where? when? how?* and *who?* are an effective way to explore any topic. As with freewriting and brainstorming, write any question that comes to mind. Don't worry if it seems silly, and don't stop to evaluate whether it is really related to the topic. If you can think of answers, include them as well, but don't limit yourself to questions for which you know the answers. When you have finished, reread what you have written and underline questions or answers that you might be able to use in writing your paper. Here are the questions one student wrote on the topic of television talk shows.

Sample Questions

Why do people watch them?

Does it make them feel better to see others with problems?

Do viewers get hooked on talk shows?

Why aren't they doing more important things, like working?

Do the shows help them forget their own problems?

How are participants chosen?

Are they paid?

Why do they participate?

What do the participants' families think of them?

Why are these shows so popular?

How do they affect those who watch?

When to Use Which Technique

Now that you have tried freewriting, brainstorming, branching, and questioning, you are probably wondering when to use each technique. In general, there are no rules to follow. The best advice is to use the technique that you find most comfortable. Try to use each more than twice before deciding which you prefer. You may find that for certain topics, one technique works better than the others. For example, suppose you decided to write an essay about your mother's sense of humor. While it might be difficult to think of questions, freewriting might help you remember important, humorous events in your life together. In a different situation, however, questioning might be the most effective technique. Suppose you are studying religious institutions in your sociology class, and your instructor has assigned a paper that requires you to explain your personal religious beliefs. Asking questions about your beliefs is likely to produce useful ideas that you can include in your paper.

Sorting Usable Ideas

Freewriting, brainstorming, branching, and questioning each produce a wide range of usable ideas, but you shouldn't feel as if you need to write about all of them. You can sort through them to decide which ones you can put together to produce your paper. Sometimes you may find that you would like to narrow your topic and develop just one idea in your paper, as did the student who made the branching diagram on the value of sports.

Organizing Ideas

Once you have used freewriting, brainstorming, branching, or questioning to generate ideas about your topic, the next step is to decide how to organize these ideas. Ideas in an essay should progress logically from one to another. Group or arrange your ideas in a way that makes them clear and understandable. Your essay should follow a logical plan. Turn to **Writing Success Strategy #2, "Follow an Organizing Plan for Your Essay,"** and study it carefully. It shows how to organize your essay and what parts to include.

Suppose you used brainstorming to generate ideas on the topic of television talk shows, as was done on the previous page. Then you decided to focus on the narrower topic of reasons why people watch talk shows. From a second brainstorming, you identified the following ideas for possible use in your essay:

shows can be informative
forget your own problems
can't stop watching
offer a place to belong, feel part of something
shows fill empty time
people like to hear about other people

learn how other people solved their problems
get "hooked"
like to watch people be exploited by host
like to watch audience reactions

In rereading your list, suppose you decide to organize your ideas by arranging them from most to least obvious or well known. The next step is to rewrite your list, listing your ideas in the order in which you will discuss them in your paper. Then reread your new list and cross off ideas that you don't like, or ideas that are too similar to another idea. For example, "get 'hooked'" is similar to "can't stop watching," so cross it out. Here is a revised list of ideas, arranged from most to least obvious.

1. *people like to hear about other people*
2. *like to watch audience reactions*
3. *learn how other people solved their problems*
4. *shows can be informative*
5. *forget your own problems*
6. *like to watch people be exploited by host*
7. *offer a place to belong, feel part of something*
8. *can't stop watching*

Your ideas will not always sort out as neatly as these, but trying to organize your ideas will help you develop a well-structured essay. Sometimes new ideas will grow out of your efforts to rework and rearrange other ideas.

Writing a Strong Thesis Statement

After you have thought carefully about the ideas in your list, try to write one sentence that expresses your overall main point. This is your thesis statement. A thesis statement tells your reader what your essay is about and provides clues to how the essay will unfold. It generally does three things:

- It identifies the topic.
- It expresses a main point about that topic that your essay will explain or support.
- It may also suggest your approach, organization, or direction of development.

Thesis statements usually change as writers generate and organize ideas, draft, and revise. An effective thesis statement should follow these guidelines:

1. **It should state the main point of your essay.** It should give an overview of your approach to your topic.

Does not state a main point:	A well-written business letter has no errors in spelling.
Revised:	To write a grammatically correct business letter, you should follow three simple rules.

2. **It should assert an idea about your topic.** Your thesis should express a viewpoint or state your approach to the topic.

Lacks an assertion:	Advertising contains images of both men and women.

Revised:	Advertising contains images of both men and women, but men are usually presented more favorably than women.

3. **It should be as specific as possible.** For this reason, is important to review and rework your thesis after you have written and revised drafts.

Too general:	Advertisers can influence readers' attitudes toward competing products.
Revised:	Athletic shoe advertisers focus more on attitude and image than on the actual physical differences between their products and those of their competitors.

4. **It may suggest the organization of your essay.** Mentioning key points that will be discussed in the essay is one way to do this. The order in which you mention them should be the order in which you discuss them in your essay.

Does not suggest organization:	Public school budgets will negatively affect education.
Revised:	Public school budgets will negatively affect academic achievement, student motivation, and dropout rate.

5. **It should not be a direct announcement.** Do not begin with phrases such as "In this essay I will" or "My assignment was to discuss."

Direct announcement:	The purpose of this essay is to show that businesses lose money because of inefficiency, competition, and inflated labor costs.
Revised:	Businesses lose money because of inefficiency, competition, and inflated labor costs.

6. **It should offer a fresh, interesting, and original perspective on the topic.** A thesis can follow the guidelines above, but if it seems dull or too predictable, it still needs more work.

Predictable:	Circus acts fall into three categories: animal, clown, and acrobatic.

Revised: Each of the three categories of circus acts—
                            animal, clown, and acrobatic—is exciting
                            because of the risk it involves.

Writing a First Draft

Having formulated a working thesis statement, you now can begin writing. Drafting is a way of trying out ideas to see if and how they work. When drafting, before you settle on what your final essay will say, you can experiment with expressing your ideas one way, then expressing them differently. In your first draft, you might use examples to explain your idea; if that does not work, you might switch to using reasons.

A first draft expresses your ideas in sentence and paragraph form. Review the parts of an essay and a paragraph by studying *Writing Success Strategies #2* and *#3*. Work from your organized list of ideas, focusing on expressing and developing each one more fully. Don't be concerned with grammar, spelling, or punctuation at this stage; instead, concentrate on what you are saying. Use the following suggestions for writing a first draft:

1. **Express the ideas from your list in sentence form in the order in which you organized them.** If you are not sure whether you should include an idea from your list, include it. You can always delete it later. Add new ideas as you think of them.
2. **Do not get bogged down in finding the best wording for an idea.** Just write the idea as you think of it. You will have time to fix it later as you revise.
3. **Think of a first draft as a chance to experiment with different ideas and methods of organization.** While you are working, if you think of a better way to organize or express your ideas, make changes or start over.
4. **As your draft develops, feel free to change your focus or even your topic.** If you decide to change your draft, use freewriting, brainstorming, branching, or questioning to develop new ideas.
5. **Be prepared to change things around later.** What you write as your last sentence might turn out to be a good beginning.
6. **If your draft is not working, don't hesitate to throw it out and start over.** Most writers have many false starts before they produce a draft with which they are satisfied.
7. **If you think you need more ideas, go back to the generating ideas step.** It is always all right to go back and forth among the steps in the writing process.

8. **When you finish your first draft, you should feel as if you have the beginnings of an essay you will be happy with.**

Here is a sample early draft of an essay on why people watch talk shows.

First Draft

It seems like every time I turn on my television, some kind of talk show is on. A few years ago, they were on mornings or late evenings, but now talk shows are on at all hours of the day. Why do people watch them? They watch them for a number of reasons, some good, some not so good.

The most obvious reason is that people find talk shows relaxing and entertaining. They also like to hear about other people. They like to get involved with other people, their problems, the details of their lives. And certainly talk show participants do tell you everything about their lives. Part of this involvement with other people comes from watching the audience and listening to their reactions and questions. Watching a talk show gives people ideas of how to solve their own problems and to get a sense of where a particular situation is headed if it is not corrected.

Talk shows can be informative. Viewers learn sources of help with personal problems. They may learn something about what to do or not to do to improve a personal relationship.

Talk shows help the viewer forget his or her own problems. By getting involved with someone else's problems, viewers tend to forget their own. Also, the problems on the show are so terrible that the viewer's own problems seem small by comparison.

Talk shows appeal to the instinct that many of us have for enjoying watching other people. We like to watch the participants, but we also like to watch the host exploiting, embarrassing, or taking advantage of the participants.

People like to feel as if they are part of something. Some friends of mine are on a first-name basis with several talk show hosts and talk as if they are personal friends with them.

Finally, some people watch talk shows because they can't help themselves—they're addicted. Before I started back to school I was a talk show addict. I would watch talk shows all morning and a good part of the afternoon. Then I would wonder what happened to my day and why I didn't get anything done. Although talk shows do have benefits, and there are plenty of good reasons people watch them, I feel they are dangerous!

Revising and Rewriting

Revision is a process that involves evaluating a draft and changing it to make it more effective. When you finish a first draft, you are more or less satisfied with it. Then, when you reread it later, you see you have more work to do.

Before you submit a paper, you may need to write two, three, or even four drafts. Revising often involves much more than changing a word or rearranging a few sentences. (See the Revision Checklist on page 288.) Revising requires that you *rethink* your ideas. It might mean changing, deleting, or rearranging some of them and adding to them. Revision is not concerned with correcting spelling and punctuation errors, or with making sentences grammatical. Make these changes later when you are satisfied with your ideas. Here is a later draft of the first draft shown on the preceding page.

Later Draft

It seems as if every time one turns on the television, some kind of talk show is on. A few years ago, they were on mornings or late evenings, but now talk shows are on at all hours of the day. Why do people watch them? They watch them to relax, to watch others, and to feel part of something.

The most obvious reason that people watch talk shows is that they find talk shows relaxing and entertaining. The shows provide a welcome relief from daily hassles. By getting involved with someone else's problems, viewers tend to forget their own. Also, the problems on the show are so terrible that the viewer's own problems seem small by comparison. Who could worry about being able to make a car payment when a man on the show has just discovered that his wife is also married to his brother?

Talk shows are also popular because they appeal to our instinct to enjoy watching other people. This instinct is sometimes called voyeurism. People like to watch and hear about other people. They like to hear about their problems and the details of the lives of others. Certainly talk show participants do tell you everything about their lives. Viewers like to watch the participants, but they also enjoy watching the host exploiting, embarrassing, or taking advantage of them. Viewers enjoy watching the audience react and question the participants.

Finally, people watch talk shows because they like to feel as if they are part of something. Some friends of mine are on a first-name basis with several talk show hosts and talk as if they were personal friends with them. They become personally involved with the participants and act as if they are part of the audience.

There is one last reason why people watch talk shows—because they can't help themselves. They are addicted. Before I started back to school, I was a talk show addict. I would watch talk shows all morning and a good part of the afternoon. Then I would wonder what happened to my day and why I didn't get anything done. Although talk shows do have benefits, and there are plenty of good reasons people watch them, they are dangerous!

In making the above revision, the writer decided that the first draft seemed like a list with many very short paragraphs, and so he decided to group the ideas into three main categories: the need to relax, the need to watch, and the need to feel part of something. Then he reorganized the essay and reworked several paragraphs. The author also removed the idea that talk shows provide information, since it did not seem to fit into any of his new categories.

Use the following suggestions for revising and rewriting:

1. **Try to let your first draft sit a while before you begin revising it.** If possible, wait until the next day, but even a few hours away from the draft will be helpful.
2. **Reread the sentence that expresses your main point.** It must be clear, direct, and complete. Experiment with ways to improve it.
3. **Reread each of your other sentences.** Does each relate directly to your main point? If not, cross it out or rewrite it to clarify its connection to the main point. If all of your sentences relate to a main point that is different from the one you've written, rewrite the sentence that expresses the main point.
4. **Read your draft again to see whether your sentences connect to one another.** If necessary, add words or sentences to connect your ideas.
5. **Delete or combine sentences that say the same thing.**
6. **Replace words that are vague or unclear.** Add more descriptive words.
7. **Get help if you get stuck at any of these stages and cannot see what changes are needed.** Ask a friend to read your essay and mark the ideas that are unclear or need more explanation.
8. **After you have made one set of revisions, wait a few hours and then repeat all of these steps.**
9. **When you have finished revising, you should feel quite satisfied both with what you have said and with the way you have said it.**

Writing an Effective Introduction

The final steps in revision are to refine your introduction and conclusion and to start thinking about a title. A strong introduction leads your reader into the essay. It has three main purposes:

- It presents your thesis statement.
- It interests your reader in the subject of your essay.
- It provides any necessary background information.

Although your introductory paragraph appears first in your essay, it does *not* need to be written first. In fact, it is sometimes best to write it last, after you have developed your ideas, written your thesis statement, and drafted your essay.

Here are some suggestions for writing an effective, interesting introduction:

Technique	*Example*
Ask a provocative question or raise a controversial issue.	What would you do if you were sound asleep and woke to find a burglar in your bedroom?
State a startling fact or statistic	Did you know that the federal government recently spent $____ for a toilet seat?
Begin with a story or anecdote.	Mark Evans, a photojournalist, has spent several evenings riding in a police cruiser to document neighborhood crime.
Use a quotation.	Oscar Wilde once said, "Always forgive your enemies—nothing annoys them so much."
State a little-known fact or misconception.	It's hard to lose weight and even harder to keep it off. Right? Wrong! A sensible low carbohydrate diet will help you.

Your introduction should also provide the reader with the background needed to understand the essay. For example, you may need to define the term *genetic engineering* for an essay on that topic. Or for an essay on extending the public school year, you might need to provide information about its current length in different states.

Writing the Conclusion

The final paragraph of an essay has two functions:

- It reemphasizes the thesis statement (but does not just repeat it).
- It draws the essay to a close.

Many writers revise their essays at least *once* before working on their conclusion. During your first and second revision, you often make numerous changes in both content and organization that may affect your conclusion. Here are a few effective ways to write a conclusion. Not all will work for every essay; choose one that fits your essay.

1. **Suggest a new direction of thought.** Raise a related issue that you did not address in the essay, or ask a related question.
2. **Look ahead.** Project into the future. Consider outcomes or effects.
3. **Call for action.** If your essay is written to prove a point or convince your reader of the need for action, it may be effective to conclude with a call for action.
4. **Summarize key points.** Especially for lengthy essays, briefly review your key supporting ideas. In shorter essays, this is usually unnecessary.

If you have trouble writing your conclusion, it's probably a signal that you need to work further on your thesis or organization.

Choosing a Title

Although the title appears first in your essay, it is often the last thing you should write. The title identifies the topic in an interesting way, and it may also suggest your focus. To select a title, read your final draft, paying particular attention to your thesis statement and your organization. Here are a few examples of catchy titles:

> "Surprise in the Vegetable Bin" (for an essay on vegetables and their effects on cholesterol and cancer)
> "Babies Go to Work" (for an essay on corporate-sponsored day-care centers)
> "Denim Goes High Fashion" (for an essay describing the uses of denim for clothing other than jeans)

To write accurate and interesting titles, try the following tips:

1. **Write a question that your essay answers.** For example, "Why Change the Minimum Wage?"
2. **Use key words that appear in your thesis statement.** If your thesis statement is "The international trading ruling seriously threatens the safety of dolphins, one of our most intelligent animals," your title could be "Serious Threat to Dolphins."

Don't necessarily go with the first title that pops into your mind. If in doubt, try out some options on a classmate to see which is most effective, or use some brainstorming.

Proofreading

Proofreading is checking for errors, a final polishing of your work. Don't be concerned with proofreading until all your rethinking of ideas and other revisions are done. Check for each of these types of errors:

- Run-on sentences
- Sentence fragments
- Spelling
- Punctuation
- Grammar
- Capitalization

When you proofread, keep the following suggestions in mind:

1. **Review your essay once for each type of error.** First, read it for run-on sentences and sentence fragments. Then read it four more times, each time paying attention to only one thing: grammar, spelling, punctuation, and so forth.
2. **To spot spelling errors, read your essay from last sentence to first sentence and from last word to first word.** The flow of ideas will not matter, so you can focus on spotting errors.
3. **Read each sentence aloud, slowly and deliberately.** This will help you catch missing words, endings you have left off verbs, or missing plurals.
4. **Check for errors again as you rewrite or type your essay in final form.** Don't do this when you are tired; you might introduce new mistakes. Then proofread your final paper one last time.
5. **Use the grammar and spell checks on your computer.** These programs may not catch all your errors, but they may find some you have overlooked.

Chapter 1

Decisions That Shape Our Lives

Each day we make hundreds of decisions. We decide what time to get up, what to wear, where to sit on the bus or train or in a classroom, which assignment to read first, what to eat for dinner, and so forth. Many of these decisions are not very important in the long term. What you choose for dinner tonight will have little impact on your life two years from now, for example.

Other decisions have a more immediate and direct impact on your life. A decision to attend college, to marry, to take a certain job, to have children, to move, or to change careers clearly has long-term effects. Suppose, for instance, that the father of three small children decides to return to school so that he can get a more interesting and better-paying job. Since his family still needs his current income, he attends school at night so that he can keep working during the day. This decision means that he will be able to spend much less time with his family now, but that they will all have a better life a bit later. When we are faced with major decisions, we usually go through a process of weighing our options, looking at the pros and cons, and trying to evaluate the best course of action. The alternative is acting impulsively, which is another kind of decision that shapes people's lives, for better or worse.

The readings in this chapter will give you perspectives on some decisions that other people have made and how their lives have been shaped accordingly. You will read about personal choices involving family, such as a woman who travels to China and must choose which infant to adopt ("The Chosen One"); a woman who must decide whether to leave her fiancé ("Saying Good-bye to Eric"); a man who decides to learn at the age of 98 to read ("Life Is So Good"); and a student's decision to leave her family in Honduras to attend school in the United States ("The Gift of Sacrifice"). You will read about a well-known athlete's decision to enlist in the Army to fight the war in Iraq ("A Heroic Life"). You will also consider the issue of vegetarianism ("Why Go Veg?") and read about the fast food industry's decision to attempt to decrease portion size and offer healthier foods ("Hold the Fries. Hey, Not All of Them!").

Brainstorming About Decisions

Class Activity: The following circumstances are situations that require choices. Choose one situation, analyze it, and make a decision. Then write a description of what you think would happen.

Situation 1: If you could acquire one new skill or talent by simply asking, what would you ask for?

Situation 2: If a drug that made it possible for you to sleep only one night per week became available, would you decide to take it?

Situation 3: If you could exchange places for a day with anyone in history, dead or alive, famous or infamous, whom would you choose to be?

The Chosen One

▸ Laura Cunningham

In this reading, the author describes one of the most important decisions in her life—which baby to adopt. This essay originally appeared in the "Hers" column of the New York Times Magazine.

Journal Writing

Write a journal entry explaining how you feel about cross-cultural adoptions.

Reading Strategy

This is a personal essay in which the author expresses her feelings, doubts, and fears about adoption. As you read, highlight statements that reveal Cunningham's attitude toward the adoption process and the decision she made.

Vocabulary Preview

articulate (5) put into words
simpatico (6) compatible; holding similar attitudes and
            beliefs
hydraulic (7) forceful
unprecedented (7) unlike anything before
ambiguous (8) unclear, having more than one meaning
emissary (8) an agent representing someone else
paraphernalia (10) equipment; all the objects or items used
                in a place or with an object
staccato (16) abrupt sounds
fetid (19) having an offensive odor
luminous (22) bright

A year ago, I boarded a flight to Shanghai during a gale force wind.   1
The plane shivered and taxied back to the hangar twice before takeoff.
It is testimony to my anxiety about the purpose of my journey that I
felt no fear of flying. I carried with me an empty infant car bed (aptly
named the Dream Ride), a three-week supply of diapers, wipes, pediatric antibiotics, bottles and disposable nipples. I was on my way to
adopt one of the tens of thousands of baby girls abandoned in China
each year.

Today as I write, my 1-year-old daughter sleeps in a crib in the next   2
room. She lies in the position of trust—on her back, her arms widespread, her face tip-tilted as if for the next kiss.

A happy ending, so far, for my darling Chinese daughter, and for   3
me. But the journey to Shanghai has somehow not ended. Many
nights, I wake at 3 A.M.—yanked from my dream, my heart hammering
alarms. At that silent, moonlit time, I remember my choice.

I am embarrassed now to recall the doubt that accompanied me to   4
China. The orphanage had sent a fax (yes, in the new China, orphan-
ages send faxes): "We have a baby for you. We would have taken her
picture but it was too cold."

My concern, if I can articulate the chill gut slide of panic as a "con-   5
cern," was that somehow I would walk into the orphanage and fail to
respond to the baby; that somehow she would not feel like "the right
one." I would have to go ahead with the adoption out of momentum,
some grim sense of decency, but without the hoped-for love at first sight.

The baby, it seemed from the fax, was already chosen. And while I   6
claimed to love all babies, in my secret, cowering heart I had to admit
that I was more drawn to some babies than to others. It wasn't beauty
or even intelligence that I required of a baby, but some sign of being,
well, simpatico.

I could not see her until the orphanage opened Monday morning. I   7
had arrived in Shanghai on Saturday night. The interval was the high
tide of my fear—suspense seemed hydraulic; blood rushed through me
at unprecedented speed.

Until Monday I had only the ambiguous answers of Ms. Zhang, the   8
orphanage's emissary who had greeted me at the airport. When I
asked: "How old is the baby? How big?" Ms. Zhang answered only with
another question: "What size baby clothes have you brought with you?"

Her response raised some possibility of control, or at least influ-   9
ence. Maybe the baby was *not* yet chosen. In my sneaking secret
chicken heart, I could still pick the best and the brightest star of abandoned baby girlhood in Shanghai.

Passing the time until I could meet "my baby," I met another   10
baby at the hotel, already adopted by a single man. (China permits
adoptions by foreigners, whether married or unmarried. Its adoption policy is unusual in that citizens, as well as foreigners, must be
at least 35 years old to adopt.) She struck me, however, as not meant
to be my baby. She did seem just right for her new father, an American psychologist, who carried with him a sitcom's supply of baby
paraphernalia.

Next I went to the nearest tourist attraction, the Temple of the Jade   11
Buddha, where there was said to be a Buddha to whom mothers pray
for a good baby.

The Buddha glowed in the dim temple. It wasn't jet lag that sent me   12
reeling to my knees before the Buddha. Half-Jewish, half-Southern Baptist, all doubt, I knelt in truest prayer. *Let the baby be one I can truly love.*

At 9 sharp the next morning I waited in the orphanage, wearing my   13
winter coat indoors (now I understood the fax). Even in midwinter
there was no heat. Vapor rose from the thermoses of hot tea carried by
the female employees. The translator announced that the baby was being carried in from the nursery building.

"You will have a choice," she said.   14

I looked out the window as she pointed across a courtyard filled   15
with dead bamboo and gray laundry. The window itself was grimy, but
through it I saw two women in blue smocks, running toward me. Each
held a bundle. There were *two* babies.

They were swaddled in comforters, their heads completely draped   16
in towels. The first baby was unveiled. There was a staccato of Chinese,
translated as: "Pick this one. She is more beautiful. She is more intelligent." Baby No. 1 was the nurses' favorite, a 2-month-old of unsurpassed good looks and robust health. She smiled.

But I couldn't take my eyes from the second baby, who was   17
revealed almost as an afterthought. She was thin, piteous, a green-complexioned elf, with low-set ears that stuck out. She wheezed. In a
pocket of my coat, I held a vial of antibiotics, carried on good advice
from a friend.

I had no choice. The second baby was sick. I had medicine impossible to obtain here. I accepted the tiny green baby, gasping and oozing, into my arms. I noticed she also had a bald spot, from lying
unmoved in her crib.   18

Shame over my earlier indecision blew from the room like a fetid   19
draft of disease and poverty.

Was it love at first sight? I knew in that instant that we were at the   20
start of our life together.

Love overtakes you at odd moments. I was trying to collect a urine   21
sample, required for a medical test. I held her, her little purple fanny
over a rice bowl, in my arms all night. I drew the blankets around us
both as a tent to keep away the cold. We waited, silently, all night, until she took a literal "tinkle." Her eyes met mine, on the other side of
the world, and I knew Little-Miss-Ears-Stick-Out, With-Tears-in-Her-Eyes was mine, all right.

Within 24 hours, the medicine had taken effect: she turned ivory   22
pink; her eyes cleared. She was beyond my dreams, exquisite, a luminous old soul with contemporary wit. I gazed at her and saw the fatefulness of every mother's choice. It is not the beautiful baby who is
chosen, but the chosen baby who becomes beautiful.

To enter a house filled with unwanted babies is to pass through a   23
door that you can never shut. At 3 A.M., I see the others—the aisles of

green cribs holding bundled babies. I try to close my eyes to them, but they refuse to disappear. They are lying there. They are cold; they are damp. I see one baby girl especially. She had an odd genetic defect: the skin of her body was coal black, but her face had no color. She looked as if she were wearing the white theatrical mask of tragedy.

Last Christmas, I was able to choose the green, sick baby over the laughing, healthy one. Would I have had the courage to take one of the others? Would someone? I wake up and see the small faces. They are lying there waiting, waiting to be chosen. 24

Examining the Reading

Finding Meaning

1. Why was the author on her way to China?
2. What was the author's greatest concern before she met the baby?
3. Why did she choose one baby over the other?
4. Describe the baby's state of health by the time the author left Shanghai.
5. Describe the conditions in the orphanage.

Understanding Technique

1. Cunningham uses sensory details (details that appeal to the senses: sight, sound, taste, smell, and touch) in her writing. Underline several places where the sensory details are particularly powerful.
2. Highlight the transitions Cunningham uses to move from one event to the next.

Thinking Critically

1. If you were in the author's place and had a choice of two babies to adopt, which one would you choose? Why?
2. The Chinese government has a policy that adoptive parents must be at least 35 years old. Do you think this is a good policy? Why or why not?
3. Why do you think the orphanage gave the author a choice of two babies to adopt?
4. What did the author mean when she said, "It is not the beautiful baby who is chosen, but the chosen baby who becomes beautiful"?

Writing About the Reading

A Paragraph

1. Write a paragraph describing whether or under what conditions you might consider adopting a child.
2. Cunningham seemed to have little difficulty making her decision. She seemed to know intuitively which baby to choose. Write a paragraph describing a similar situation in which you seemed to know the right decision to make.

An Essay

1. The author suggests that all mothers think their own children are beautiful. From your experience as a child, as a parent, or as both, write an essay agreeing or disagreeing that parents see beauty (physical or otherwise) in their children and tend to overlook their children's faults. Support your position with examples from your experience.
2. Cunningham felt doubtful and anxious as she awaited the important moment when she would see her baby. Write an essay describing an event about which you felt anxious or nervous. Explain why you were anxious and how the event turned out.

A Creative Activity

Suppose the author decided to write a letter to the other baby, explaining why she had not chosen her. What do you think she would have said? Write a first draft of the letter.

A Heroic Life

▶ **Dirk Johnson, Andrew Murr, Robina Riccitello, Karen Breslau, Ronald Moreau, Owen Matthews, T. Trent Gegax, and Randy Collier**

This article describes an unusual decision made by a professional athlete. Pat Tillman, a strong safety for the Arizona Cardinals professional football team, left a successful and lucrative NFL career to enlist in the United States Army with the intention of "laying himself on the line" in the war against terrorism. Unfortunately, Pat was killed in an ambush in Afghanistan in April 2004 at the age of 27. This article first appeared in Newsweek *magazine May 3, 2004.*

Journal Writing

Think about a time when you "laid yourself on the line." Describe what you did and why your action was worth the physical or emotional risk.

Reading Strategy

As you read this story, try to determine if the authors of the story have an opinion about the war on terrorism being fought in Afghanistan and Iraq. Identify passages that reveal the authors' feelings about the war.

Vocabulary Preview

buttes (1) isolated hills or mountains
mosque (2) a Muslim building for worship
rife (2) prevalent to an increasing degree
enclave (4) a distinctly bounded area enclosed within a larger
    unit
divulge (5) to make known
candor (6) frankness, sincerity
harrowing (7) agonizing
intolerable (7) not endurable

Pat Tillman

When nobody was around, Arizona State University football star Pat   1
Tillman would climb the 10-story light tower at Sun Devil Stadium,
certainly without permission, just to gaze at the buttes, the desert, the
glow of Phoenix—and ponder the state of the world. A roughneck with
a philosophical bent, Tillman never followed convention. This was a
college kid who, as a freshman, defied the advice of coaches to "red-
shirt" and delay his football career a year. He told coach Bruce Snyder
he'd be gone in four years. "He said, 'I've got other things I'm going to
do with my life.'"

He went pro with the Arizona Cardinals and became known for his   2
hippielike, shoulder-length hair—and his bone-rattling hits as a strong
safety. But days after the terror of September 11, 2001, Tillman saw him-

self as just another millionaire athlete. "You know, my great-grandfather was at Pearl Harbor, and a lot of my family have . . . fought in wars," he told a team camera crew, almost in shame. "And I haven't really done a damn thing as far as laying myself on the line like that." Six months later, Tillman shocked the sports world by enlisting in the Army and shipping out. Last Thursday, he laid it all on the line. He was killed in an ambush near Spera, a tiny town of mud huts and a new mosque, in a region rife with Qaeda warriors. He was 27 years old.

This is the cost of war in Afghanistan and Iraq: the loss of so much promise and potential. More than 800 American men and women have now died in the military effort, and thousands have been wounded. American troops tend to be honorable but anonymous—working-class or poor, disproportionately black, brown or rural. If they come home, they often return to quiet lives as clock punchers. But in Tillman, the sacrifice of war suddenly bears a face of stardom. The Pentagon can try to block images of flag-draped coffins. But Tillman's death is a startling billboard of grief, a reminder that these lost soldiers—all of them, famous or not—had so much left to give.

Tillman had everything: riches, smarts, good looks. An academic All-American, he had a 3.84 grade-point average in marketing at Arizona State. He joined the service just after a honeymoon to Bora Bora with his high-school sweetheart, Marie. He and a younger brother, Kevin, slipped off to enlist in Denver, where they could avoid publicity. Kevin, who gave up a budding minor-league baseball career, remains in the Army. Pat Tillman wanted no attention, no glory, for joining the rank and file. He "didn't want to be singled out from his brothers and sisters in the military," says former Cardinals coach Dave McGinnis. Tillman apparently had made a pact with his family to stay silent about his service, a promise they have kept. They have gathered to grieve inside the comfortable family home in a leafy enclave of San Jose.

His was no simple case of patriotism; Tillman was never known as a flag-waver. His agent, Frank Bauer, told reporters he had suspected that Tillman might quit to teach or to practice law like his father, Patrick Sr., but not to join the military. Snyder, his college coach, said Tillman never used the word patriotism when he explained his plans to enlist. "He just seemed to think something had to be done." When players asked why he enlisted, he didn't want to talk about it. McGinnis says there were "reasons Pat said he had that he didn't want to divulge," and the coach respected his view and his right to make his own path. Tillman had always been different. When he joined the pros, he rode a bicycle to practice because he didn't own a car. He refused to buy a cell phone. A sports publicist at Arizona State once described him as "a surfer dude."

Growing up in San Jose, Tillman went to Leland High School. "All the girls loved him," says a former classmate, "and all the guys wanted to be him." But he was not perfect. His Spanish teacher, Carla Lucarotti, recalls that he had a mischievous streak about him. "They were all young and crazy," Lucarotti says. In high school Tillman got into a fight—defending a friend—and ended up being charged with felony assault as a juvenile. He pleaded guilty and served time on a work farm the summer before entering Arizona State. A sports reporter, Tim Layden, wrote about Tillman's candor when asked if he'd ever been arrested or gotten into trouble. "Nickel and dime stuff—he didn't have to tell me the truth," Layden wrote.

Tillman gave up a $3.6 million contract to join the harrowing world   7 of life as an Army Ranger. The training alone is nearly intolerable: working to exhaustion—in conditions of swamps, jungles, mountains— about 20 hours a day. Rangers are sent to places where the danger is the worst. That's where Tillman was on Thursday. Dusk was falling and the new moon hadn't risen yet—the darkest time of the night for eyes still smarting from the blinding mountain sun and daytime temperatures of 105 degrees. Military officials say that Tillman's unit was ambushed in a region where Qaeda forces sneak across from Pakistan. The coalition returned fire. Two other Americans were hurt. One Afghan soldier was killed.

On a trip home in December—after serving in Iraq—Tillman made   8 a surprise visit to his old Cardinals teammates at a game in Seattle. Again he refused to explain why he gave it all up for the harsh life of a soldier. His intensity was not unexpected. . . . He told his pals he intended to return to football after his tour of duty. Just before he left, he thanked McGinnis for letting him come to visit. "No—thank you," said McGinnis. And then Tillman slipped out a side door, intent on avoiding attention.

Known for engaging his teammates in deep talks in the weight   9 room, Tillman had always looked for a hurdle to jump. Bored during one off-season, he ran a marathon. Next he did a triathlon. Renowned for his toughness, Tillman seemed bulletproof. Bauer, his agent, says NFL coaches and execs would joke that if anybody was going to find Osama bin Laden, this was the guy to do it. He died trying.

Examining the Reading

Finding Meaning

1. How did Pat Tillman shock the sports world?
2. Why did Tillman and his brother Kevin drive to Denver to enlist in the military?
3. What type of pact did Tillman make with his family? Why do you think he made this pact?

4. What evidence do the authors give to support their comment that "Tillman had always been different"?
5. Describe Tillman's visit to his Cardinals teammates after serving in Iraq. How do the details of his visit support the idea that Tillman "didn't want to be singled out from his brothers and sisters in the military"?
6. What types of activities did Tillman engage in when he was "bored" in the football off-season?

Understanding Technique

1. Why do the authors begin the article with the description of Tillman climbing the light tower at Sun Devil Stadium? What does this story tell you about Tillman's personality and priorities?
2. Identify a few of the vivid descriptions the authors use in the article. What impression do these details create?
3. Why did the authors include the detail that Tillman served time in a work farm?
4. How does the authors' use of quotations enhance the article?

Thinking Critically

1. What do the authors mean when they say, "Tillman's death is a startling billboard of grief"?
2. Why do you think that American troops tend to be "honorable but anonymous"?
3. Why do you think Tillman refused to explain why he gave up his football career for the harsh life of a soldier?
4. Why is it ironic that "Tillman seemed bulletproof"?

Writing About the Reading

A Paragraph

1. Write a paragraph evaluating Pat Tillman's decision to enlist in the Army.
2. Write a paragraph explaining your position on U.S. military involvement in Iraq and the Middle East.
3. Write a paragraph describing a decision you made based on events happening around you.

An Essay

1. Was Pat Tillman a hero? Explain your response by defining what a hero is and using details from the article to support your position.

2. How is the life of an Army Ranger similar to the life of an NFL player? How is it different? Do you think Tillman's football career prepared him for his career as a Ranger? Why or why not? Write an essay answering these questions.
3. Write an essay describing a time when you made a choice to give up, forgo, or postpone something you would have enjoyed, valued, or profited from.
4. Describe your position on the use of force in response to a conflict. When, if ever, do you think force is justifiable? Write an essay explaining your position.

Creative Activities

1. Design and describe a fitting memorial for Tillman. Try to consider the wishes and desires of Tillman's family, his fans, and Tillman himself.
2. Write a different ending to Tillman's enlistment. Suppose, for example, he returned safely from the war.

Life Is So Good

▶ **George Dawson and Richard Glaubman**

An elderly man tells of his decision to learn to read after a long life of working and raising a family. He wrote a book titled Life Is So Good *with the assistance of Richard Glaubman, who is mentioned in this excerpt from the book.*

Journal Writing

Write a journal entry about something you have accomplished after a long struggle.

Reading Strategy

In a story with dialogue, sometimes it is hard to tell who is speaking. As you read, note each speaker when you come across conversation.

The old man who could not read lives alone in a house that is small 1
and square, in an area that some people call the ghetto. . . . The old man got by until 1996, when a young man knocked on his door and said he was recruiting people for the Adult Basic Education classes at the old high school.

"*I've been alone for ten years," the old man told him. "I'm tired of* 2
fishing. It's time to learn to read."

—*Seattle Times,* Larry Bingham, February 1, 1998

I always had a dream that I would learn how to read. It was my secret, 3
that I couldn't read. There was nothing I couldn't do and my mind was as good as anyone's. That's just how it was. All my life, I had been just too busy working to go to school. I kept it a secret that I couldn't read.

My mind worked hard. When I traveled somewhere, I could never 4
read a sign. I had to ask people things and had to remember. I could never let my mind forget anything, never let my mind take a vacation.

I listened to the news and had to trust what I heard. I never read it 5
for myself. My wife read the mail and paid our bills. I made sure that each of the children learned to read. When they came home from school, there was milk and cookies on the kitchen table. They would

---

tell me what their classmates did and what the teacher said. I made sure they told me what they had learned that day. I always listened. I always asked if they had worked hard.

The answer was always yes, because they knew I would be waiting   6
to find out. They knew what I expected: hard work. I would tell them, "School is important and there is a lot to learn."

To each of them I would say, "I'm proud of you."   7

I helped them with their homework.   8

"How could you do that," Richard asked, "if you couldn't read?"   9

Just then the screen door banged open and Junior came in. His   10
jacket was dripping with water. "Tell Richard here how I helped you with your schoolwork. He don't believe me."

Junior laughed and said, "Every night, Daddy made us sit down at   11
the kitchen table and do our homework. We had to show it to him when we were done. We didn't know he couldn't read. Daddy would say, 'Read back what you got. You'll learn it better that way,' and that was probably true. I graduated fourth in my class! Daddy, and our mother too, they didn't want to hear about excuses. It was that simple," Junior said.

"When did you find out that your father couldn't read?"   12

"I was in high school when my father told me."   13

"What did you think?"   14

"He was our father and it didn't change anything, but we kept it a   15
secret for him."

"Why?"   16

"Well, some folks don't understand things like that and we just   17
wanted to protect him."

"So, it became more of a family secret?"   18

"That's a good way to put it."   19

"Back then, did you ever think your father would learn to read?"   20

"I knew he would have liked to. He thought reading was so impor-   21
tant. But back then, there were more people his age that never learned to read than there is today."

"So it wasn't so uncommon?"   22

"I don't know for sure. It wasn't something people would talk   23
about either."

I listened to the two of them talk, but I know that a lot of people   24
still don't understand. They be thinking I spent my life just waiting to learn to read. That's not it at all. I didn't think about things I couldn't do nothing about. Things were just the way they were. And that's that.

People wonder why I didn't go back to school earlier. After I re-   25
tired, I finally had the time. I was proud to get my children through school and raise them properly. But I understood that school was there for the children. When I was young, I had missed my turn to go. I had never heard of these adult education classes. I've never had any extra money to hire a special teacher. People that been in my house have

seen the sagging ceiling, the cracked window, the broken plaster on the wall and they know that. So I didn't expect nothing.

One day, out of the blue, a man came to the door. He handed me a piece of paper. Good thing I was home or I would have thrown it out like most fliers that I couldn't read. But he said there were some classes for adults. They taught reading. The school, the same one my own children had gone to, was close enough to walk to. It's maybe six blocks away. 26

Junior thinks that man might have thought there might be some of Daddy's grandchildren living in the house. 27

No matter. I live by myself now. I shook his hand and told him, "I will be coming to school!" 28

My turn had come. My first day of school was January 4, 1996. I was ninety-eight years old and I'm still going. Except for three funerals, I've gone to school every day for three years. School starts at nine. 29

© Richard Glaubman

George Dawson

I can't wait and I'm up by five-thirty to make my lunch, pack my books, and go over my schoolwork. Since I started school, I'm always early. I haven't ever been late.

"I was just thinking," Richard said, "how hard it is to learn to read   30
at any age. Not everybody succeeds. Mr. Dawson, were you a little afraid that you wouldn't make it? Didn't you have any doubts?"

"Son, I always thought I could drive a *spike*[1] as good as any man   31
and cook as good as any woman. I just figured if everybody else can learn to read, I could too."

"Was it hard to learn to read?"   32

"Sure, it was. But I been working hard all my life. I'm used to it and   33
it don't scare me none. Mr. Henry, my teacher, he's a good man and he's a good teacher. Tomorrow, you come to class with me." . . .

I came to school to learn something, but I'm happy to be helping   34
people. Sure, it makes me feel good. You bet I like school! Every morning I get up and I wonder what I might learn that day. You just never know. I am so grateful to have this chance to go to school.

I have to admit, it's easier for me to do silent reading than it is for   35
me to read out loud. To see how I'm doing, Mr. Henry has me read out loud to him, but I stumble a lot over words when I read that way. The day Richard was there, he was sitting at my table. Him being a teacher too, when I was done I said, "My reading is getting better and better, but when I read out loud it's harder."

Richard shrugged. "Probably, it's like when you first rode a bicycle.   36
It was hard to keep your balance and then one day it just got easier. Do you remember how that felt?"

"No. I remember what it felt like the first time I rode a mule."   37

It's like we both speak English, but sometimes we just got to start   38
over so we can understand each other. It's not easy for either of us, but we keep trying. I showed him the cafeteria where we have lunch. I unpacked my barbecued beef sandwich, and from a paper sack he took out a turkey sandwich.

I get hungry at school and besides a sandwich, I bring dessert. Pie   39
is good and if I don't want it I can always trade a slice of pie with someone at my table for some cookies or cupcakes. I do that sometimes. Richard didn't bring any dessert.

I said, "See, if you don't have any dessert then you don't have nothing to trade."   40

"Next time."   41

Junior stopped by at lunch and he and Richard went over to my   42
house when I went back to class. I followed later. When Richard comes, he rents these shiny little cars or a van and we drive around

---

[1]Work on the railroad; work hard.

town in those. P.J. [one of Dawson's classmates] gave me a ride. He usually takes me home. P.J. has got a big old car. But nowadays cars are all the same to me. Thing is, it's hard to tell a Chevy from a Ford, plus there's all the other brands that people drive. One thing is they all got radios now. That's not so special like it used to be.

Junior and Richard were already at my house. Junior usually comes by after school anyway. I joined them at the kitchen table. Junior told Richard, "I used to come by almost every day. Now I come by after school. It's nice. It seems that it gives us more to talk about."   43

"I tell him about my classmates and what the teacher said."   44

Junior said, "He even tells me what they all had for lunch. I always ask, 'Daddy, did you work hard at school?'"   45

I said, "The answer is always yes."   46

Junior said, "I tell my dad, 'School is important. There is so much to learn. I'm proud of you.'"   47

Examining the Reading

Finding Meaning

1. What was Mr. Dawson's secret?
2. How did Mr. Dawson cope with daily life without being able to read?
3. What did Mr. Dawson expect from his children?
4. How did Mr. Dawson finally go back to school?
5. How did Mr. Dawson feel about learning to read?
6. Why does Mr. Dawson bring dessert to school?
7. What do Junior and his dad talk about after school?

Understanding Technique

1. The story begins with an excerpt from a *Seattle Times* article. Is this an effective introduction? Why or why not?
2. Mr. Dawson's story is told in the first person (the writer is the speaker in the story). What effect does this style have? Would it be as effective if the story were told by another person?
3. How do Richard and Junior help tell the story?
4. What special details does Mr. Dawson use to add depth to his story? Why are they effective?

Thinking Critically

1. Why did Mr. Dawson and his family keep the fact that he couldn't read a secret?
2. Why did Mr. Dawson tell his children to "read back" their homework to him? How did it help the children?

3. Mr. Dawson writes that he missed only three days of school and has never been late. What makes him so enthusiastic about school?
4. How would you describe Mr. Dawson's attitude toward life?
5. Mr. Dawson was illiterate until he was ninety-eight years old. What other issues do you think he faced as an older person?

Writing About the Reading

A Paragraph

1. Write a paragraph identifying and discussing one skill other than reading that is needed for academic success. Why is this skill important?
2. Teachers can make a great difference in a student's life. Write a paragraph describing one important quality that a teacher should possess.

An Essay

1. People who cannot read face many challenges. Assume you are illiterate. Write an essay describing some of the daily problems you face. Explain at what points you feel vulnerable or dependent on others.
2. Mr. Dawson made the decision to learn to read, although it was a difficult task. Write an essay describing a decision that meant facing a challenging task.
3. If you could be any kind of teacher in any location, what would you choose and why? Where would you teach? Why? Write an essay answering these questions.

A Creative Activity

Imagine what it would be like to teach someone to read. Create a plan for your first day. Include how you would start the lesson and how you would introduce yourself.

Saying Good-bye to Eric

> ◗ Jennifer S. Dickman

In this essay, published in Nursing *magazine, Jennifer S. Dickman describes how a personal tragedy motivated her to become a nurse.*

Journal Writing

Write a journal entry about a difficult decision that you were forced to make.

Reading Strategy

Eric's accident and what happened afterward certainly took a terrible emotional toll on the author. Review the essay and underline those sections where the author expresses her feelings about the events connected to this tragedy.

Vocabulary Preview

intubated (5) had tubes inserted to assist bodily functions
ventilation (5) breathing
evacuate (5) to remove the contents of
hematoma (5) a localized swelling filled with blood resulting from a break in a blood vessel
debride (5) surgically remove unhealthy tissue
temporal lobe (5) section of the brain containing the sensory area associated with hearing
frontal lobe (5) section of the brain responsible for higher thought
intraventricular catheter (5) a tube inserted into a ventricle, or small cavity in the brain
intracranial (5) within the skull
neurology (6) the science dealing with disorders of the brain and nervous system
irony (7) strange twist; joke or a turnaround of events
secretions (8) fluids
weaned (9) gradually removed from

As Eric rode off on his motorcycle that crisp November day, he turned and gave me a smile and a wave. I never dreamed that would be the last expression I'd ever see on my fiancé's face.

A few hours later, I was driving to the regional trauma center, my 2
hands trembling on the steering wheel, my eyes blurred with tears.
Eric's bike had skidded out of control on wet pavement and he'd been
thrown into a field.

Please let him be okay, I prayed. *We're in the middle of planning our* 3
wedding.

When I arrived at the trauma center, my worst fears were immedi- 4
ately confirmed. He'd suffered a serious brain injury.

Caring for Eric

Eric had been intubated in the ED and required assisted ventilation. 5
He was initially admitted to the neurology ICU—later that day he un-
derwent surgery to evacuate a hematoma and to debride damaged parts
of his temporal and frontal lobes. During surgery, an intraventricular
catheter was inserted to continuously monitor his intracranial pressure.

I stumbled through those first few hours—and then days—in a fog 6
of shock and disbelief. I never left the hospital, choosing to sleep in the
visitor's lounge. When Eric was finally moved to a private room in the
neurology unit, I slept on a cot next to him.

Grief prevented me from seeing the irony in my situation. I'd taken 7
a semester off from nursing school because I wasn't sure if I wanted to
be a nurse—I didn't know if I was up to it. And now I was devoting all
of my time to caring for Eric.

I bathed him, turned him, did his catheter care, and learned to give 8
his tube feedings. I read to him, talked to him, and played all of his favorite music. I even convinced his doctors to let me give herbal tea
through his feeding tube cause I'd read that certain herbs help decrease lung secretions.

After 4 months, Eric's condition improved slightly. He began blink- 9
ing his eyes, making small hand and foot movements, and trying to
breathe on his own. I was thrilled, even though deep down I knew that
these weren't signs of recovery. When Eric was finally weaned from the
ventilator and began breathing on his own, I felt like shouting for joy.
That's when his doctor took me aside.

"You'd better get on with your life, Jennifer," he said gently but 10
firmly. "Eric's reached a plateau, and he'll be this way as long as he lives."

Confronting Reality

At first, I refused to believe him. But then, with the help of my family 11
and friends, I took an honest look at the situation. For 6 months, I'd
given up everything to devote my energy to Eric. I'd lost a lot of weight
and was mentally and physically exhausted. I knew the time had come
to accept his condition and start living my own life—which, I decided,
included returning to nursing school.

A few weeks after I'd reached my decision, Eric was transferred to   12
a long-term-care facility. Before he left I said a final good-bye.

I still feel the pain of losing Eric—and I'm sure I always will. But I   13
also remember how caring for him helped clear up any confusion over
my career choice. Although I couldn't bring Eric back, his tragedy
brought me back to nursing.

Examining the Reading

Finding Meaning

1. How did Eric's accident occur?
2. Describe the injuries he suffered.
3. How did the author provide care for Eric?
4. What effect did caring for Eric have on Dickman's life and health?
5. What did the author decide to do after six months of caring for Eric?

Understanding Technique

1. What techniques does Dickman use to make her story real and compelling?
2. Why do you think she included in paragraph 5 the technical details of Eric's medical condition?

Thinking Critically

1. Evaluate how Eric's accident affected Dickman at first. Is this a typical first reaction? Why or why not?
2. What did the author mean by "Grief prevented me from seeing the irony in my situation"? What was this irony?
3. Why did the doctor tell the author that she should get on with her life just when Eric seemed to be improving?
4. Was there a chance that Eric might have recovered completely from his accident?
5. Do you think the author's decision to return to nursing school is logical and reasonable?

Writing About the Reading

A Paragraph

1. Someone might say that if Dickman had truly loved Eric, she would have continued to care for him for the rest of his life. Write a paragraph defending or rejecting this idea.

2. Write a paragraph on what you imagine would be the hardest part of being a nurse and why.

An Essay

1. The author had some difficulty deciding whether or not to become a nurse, but her experiences after Eric's accident helped her make that decision. Write an essay describing an experience in your life that helped you discover your career goals.
2. Sometimes it takes a tragic event to remind us of our blessings or to awaken us to a new, important direction for our lives. Write an essay about how such an experience made you a better person.

A Creative Activity

Imagine that Eric would have survived with only minimal brain damage. How do you imagine this might have changed the ending for the author? Rewrite the ending as though this were the case.

Why Go Veg?

▶ **Barbara Tunick**

The author describes some of the personal, social, and environmental reasons that people adopt a vegetarian lifestyle. This article first appeared in Vegetarian Times *magazine in July of 2002.*

Journal Writing

1. Are you or have you ever considered becoming a vegetarian? Write a journal entry explaining your reasons.
2. Do you follow a healthy diet? Write an entry describing what you could do to improve it.

Reading Strategy

As you read, highlight the six reasons why the author believes people should become vegetarians.

Vocabulary Preview

abundance (3) an ample quantity
chronic (6) marked by long duration or frequent recurrence
degenerative (6) tending to cause the progressive deterioration of a tissue or organ
mortality (7) the state of being subject to death
arresting (7) stopping
eschew (13) to avoid; shun
intolerant (14) unable or unwilling to endure
sentient (17) having sense perception; conscious
wreak havoc (19) to cause general confusion
vogue (20) the leading place in popularity or acceptance
pacifist (21) a person who is strongly and actively opposed to conflict

*I*t's hip to be vegetarian today—and we don't mean hip as in hippie.   1
Sure, some of us might have love beads still hanging in the closet, but for the estimated 5 million Americans who have chosen a meat-free diet, reasons for going veg are as varied as our favorite '60s rock stars.

Some of us want to live longer, healthier lives or do our part to re-   2
duce pollution. Others of us have made the switch to preserve the earth's
natural resources or because we've always loved animals and are ethi-
cally opposed to eating them.

Thanks to an abundance of scientific research that demonstrates   3
the health and environmental benefits of a plant-based diet, even the
federal government is recommending that Americans consume the majority of their calories from grain products, vegetables and fruits.

Why go veg? Here are six great reasons.   4

Get Healthy

The No. 1 reason most of us switch to a plant-based diet is because   5
we're concerned about our health, says the Baltimore-based Vegetarian Resource Group. And there's good reason: An estimated 70 percent
of all diseases—including one-third of all cancers—are related to diet.

A vegetarian diet reduces the risk for several chronic degenerative   6
diseases, such as obesity, coronary artery disease, high blood pressure,
diabetes and certain types of cancer—including colon, breast, prostate,
stomach, lung and esophageal cancer. The China-Cornell-Oxford Project, a study of the diet and health of 6,500 people from 65 countries,
found in the 1980s that rural Chinese people who consumed the least
amount of fat and animal products had the lowest risks of cancer,
heart attack and other chronic degenerative diseases, compared to
those who consumed more animal products.

As for cardiovascular disease—the leading cause of death in the   7
United States—not only is mortality lower in vegetarians than in non-
vegetarians, but vegetarian diets have also been successful in arresting
and reversing coronary artery disease, says Joel Fuhrman, MD, spokes-
person for Physicians Committee for Responsible Medicine and author
of *Eat to Live: The Revolutionary Plan for Fast and Sustained Weight Loss.*

Feel Younger; Live Longer

"If you switch from a normal American diet to a vegetarian diet, you   8
can add about 13 healthy years to your life," says Michael F. Roizen,
MD, dean of the School of Medicine, SUNY Upstate, Syracuse, New
York, and author of *The Real Age Diet.* "People who consume saturated,
four-legged fat have a shorter life span and more disability at the end
of their lives. Animal products dog your arteries, zap your energy and
slow down your immune system. Meat-eaters also experience acceler-
ated cognitive and sexual dysfunction at a younger age."

In a 1976–1988 study of 34,000 Seventh-Day Adventists, researchers   9
at Loma Linda University in California found that vegetarians live about
seven years longer than meat-eaters, and vegans—people who consume no animal products—live about eight years longer.

Lose Weight

Meat consumption is linked to obesity. According to the National Center　10
for Health Statistics and the American Society for Clinical Nutrition, 61
percent of adults and 20 percent of U.S. children are overweight.

A study from 1986–1992 by Dean Ornish, MD, a *Vegetarian Times*　11
board member, found that overweight people who followed a low-fat,
vegetarian diet lost an average of 24 pounds in the first year and had
kept off that weight five years later.

Overweight people who adapted a low-fat, vegetarian diet lost　12
weight without counting calories, measuring portions or, most impor-
tantly, feeling hungry. "It makes sense that you'll lose weight if you follow a low-fat, plant-based diet since you're eating less fat, no cholesterol
and higher fiber," says Fuhrman. "Eliminating dairy from your diet is
the first step to losing weight."

Resolve Digestive Difficulties

A number of people who become vegetarians eschew all milk and dairy　13
products because they cause digestive complaints.

According to the American Gastroenterological Association, close　14
to 50 million Americans are lactose-intolerant or have trouble digest-
ing the sugar, or lactose, found in milk and dairy products. As a result,
they may experience abdominal bloating, flatulence, nausea or diarrhea
after consuming milk or dairy products.

"Many people are also sensitive to milk protein," says John Mc-　15
Dougall, MD, author of *The McDougall Program for Women*, which ad-
vocates a low-fat, vegetarian diet for optimum wellness. "Your immune
system recognizes cow protein as foreign and makes antibodies against
it. Unfortunately, these same antibodies attack our own tissues and
cause problems like severe arthritis and even Type-1 diabetes."

Spare Animals

Many vegetarians give up meat because of their concern for animals.　16
Eight billion animals are slaughtered for human consumption each
year. And, unlike farms of yesteryear where animals roamed freely, today most animals are "factory farmed"—crammed into cages where
they can barely move and fed a diet tainted with pesticides.

"If you believe that animals are sentient beings, how can you sim-　17
ply disregard their needs and comfort?" asks Polly Walker, MD, MPH,
associate director for programs at Johns Hopkins University's Center
for a Livable Future.

Reduce Pollution

Some people become vegetarian after realizing the devastation the　18
meat industry is having on the environment. According to the U.S.

Environmental Protection Agency, chemical and animal waste runoff from factory farms is responsible for more than 173,000 miles of polluted rivers and streams.

"By concentrating thousands of animals into a small area, industrial animal production creates threats to both the environment and human health," says Walker. "Factory farms have the potential to wreak havoc on the environment, as was experienced in North Carolina during Hurricane Floyd in 1999."   19

Health reasons, environmental concerns, ethics—whatever your motivation for choosing vegetarianism, you're in good company. Even though your love beads probably won't come back into style, good health will always be in vogue.   20

Beverly Cappel, DVM, always knew she wanted to be a veterinarian. "Even as a little girl I collected sick or injured animals," says Cappel, who runs a holistic veterinary care center in Chestnut Ridge, New York. "Our basement was filled with boxes and cages and crates of hurt birds, squirrels, chipmunks, cats and dogs." Cappel became a vegetarian in 1969, during her pre-veterinary training. "I've always loved animals, and I've always been a pacifist, so it makes perfect sense that I would be a vegetarian" she says. "I have to say, though, that while I became a vegetarian solely for ethical reasons, I would now have to include the health benefits as well."   21

Examining the Reading

Finding Meaning

1. Approximately how many Americans are currently vegetarians?
2. What is the number one reason why people switch to a plant-based diet?
3. List some of the diseases for which a vegetarian diet can reduce your risk.
4. What is a vegan?
5. What are some of the advantages of avoiding dairy products?
6. According to the article, how has animal farming changed in recent years?
7. How can becoming a vegetarian have a positive influence on the environment?
8. How have Dr. Cappel's reasons for becoming a veterinarian changed?

Understanding Technique

1. Highlight and evaluate the author's thesis statement.

2. What types of evidence does Tunick use to support each of her reasons? Evaluate the effectiveness of each.
3. Describe the tone of the essay. How does the author attempt to connect to her audience and gain their interest?
4. Notice that Tunick identifies each of the reasons for becoming a vegetarian in the opening paragraph. What are the advantages and disadvantages of this technique?

Thinking Critically

1. If adopting a vegetarian lifestyle is healthier than a traditional American diet, why aren't more Americans vegetarians?
2. What does the author mean when she writes, "It's hip to be vegetarian today—and we don't mean hip as in hippie"?
3. Do you think Tunick presents a convincing case for vegetarianism? What could the author have done to make her argument more compelling?

Writing About the Reading

A Paragraph

1. As mentioned in the article, obesity is becoming a serious problem in America. Write a paragraph describing other ways that obesity can be combated.
2. Dr. Cappel describes how she loved animals as a child, which led her to become a veterinarian. Describe a hobby or interest you had as a child that might lead you to a particular profession or position on an issue.
3. Write a paragraph describing a decision you have made about the types or kinds of food you eat.

An Essay

1. Play devil's advocate (take the opposing view) and write an essay explaining some reasons why people should *not* choose a vegetarian lifestyle.
2. Think about a personal choice that you have made, such as choosing to exercise regularly, choosing not to smoke or drink alcohol, or choosing to avoid certain types of consumer products. Write an essay explaining why people should adopt your choice.

A Creative Activity

Write the script for a public service television commercial encouraging people to make a particular lifestyle choice. For example, you might encourage people to stop smoking, practice safe sex, avoid drugs, pursue an education, or develop an exercise program.

Hold the Fries.
Hey, Not All of Them!

▶ **Marian Burros**

Marian Burros is a well-known cookbook author and journalist for the New York Times. *She often writes about health and food-related issues. In this essay she discusses changes that restaurants and food companies are making in their products and explores the companies' motivation for making such changes. The article first appeared in the* New York Times *on March 10, 2004.*

Journal Writing

Write a journal entry describing your habits and attitudes toward fast food consumption.

Reading Strategy

In this article, the author identifies several reasons why restaurants and food companies have decided to promote healthier images. As you read, highlight each reason. Which of these is most likely to be motivating the change?

Vocabulary Preview

edicts (2) orders or commands
looming (2) coming into sight in an impressively great or
              exaggerated form
castigated (7) severely criticized
churlish (7) difficult to deal with

Add Morgan Spurlock to the list of those eager to take credit for the   1
McDonald's Corporation's decision to discontinue its supersize soft drinks and French fries. In his new movie, *Super Size Me,* Mr. Spurlock documents his 30-day diet of nothing but McDonald's food and his gain of 25 pounds. But responsibility for the changes that restaurants and food companies are making to improve the nutrition of their products is also claimed by groups like the Center for Science in the Public Interest, which has criticized fast-food restaurants for years, saying

their food is unhealthy, and lawyers for people who claim in lawsuits that fast food made them fat.

The companies deny that such criticism has anything to do with 2 their decisions to reduce portions, improve labeling, remove trans fatty acids from chips and crackers or offer cookies and ice cream with fewer calories and hamburgers and pizzas with less fat. "I think what's driven this is consumer demand, not government edicts or lawsuits," said Steven Anderson, president and chief executive of the National Restaurant Association. Not everyone in the food business agrees. In a letter to the industry publication *Nation's Restaurant News*, Jim Funk, the chief executive of the Louisiana Restaurant Association, called the criticisms and potential lawsuits "looming threats."

Whether prompted by consumer demand or regulatory threat, 3 changes are occurring. Two bills before Congress would require restaurants to provide diners with nutritional information about meals. Last week, Ruby Tuesday announced that in April it would become the first chain to provide such information on menus in its 700 casual-dining locations. The amounts of fat, calories, net carbohydrates and fiber will be provided for every dish. "Instead of saying you can't give full nutrition information, we saw this as a way to get ahead of our competition," said Sandy Beall, founder and chief executive. McDonald's has begun providing similar information on tray liners in its Maine stores. "We have been very responsive and responsible," said Walt Riker, a McDonald's spokesman.

In two years, the Food and Drug Administration will require companies to list how much trans fatty acid is in their products. That won't exactly be a selling point, since scientists say that trans fats are at least as bad for the heart as saturated fats, and possibly worse. Some companies are taking the next step and removing trans fatty acids. Frito-Lay is taking them out of its Doritos, Tostitos, Santitas and Chee-tos. (Its potato chips, it says, never had trans fats.) "When we learned from the scientific community that trans fats were as bad or worse than saturated fat," said Lynn Markley, a spokeswoman for Frito-Lay, "we took action by eliminating them from our core products."

Kraft has already begun to remove trans fats from Triscuits and in 5 the coming weeks will begin distributing a new line of Oreos, Chips Ahoy, Cheese Nips and Wheat Thins without trans fatty acids. Nancy Daigler, a spokeswoman for Kraft, said the company acted in response to a National Academy of Sciences study concluding that trans fats raise low-density lipoproteins, the bad cholesterol. "In general," Ms. Daigler said, "we are responding to overall growing focus by consumers on health and wellness."

The increase in low-carb items is clearly a result of consumer demand, but most scientists question how healthful some of them are. A double cheeseburger wrapped in lettuce still has as much fat and saturated fat as it would inside a bun. But low-carb dieters care little about calories and fat.

The elimination of supersizes by McDonald's has won qualified praise from its critics. Michael Jacobson, executive director of the Center for Science in the Public Interest, which has castigated fast-food restaurants for years, citing their high-fat, high-calorie food and their resistance to nutrition labeling, said that the removal of the seven-ounce, 610-calorie supersize French fries from menus still leaves a six-ounce, 540-calorie serving, and the removal of the 42-ounce supersize soft drink leaves a 32-ounce drink with 310 calories. But Mr. Jacobson added, "I don't want to be churlish, because I think it's good that McDonald's is dropping these products."

Richard Martin, a longtime observer of the industry, says that whatever McDonald's reasons for removing the supersizes, such a decision is never simple. "You don't know if their actions were to deflect criticism from nutrition activists and anti-obesity critics or something more calculated," said Mr. Martin, the managing editor of *Nation's Restaurant News*. Sales of French fries, he noted, have been way down, perhaps because they are not on anyone's low-carb diet, perhaps because they contain trans fatty acids or maybe even because they have French in the name. "So maybe it's a losing battle," he said. "Supersizing has been a lightning rod for criticism, and maybe McDonald's figures, 'Let's neutralize this,' but they wouldn't do something just to blunt criticism—there is a strategic advantage in this somehow."

McDonald's says its motive is quite simple: supersizes haven't been selling well. "Supersize fries were a slow-moving item," Mr. Riker said. "Certainly sales of supersize soft drinks were nowhere near the sales of other drinks." Dr. Marion Nestle, former chairwoman of the department of food studies and public health at New York University, said that even though plenty of large portions will remain, "added together, McDonald's action could amount to an important change and a step in the right direction with people becoming more accustomed to smaller-size portions again." "If people want to be smaller," Dr. Nestle said, "they have to eat smaller amounts."

While the food industry is trying to promote a more healthful image, that effort is often undercut by its simultaneous addition of new higher-fat, higher-calorie items. The Subway restaurant chain, which features seven sandwiches with less than six grams of total fat, has now added wraps that, while low in carbohydrates, contain bacon, cheese and nine grams of saturated fat—almost half the recommended daily allowance. Burger King, unhappy with sales of its new low-fat fire-roasted chicken on a baguette, has increased the size of the baguette and added a version called Chicken Caesar Club with bacon, Caesar dressing and Parmesan cheese, raising the fat to 14 grams from 5. In the next several weeks Kraft will introduce Oreos without the filling in

100-calorie single-serving packs. It had previously introduced Oreos that are frosted as well as filled—each with 110 calories, twice as many as in the original cookie.

Examining the Reading

Finding Meaning

1. Why have groups like the Center for Science in the Public Interest criticized fast food restaurants?
2. Why has Ruby Tuesday decided to provide nutritional information about its meals?
3. Why are companies deciding to remove trans fatty acids from some products?
4. Explain what is meant by the phrase "Supersizing has been a lightning rod for criticism."
5. According to Dr. Marion Nestle, what do people need to do to lose weight?
6. How is the fast food industry undercutting its own efforts to promote healthier food choices?

Understanding Technique

1. The author frequently uses quotations from experts in the industry in her article. What effect do the quotations have?
2. Why do you think the author concludes her article with three examples of companies that are introducing less healthy food alternatives?
3. The author mentions Morgan Spurlock's movie *Super Size Me* at the beginning of the essay. Is this an effective way of introducing the topic?
4. Explain the meaning of the title and evaluate its effectiveness.

Thinking Critically

1. What are the advantages for food companies and restaurants of offering nutritional information? What are the disadvantages?
2. Do you think the government should regulate food content? Why or why not?
3. What effect might the availability of nutritional information about menu items have on diners' choices?
4. Do you think people should be allowed to sue restaurants or food companies for making them overweight or unhealthy? Why or why not?

Writing About the Reading

A Paragraph

1. Brainstorm a list of the factors that people consider when they make food choices. Write a paragraph explaining which factors are most influential in your own food selections.
2. Write a paragraph that explains the popularity of fast food restaurant chains such as Burger King and McDonald's. Explain why people eat there.

An Essay

1. The article mentions the low-carb dieting trend and the many products the food industry is offering to people who are adopting this lifestyle. What other diets have been popular in the past? Have they been successful? Write an essay about dieting trends or fads. Include your own or others' experiences.
2. Substances such as marijuana and cocaine are illegal in the United States because the government has determined that these substances are harmful to people's health and well-being. However, cigarettes, alcohol, and unhealthy foods are available to adults in most communities. Explain why you think some unhealthy products continue to be offered to the public and other products are banned.

A Creative Activity

Obtain nutritional information from a fast food restaurant. Create a brochure explaining how a person can occasionally eat at the restaurant and still maintain a healthy lifestyle.

The Gift of Sacrifice

▶ **Blanca Matute**
Student Essay

*In this essay, a young woman describes a childhood decision to
leave her parents and move to the United States. Matute wrote
this essay while she was a student at college.*

When we make decisions, we have to live with the consequences.   1
Hopefully, we like the decisions and are grateful that we made them,
but in some cases, we regret the decision. Unfortunately, we cannot go
back in time and change our original choice, even though the decision
we made put us in a difficult or challenging position. Eight years ago,
I learned that when a person makes a decision, he or she must stick
with the choice and persevere.

When I was ten years old, I made a decision that greatly affected   2
my life. I had to decide whether to move to the United States to continue my education or stay in Honduras with my family. The idea of
studying in the United States sounded like a wonderful opportunity,
but it meant growing up without my mother's constant presence and
guidance. I decided to leave my mother in Honduras with the rest of
my family to journey to New York to pursue a better education. My
family supported this decision because they knew it was a good opportunity for me. They were also sad because I would be away for
many years.

I came to the United States because I believed it was going to make   3
a difference in my life. At first I found it difficult to understand how my
family expected me to get a good education without my mother's support. In the beginning, I regretted my decision to come to this country.
Adjusting to the different languages, the diverse cultures, and the
crowded surroundings was an enormous challenge. With the help of
the family I lived with, my sisters and their mother, I worked hard to
adjust to my new life. I still, however, missed my mother.

As time passed, I was often sad because I had not seen my mother   4
for many years. I doubted my decision and questioned my mother's
motives for encouraging me to come to the United States. At times, I
felt as if my life was over because I thought that she had just wanted to
get rid of me. Eventually, I learned that I had made the right decision

and that my mother had supported it because she loved me. I realized that our separation had been just as difficult for her as it had been for me. Because of her love for me, she was willing to let me go so that I could have better opportunities in life. Ultimately, she taught me an important lesson in life, the gift of sacrifice.

As I became accustomed to my new life, many wonderful things 5 began to happen; I learned a new language; I made new friends; I started to do well in school. Because of my academic achievement, I represented my junior high school at various assemblies in New York State. For example, I traveled to upstate New York as a school representative to receive an award for my school's having the best bilingual program in the public schools' twelfth district.

In 1990, I was awarded a scholarship to Aquinas High School for 6 high achievement in junior high school, and I was selected to participate in the Student/Sponsor Partnership Program. This program sponsors academically gifted students through high school. At Aquinas I met teachers who really cared about their students' education. A new world opened up to me. I joined the Spanish Club, the Math Club, the String Ensemble, where I learned to play the viola, and the Concert Band, where I played the clarinet. I became class president in my senior year.

Each time I wrote my mother to tell her how well I was doing, she 7 wrote back expressing her pride in me and my accomplishments. Even in my second year at Aquinas, when my grades were not as good as they could have been, my mother was still proud of me. With the help of a special teacher at Aquinas and hard work, I was able to bring my grades back up again. Now, I look back on all I have learned and what I have accomplished since I left Honduras and my mother eight years ago. It seems impossible that I ever regretted my decision to come to the United States.

I have learned that making a decision can sometimes lead to happiness and sometimes to sadness; in my case it led to both. At first I regretted coming to this country, but now I see that I made the right decision. It gave me not only a chance for a good education, but also a good opportunity to succeed in life. Even though I still miss my mother, I know that she is happy and proud to know of my college plans. I look to the future with awe and excitement.

Examining the Essay

1. How did Matute organize her ideas?
2. In which paragraph(s) do you think more detail is needed?
3. Evaluate the author's use of descriptive language—words that help you visualize and imagine people, places, or objects.

Writing an Essay

1. In "The Gift of Sacrifice," Matute describes the sacrifice that her mother made for her. Write an essay evaluating a sacrifice you made or one that was made for you. Was it worth it?

2. In leaving Honduras, Matute faced numerous challenges and difficult situations, including learning a new language, meeting new friends, and so forth. Write an essay discussing a difficult situation you faced and how you handled it.

 ## Making Connections

1. Both Matute in "The Gift of Sacrifice" and Dickman in "Saying Good-bye to Eric" make a decision and experience its consequences. Write an essay comparing the type of decisions they made and the importance and possible outcomes of these decisions.

2. Some decisions take longer than others to make. Examine the role that time plays in the decision-making process described in Dawson and Glaubman's "Life Is So Good" and Cunningham's "The Chosen One."

3. Cunningham in "The Chosen One," Dickman in "Saying Good-bye to Eric," and Matute in "The Gift of Sacrifice" face difficult decisions. Compare how each author made her decision. Was it primarily rational or emotional? Was it well thought out or impulsive, and is one approach better than the other? Why or why not?

 ## Internet Connections

1. Examine the "25 Facts About Organ Donation and Transplantation" at the National Kidney Foundation's web site **http://www.kidney.org/general/news/factsheet.cfm?id= 30.** Write a paragraph evaluating the effectiveness of this list. Which facts lead to the most compelling reasons for organ donation?

2. On the web site of the National Adoption Information Clearinghouse (**http://naic.acf.hhs.gov/parents/crisis/cfm**) there is a fact sheet about "adopting children from areas of cri-

sis or disaster." Evaluate the recommendations made there. Are the reasons for not adopting these children convincing? Why or why not?

3. Visit this site, which lists the steps to making decisions: **http://www.selfhelpmagazine.com/articles/growth/ decisionmaking.html.** Write an essay evaluating your own decision-making process. Do you have a system? How well does it work for you? Do you use any of the steps outlined at the web site you just visited? What is the most important decision you have had to make?

(If any of these web sites are unavailable, use a search engine to locate another appropriate site.)

Chapter 2

Events That Shape Our Lives

Many daily events—conversations, meals, classes, purchases, interactions with friends—seem important at the time but are not particularly memorable in the long term. Occasionally, however, a single event will make a difference and leave a lasting impression. It may be a landmark event, such as meeting your future spouse, getting a job, playing in a big game, celebrating a big birthday in a notable way, or receiving an important prize or award. Or perhaps something happened to your health that led you to make a change in your habits or behavior.

Other times, it may be a much smaller, more ordinary, and seemingly less significant event that has a dramatic or meaningful effect on the direction of your life or contributes to making you who you are. For example, the first time you picked up a guitar or heard a piano, you may have realized that you wanted to be a musician. One friend's frank comment might have caused you to reexamine your priorities and decide to pursue a more practical way to make a living. But another friend might have encouraged you to work hard at your music, and you could go on to have a successful recording career. Watching children play on a playground might help you realize that having a child must be an important part of your future plans.

The selections in this chapter describe how events, both large and small, both chance and planned, can have a shaping effect on people's lives. Each reading will help give you a perspective on the importance of events in the human experience. You will read about encounters with birth ("A Letter to My Daughter") and death ("Desert Storm and Shield"). You'll also read about how an academic award shaped a young girl's attitude toward the world ("The Scholarship Jacket") and how a date chosen for a marriage ceremony connects the bridegroom to his past ("Breaking Glass"). You'll read about an important event in a blind man's life ("Blind to Faith") and a young black man's experience with an incident of racial profiling ("Ragtime, My Time"). You will also read about a psychological reaction to an event that has changed the lives of many people—the terrorist attacks of September 11, 2001 ("Naked Terror").

Brainstorming About Events

Class Activities:

1. Working in groups of three or four, list events that are *supposed* to be memorable (graduations, birthdays, etc.).
2. Prepare a second list, including only events that made a difference in your life.
3. Compare the two lists. How frequently does the same event appear on both lists?
4. Discuss conclusions that can be drawn.

The Scholarship Jacket

▸ Marta Salinas

This fictional story describes a young girl's experience in which she struggles to receive an award she has earned. The essay was reprinted from Cuentos Chicanos: A Short Story Anthology.

Journal Writing

1. Write a journal entry exploring your attitudes about winning games, prizes, or awards. Is this important to you? Why or why not?
2. Write a journal entry that identifies and explains a time in your life when you were cheated out of something you deserved.

Reading Strategy

When reading short stories such as this one, try to identify the following elements:

- Setting—Where and when does the story take place?
- Characters—Who are the important people involved in the story?
- Point of view—Through whose eyes is the story being told?
- Plot—What major events occur?
- Theme—What is the meaning of the story? What is its message?

Vocabulary Preview

agile (2) coordinated; easy in movement
eavesdrop (4) listen secretly
rooted (4) held uncontrollably; firmly established
filtered (7) passed through
fidgeted (8) moved about nervously
muster (12) gather
mesquite (15) a spiny plant with sweet pods
gaunt (25) extremely thin
vile (29) foul; repulsive
adrenaline (31) a hormone secreted by the body, causing the stimulation of heart action and an increase in blood pressure

*T*he small Texas school that I attended carried out a tradition every   1
year during the eighth grade graduation; a beautiful gold and green
jacket, the school colors, was awarded to the class valedictorian, the
student who had maintained the highest grades for eight years. The
scholarship jacket had a big gold **S** on the left front side and the win-
ner's name was written in gold letters on the pocket.

My oldest sister Rosie had won the jacket a few years back and I   2
fully expected to win also. I was fourteen and in the eighth grade. I had
been a straight A student since the first grade, and the last year I had
looked forward to owning that jacket. My father was a farm laborer
who couldn't earn enough money to feed eight children, so when I was
six I was given to my grandparents to raise. We couldn't participate in
sports at school because there were registration fees, uniform costs,
and trips out of town; so even though we were quite agile and athletic,
there would never be a sports school jacket for us. This one, the scholarship jacket, was our only chance.

In May, close to graduation, spring fever struck, and no one paid   3
any attention in class; instead we stared out the windows and at each
other, wanting to speed up the last few weeks of school. I despaired
every time I looked in the mirror. Pencil thin, not a curve anywhere, I
was called "Beanpole" and "String Bean" and I knew that's what I
looked like. A flat chest, no hips, and a brain, that's what I had. That
really isn't much for a fourteen-year-old to work with, I thought, as I
absentmindedly wandered from my history class to the gym. Another
hour of sweating in basketball and displaying my toothpick legs was
coming up. Then I remembered my P.E. shorts were still in a bag under my desk where I'd forgotten them. I had to walk all the way back
and get them. Coach Thompson was a real bear if anyone wasn't
dressed for P.E. She had said I was a good forward and once she even
tried to talk Grandma into letting me join the team. Grandma, of
course, said no.

I was almost back at my classroom's door when I heard angry   4
voices and arguing. I stopped. I didn't mean to eavesdrop; I just hesi-
tated, not knowing what to do. I needed those shorts and I was going
to be late, but I didn't want to interrupt an argument between my
teachers. I recognized the voices: Mr. Schmidt, my history teacher, and
Mr. Boone, my math teacher. They seemed to be arguing about me. I
couldn't believe it. I still remember the shock that rooted me flat against
the wall as if I were trying to blend in with the graffiti written there.

"I refuse to do it! I don't care who her father is, her grades don't   5
even begin to compare to Marta's. I won't lie or falsify records. Marta

has a straight A plus average and you know it." That was Mr. Schmidt and he sounded very angry. Mr. Boone's voice sounded calm and quiet.

"Look, Joann's father is not only on the Board, he owns the only   6
store in town; we could say it was a close tie and—"

The pounding in my ears drowned out the rest of the words, only a   7
word here and there filtered through. ". . . Marta is Mexican. . . . re-
sign. . . . won't do it. . . ." Mr. Schmidt came rushing out, and luckily
for me went down the opposite way toward the auditorium, so he
didn't see me. Shaking, I waited a few minutes and then went in and
grabbed my bag and fled from the room. Mr. Boone looked up when I
came in but didn't say anything. To this day I don't remember if I got
in trouble in P.E. for being late or how I made it through the rest of the
afternoon. I went home very sad and cried into my pillow that night so
Grandmother wouldn't hear me. It seemed a cruel coincidence that I
had overheard that conversation.

The next day when the principal called me into his office, I knew   8
what it would be about. He looked uncomfortable and unhappy. I decided I wasn't going to make it any easier for him so I looked him straight
in the eye. He looked away and fidgeted with the papers on his desk.

"Marta," he said, "there's been a change in policy this year regarding   9
the scholarship jacket. As you know, it has always been free." He cleared
his throat and continued. "This year the Board decided to charge fifteen dollars—which still won't cover the complete cost of the jacket."

I stared at him in shock and a small sound of dismay escaped my   10
throat. I hadn't expected this. He still avoided looking in my eyes.

"So if you are unable to pay the fifteen dollars for the jacket, it will   11
be given to the next one in line."

Standing with all the dignity I could muster, I said, "I'll speak to my   12
grandfather about it, sir, and let you know tomorrow." I cried on the
walk home from the bus stop. The dirt road was a quarter of a mile from
the highway, so by the time I got home, my eyes were red and puffy.

"Where's Grandpa?" I asked Grandma, looking down at the floor so   13
she wouldn't ask me why I'd been crying. She was sewing on a quilt
and didn't look up.

"I think he's out back working in the bean field."   14

I went outside and looked out at the fields. There he was. I could   15
see him walking between the rows, his body bent over the little plants,
hoe in hand. I walked slowly out to him, trying to think how I could
best ask him for the money. There was a cool breeze blowing and a
sweet smell of mesquite in the air, but I didn't appreciate it. I kicked at
a dirt clod. I wanted that jacket so much. It was more than just being a
valedictorian and giving a little thank you speech for the jacket on
graduation night. It represented eight years of hard work and expecta-

tion. I knew I had to be honest with Grandpa; it was my only chance. He saw me and looked up.

He waited for me to speak. I cleared my throat nervously and clasped my hands behind my back so he wouldn't see them shaking. "Grandpa, I have a big favor to ask you," I said in Spanish, the only language he knew. He still waited silently. I tried again. "Grandpa, this year the principal said the scholarship jacket is not going to be free. It's going to cost fifteen dollars and I have to take the money in tomorrow, otherwise it'll be given to someone else." The last words came out in an eager rush. Grandpa straightened up tiredly and leaned his chin on the hoe handle. He looked out over the field that was filled with the tiny green bean plants. I waited, desperately hoping he'd say I could have the money.   16

He turned to me and asked quietly, "What does a scholarship jacket mean?"   17

I answered quickly; maybe there was a chance. "It means you've earned it by having the highest grades for eight years and that's why they're giving it to you." Too late I realized the significance of my words. Grandpa knew that I understood it was not a matter of money. It wasn't that. He went back to hoeing the weeds that sprang up between the delicate little bean plants. It was a time consuming job; sometimes the small shoots were right next to each other. Finally he spoke again.   18

"Then if you pay for it, Marta, it's not a scholarship jacket, is it? Tell your principal I will not pay the fifteen dollars."   19

I walked back to the house and locked myself in the bathroom for a long time. I was angry with Grandfather even though I knew he was right, and I was angry with the Board, whoever they were. Why did they have to change the rules just when it was my turn to win the jacket?   20

It was a very sad and withdrawn girl who dragged into the principal's office the next day. This time he did look me in the eyes.   21

"What did your grandfather say?"   22

I sat very straight in my chair.   23

"He said to tell you he won't pay the fifteen dollars."   24

The principal muttered something I couldn't understand under his breath, and walked over to the window. He stood looking out at something outside. He looked bigger than usual when he stood up; he was a tall gaunt man with gray hair, and I watched the back of his head while I waited for him to speak.   25

"Why?" he finally asked. "Your grandfather has the money. Doesn't he own a small bean farm?"   26

I looked at him, forcing my eyes to stay dry. "He said if I had to pay for it, then it wouldn't be a scholarship jacket," I said and stood up to   27 leave. "I guess you'll just have to give it to Joann." I hadn't meant to say that; it had just slipped out. I was almost to the door when he stopped me.

"Marta —wait."   28

I turned and looked at him, waiting. What did he want now? I   29
could feel my heart pounding. Something bitter and vile tasting was coming up in my mouth; I was afraid I was going to be sick. I didn't need any sympathy speeches. He sighed loudly and went back to his big desk. He looked at me, biting his lip, as if thinking.

"Okay, damn it. We'll make an exception in your case. I'll tell the   30
Board, you'll get your jacket."

I could hardly believe it. I spoke in a trembling rush. "Oh, thank   31
you, sir!" Suddenly I felt great. I didn't know about adrenaline in those days, but I knew something was pumping through me, making me feel as tall as the sky. I wanted to yell, jump, run the mile, do something. I ran out so I could cry in the hall where there was no one to see me. At the end of the day, Mr. Schmidt winked at me and said, "I hear you're getting a scholarship jacket this year."

His face looked as happy and innocent as a baby's, but I knew bet-   32
ter. Without answering I gave him a quick hug and ran to the bus. I cried on the walk home again, but this time because I was so happy. I couldn't wait to tell Grandpa and ran straight to the field. I joined him in the row where he was working and without saying anything I crouched down and started pulling up the weeds with my hands. Grandpa worked alongside me for a few minutes, but he didn't ask what had happened. After I had a little pile of weeds between the rows, I stood up and faced him.

"The principal said he's making an exception for me, Grandpa, and   33
I'm getting the jacket after all. That's after I told him what you said."

Grandpa didn't say anything, he just gave me a pat on the shoulder   34
and a smile. He pulled out the crumpled red handkerchief that he always carried in his back pocket and wiped the sweat off his forehead.

"Better go see if your grandmother needs any help with supper."   35

I gave him a big grin. He didn't fool me. I skipped and ran back to   36
the house whistling some silly tune.

Examining the Reading

Finding Meaning

1. Why didn't the author participate in school sports, although she was athletic?
2. What were Marta's two teachers arguing about?

3. Why did Marta's grandfather refuse to give her the money for the scholarship jacket?
4. What kind of a person was Marta's grandfather?
5. Why did Marta's math teacher, Mr. Boone, want the scholarship jacket to go to another student?

Understanding Technique

1. Discuss Salinas's use of dialogue. What purpose does it serve in the story?
2. What is the theme of the story?

Thinking Critically

1. Why do you think the Board decided to charge for the scholarship jacket?
2. Why do you think the principal changed his mind about charging Marta for the jacket?
3. Discuss the character differences between Marta's teachers.
4. After Marta told her grandfather she was getting the scholarship jacket, what did she mean when she said his reaction "didn't fool me"?

Writing About the Reading

A Paragraph

1. The author implied that Mr. Schmidt, her history teacher, was willing to quit his job if Marta did not receive the scholarship jacket that was rightfully hers. Suppose you were Mr. Schmidt: would you have been willing to quit your job over the issue of fairness? Write a paragraph stating and defending your decision.
2. Suppose you were in a position to win a game or contest and then realized that someone else was about to win it unfairly. Write a paragraph describing how you would handle the situation.

An Essay

1. The author became so anxious while talking to her principal that she was afraid she was going to become sick. Write an essay describing a situation in your life that caused you the same level of anxiety and explain how you resolved it.
2. The awarding of the scholarship jacket is a memorable event illustrating a choice between right and wrong that the author recalls from her childhood. Write an essay recalling such an event from

your childhood, and explain how it affected you and whether it ended happily or not.

A Creative Activity

Suppose the principal had decided not to make an exception for Marta. How might she have felt? What, if anything, might she say to Joann? What might her grandfather say? Rewrite the ending of the story, answering the above questions.

Ragtime, My Time

▸ Alton Fitzgerald White

An African-American actor living in Harlem describes being unfairly arrested by police. This article first appeared in The Nation *in 1999.*

Journal Writing

Describe a time when you were victimized because of your age, sex, or social status (as a student, as a teenager) or your tastes or preferences. Describe your emotions and how you handled the situation.

Reading Strategy

The author tells his story chronologically. As you read, create a time line of his experiences.

Vocabulary Preview

naïvely (2) innocently; simply
ovation (3) thunderous applause
portraying (3) representing in a play; playing the part of
overt (4) plain to see; not hidden
charismatic (4) ability to arouse attraction
splurged (5) indulged in something extravagant
vestibule (5) entrance hall
acknowledging (7) recognizing someone's existence
ailing (8) sick; needing care
residue (9) remainder; trace amount
ordeal (10) difficult experience
pseudo (15) fake; false

*A*s the youngest of five girls and two boys growing up in Cincinnati, I   1
was raised to believe that if I worked hard, was a good person, and always told the truth, the world would be my oyster.[1] I was raised to be a gentleman and learned that these qualities would bring me respect.

---

[1] A place where great opportunities open up.

While one has to earn respect, consideration is something owed to   2
every human being. On Friday, June 16, 1999, when I was wrongfully
arrested at my Harlem apartment building, my perception of everything I had learned as a young man was forever changed—not only because I wasn't given even a second to use the manners my parents
taught me, but mostly because the police, whom I'd always naïvely
thought were supposed to serve and protect me, were actually hunting me.

I had planned a pleasant day. The night before was payday, plus I   3
had received a standing ovation after portraying the starring role of
Coalhouse Walker Jr. in the Broadway musical *Ragtime*. It is a role that
requires not only talent but also an honest emotional investment of the
morals and lessons I learned as a child.

Coalhouse Walker Jr. is a victim (an often misused word, but in   4
this case true) of overt racism. His story is every black man's nightmare. He is hard-working, successful, talented, charismatic, friendly,
and polite. Perfect prey for someone with authority and not even a
fraction of those qualities. On that Friday afternoon, I became a real-
life Coalhouse Walker. Nothing could have prepared me for it. Not
even stories told to me by other black men who had suffered similar
injustices.

Friday for me usually means a trip to the bank, errands, the gym,   5
dinner, and then off to the theater. On this particular day, I decided to
break my pattern of getting up and running right out of the house. Instead, I took my time, slowed my pace, and splurged by making strawberry pancakes. Before I knew it, it was 2:45; my bank closes at 3:30,
leaving me less than 45 minutes to get to midtown Manhattan on the
train. I was pressed for time but in a relaxed, blessed state of mind.
When I walked through the lobby of my building, I noticed two light-
skinned Hispanic men I'd never seen before. Not thinking much of it, I
continued on to the vestibule, which is separated from the lobby by a
locked door.

As I approached the exit, I saw people in uniforms rushing toward   6
the door. I sped up to open it for them. I thought they might be paramedics, since many of the building's occupants are elderly. It wasn't
until I had opened the door and greeted them that I recognized that
they were police officers. Within seconds, I was told to "hold it"; they
had received a call about young Hispanics with guns. I was told to get
against the wall. I was searched, stripped of my backpack, put on my
knees, handcuffed, and told to be quiet when I tried to ask questions.

With me were three other innocent black men who had been on   7
their way to their U-Haul. They were moving into the apartment beneath mine, and I had just bragged to them about how safe the building was. One of these gentlemen got off his knees, still handcuffed, and

unlocked the door for the officers to get into the lobby where the two strangers were standing. Instead of thanking or even acknowledging us, they led us out the door past our neighbors, who were all but begging the police in our defense.

The four of us were put into cars with the two strangers and taken to the precinct station at 165th and Amsterdam. The police automatically linked us, with no questions and no regard for our character or our lives. No consideration was given to where we were going or why. Suppose an ailing relative was waiting upstairs, while I ran out for her medication? Or young children, who'd been told that Daddy was running to the corner store for milk and would be right back? My new neighbors weren't even allowed to lock their apartment or check on the U-Haul. 8

After we were lined up in the station, the younger of the two Hispanic men was identified as an experienced criminal, and drug residue was found in a pocket of the other. I now realize how naïve I was to think that the police would then uncuff me, apologize for their mistake, and let me go. Instead, they continued to search my backpack, questioned me, and put me in jail with the criminals. 9

The rest of the nearly five-hour ordeal was like a horrible dream. I was handcuffed, strip-searched, taken in and out for questioning. The officers told me that they knew exactly who I was, knew I was in *Ragtime*, and that in fact they already had the men they wanted. 10

How then could they keep me there, or have brought me there in the first place? I was told it was standard procedure. As if the average law-abiding citizen knows what that is and can dispute it. From what I now know, "standard procedure" is something that every citizen, black and white, needs to learn, and fast. 11

I felt completely powerless. Why, do you think? Here I was, young, pleasant, and successful, in good physical shape, dressed in clean athletic attire. I was carrying a backpack containing a substantial paycheck and a deposit slip, on my way to the bank. Yet after hours and hours I was sitting at a desk with two officers who not only couldn't tell me why I was there but seemed determined to find something on me, to the point of making me miss my performance. 12

It was because I am a black man! 13

I sat in that cell crying silent tears of disappointment and injustice 14
with the realization of how many innocent black men are convicted for no reason. When I was handcuffed, my first instinct had been to pull away out of pure insult and violation as a human being. Thank God I was calm enough to do what they said. When I was thrown in jail with the criminals and strip-searched, I somehow knew to put my pride aside, be quiet, and do exactly what I was told, hating it but coming to terms with the fact that in this situation I was a victim. They had guns!

Before I was finally let go, exhausted, humiliated, embarrassed, 15 and still in shock, I was led to a room and given a pseudo-apology. I was told that I was at the wrong place at the wrong time. My reply? "I was where I live."

Everything I learned growing up in Cincinnati has been shattered.   16
Life will never be the same.

Examining the Reading

Finding Meaning

1. According to White, how does one earn respect?
2. Why did White think paramedics were coming to his building?
3. Who was finally identified as a criminal that day?
4. What reason did the police give for bringing White to the police station?
5. What was White's reaction to being handcuffed? How did he instinctively want to react?
6. How did White feel about the apology that the police finally gave him?

Understanding Technique

1. Describe how this essay is organized.
2. The author uses many descriptive details in this personal account. Highlight some that are particularly revealing and explain what they add to the story.
3. White compares himself with Coalhouse Walker Jr. How does this comparison contribute to the story?
4. The author uses many short descriptive sentences. How effective is this style?

Thinking Critically

1. Predict what would have happened if White had been Caucasian and in the same place at the same time. Give evidence to support your prediction.
2. Why didn't White's manners help him the day he was arrested?
3. The author writes that *victim* is an "often misused word." What does he mean?
4. What does the author mean when he describes Coalhouse Walker Jr. as "perfect prey for someone with authority"?
5. What factors should the police have taken into account?
6. In what ways will life never be the same for the author?

Writing About the Reading

A Paragraph

1. Write a paragraph describing a time when your actions were misunderstood or you were wrongly accused.
2. The incident shattered the lessons that White learned during his childhood. Write a paragraph describing a childhood belief that you have discovered is no longer true.
3. Write a paragraph describing a situation in which you had to put your pride aside and accept an unpleasant situation.

An Essay

1. Write an essay exploring the issue of racial profiling. First, define the issue, and then outline the points on which police, minorities, and other citizens agree and those on which they disagree.
2. White's concept of earning respect and receiving fair treatment was changed dramatically by this incident. Write an essay describing a situation that changed your attitudes or perceptions.
3. Power can corrupt. Write an essay discussing what actions might be taken to prevent police from abusing their power.
4. Write an essay describing a situation in which you felt completely powerless or in which you felt victimized.

A Creative Activity

Imagine you are a police officer in the essay. Describe why you behaved as you did.

A Letter to My Daughter

▸ **Siu Wai Anderson**

This letter, written by a mother to her infant daughter, discusses issues of cross-cultural adoptions. It was first published in an anthology of writings by women of color: Making Face, Making Soul.

Journal Writing

Write a journal entry exploring the issue of cross-cultural adoptions. How do children benefit? What problems do they face?

Reading Strategy

Anderson uses a personal letter to describe her ancestry and express her feelings toward her daughter. As you read, think about why Anderson uses the letter format. What advantages does it give her as a writer?

Vocabulary Preview

auspicious (1) favorable
travail (1) painful work; childbirth
demographical (3) conforming to the average of the
                              population
proverbial (3) as in a popular saying or proverb
legacy (3) inheritance
agonizing (4) extremely painful
ancestral (5) having to do with forebears
hail (7) welcome
deprivation (7) being kept from having
lavishing (10) giving abundantly

August 1989, Boston

Dear Maya Shao-ming,

You were born at Mt. Auburn Hospital in Cambridge on June 6, 1989, 1
an auspicious date, and for me, the end of a long, long travail. Because
you insisted on being breech, with your head always close to my heart,
you came into the world by C-section into a chilly O.R. at the opposite

end of the labor and delivery suite where, exhausted yet exuberant, I pushed out your brother in a birthing room nearly four years ago.

I couldn't believe my ears when your father exclaimed, "A girl!" All I could do was cry the tears of a long-awaited dream come true. You are so beautiful, with your big dark eyes and silky black hair. Your skin is more creamy than golden, reflecting your particular "happa haole" blend. But your long elegant fingers are those of a Chinese scholar, prized for high intelligence and sensitivity.

You are more than just a second child, more than just a girl to match our boy, to fit the demographical nuclear family with the proverbial 2.5 children. No, ten years ago I wrote a song for an unborn dream: a dark-haired, dark-eyed child who would be my flesh-and-blood link to humanity. I had no other until your brother came. He was my first Unborn Song. But you, little daughter, are the link to our female line, the legacy of another woman's pain and sacrifice thirty-one years ago.

Let me tell you about your Chinese grandmother. Somewhere in Hong Kong, in the late fifties, a young waitress found herself pregnant by a cook, probably a co-worker at her restaurant. She carried the baby to term, suffered to give it birth, and kept the little girl for the first three months of her life. I like to think that my mother—your grandmother—loved me and fought to raise me on her own, but that the daily struggle was too hard. Worn down by the demands of the new baby and perhaps the constant threat of starvation, she made the agonizing decision to give away her girl so that both of us might have a chance for a better life.

More likely, I was dumped at the orphanage steps or forcibly removed from a home of abuse and neglect by a social welfare worker. I will probably never know the truth. Having a baby in her unmarried state would have brought shame on the family in China, so she probably kept my existence a secret. Once I was out of her life, it was as if I had never been born. And so you and your brother and I are the missing leaves on an ancestral tree.

Do they ever wonder if we exist?

I was brought to the U.S. before I was two, and adopted by the Anglo parents who hail you as their latest beautiful grandchild. Raised by a minister's family in postwar American prosperity and nourished on three square meals a day, I grew like a wild weed and soaked up all the opportunities they had to offer—books, music, education, church life and community activities. Amidst a family of blue-eyed blonds, though, I stood out like a sore thumb. Whether from jealousy or fear of someone who looked so different, my older brothers sometimes tormented me with racist name-calling, teased me about my poor eyesight and unsightly skin, or made fun of my clumsy walk. Moody and impatient, gifted and temperamental, burdened by fears and night-mares that none of us realized stemmed from my early years of depri-vation, I was not an easy child to love. My adoptive mother and I clashed countless times over the years, but gradually came to see one another as real human beings with faults and talents, and as women of strength in our own right. Now we love each other very much, though the scars and memories of our early battles will never quite fade. Lack-ing a mirror image in the mother who raised me, I had to seek my iden-tity as a woman on my own. The Asian American community has helped me reclaim my dual identity and enlightened my view of the struggles we face as minorities in a white-dominated culture. They have applauded my music and praised my writings.

But part of me will always be missing: my beginnings, my personal 8
history, all the subtle details that give a person her origin. I don't know how I was born, whether it was vaginally or by Cesarean. I don't know when, or where exactly, how much I weighed, or whose ears heard my first cry of life. Was I put to my mother's breast and tenderly rocked, or was I simply weighed, cleaned, swaddled and carted off to a sterile nursery, noted in the hospital records as "newborn female"?

Someone took the time to give me a lucky name, and write the ap- 9
propriate characters in neat brush strokes in the Hong Kong city reg-ister. "Siu" means "little." My kind of "wai" means "clever" or "wise." Therefore, my baby name was "Clever little one." Who chose those words? Who cared enough to note my arrival in the world?

I lost my Chinese name for eighteen years. It was Americanized for 10
convenience to "Sue." But like an ill-fitting coat, it made me twitch and fret and squirm. I hated the name. But even more, I hated being Chi-nese. It took many years to become proud of my Asian heritage and work up the courage to take back my birthname. That plus a smatter-ing of classroom Cantonese, are all the Chinese culture I have to offer you, little one. Not white, certainly, but not really Asian, I straddle the two worlds and try to blaze your trails for you. Your name, "Shao-ming," is very much like mine—"Shao" is the Mandarin form of "Siu," meaning "little." And "ming" is "bright," as in a shining sun or moon. Whose lives will you brighten, little Maya? Your past is more complete than mine, and each day I cradle you in your babyhood, lavishing upon you the tender care I lacked for my first two years. When I console you, I com-fort the lost baby inside me who still cries out for her mother. No won-der so many adoptees desperately long to have children of their own.

Sweet Maya, it doesn't matter what you "become" later on. You 11
have already fulfilled my wildest dreams.

I love you,

Mommy

Examining the Reading

Finding Meaning

1. What does the author know about her biological mother?
2. Why did the author's brothers tease her and call her names?
3. Explain Siu Wai's reaction to being called Sue.
4. How does the author feel about her Asian identity?
5. What did the author most want to tell her daughter?

Understanding Technique

1. What type of details does Anderson include to make her essay lively and interesting?
2. Although she describes events, Anderson does not follow a strict chronological sequence. Why doesn't she and what effect does this have?

Thinking Critically

1. As a Chinese female raised by American parents and not knowing her biological mother, the author faced numerous problems in growing up. What kinds of problems do you think these were?
2. It seems to be especially important to the author that she be an excellent mother to her infant daughter. Why do you think this is?
3. What does the author mean at the end of the story when she writes to her daughter, "It doesn't matter what you 'become' later on. You have already fulfilled my wildest dreams"?
4. Suppose the author had given birth to a second son instead of a daughter. Do you think she would have written a letter? If so, how would it differ from the letter to Maya?

Writing About the Reading

A Paragraph

1. If you could see a videotape of one day of your childhood, what day would you choose? Write a paragraph explaining your choice.
2. If you could communicate briefly with only one deceased relative or friend, whom would you choose? Write a paragraph explaining your choice and what you would want to say.

An Essay

1. Write a letter to someone close to you explaining a difficult part of your childhood.

2. Suppose you have just learned that the parents who raised you were not your biological parents. Next week you will meet your biological parents. Write an essay identifying the three most important questions you want to ask them. Explain why each is important. If you are adopted, explain whether you know or want to know your birth parents.

A Creative Activity

Suppose Maya is now 15 years old and has decided to write a letter to her biological grandmother (Siu Wai's biological mother). What do you think she will say? Write the opening paragraph of the letter.

Naked Terror

▶ **Jeffrey Rosen**

In this article, the author describes the psychological reaction of the American public to a terrifying event: the September 11 terrorist attacks on the World Trade Center. The article is adapted from Rosen's book The Naked Crowd: Reclaiming Security and Freedom in an Anxious Age. *It first appeared in the* New York Times Magazine *on January 4, 2004.*

Journal Writing

Write a journal entry explaining how the terrorist attacks of September 11, 2001, have affected your life.

Reading Strategy

This essay can be seen as a call to action. As you read the essay, try to determine what the author wants from the American people.

Vocabulary Preview

disproportionate (1) not properly related in size or amount
concealed (2) hidden
prototype (2) an original model upon which something is patterned
extracts (2) takes out or pulls forth
mundane (4) ordinary, commonplace
purveyors (5) people who supply or provide something
pander (6) to cater to the weaknesses of others
fixates (7) focuses
draconian (7) harsh or cruel

When the Bush administration raised America's antiterrorism alert status from yellow to orange over the holidays, some travelers became anxious, while others took the warning in stride. If and when another attack on American soil occurs, however, everything we know about the psychology of fear suggests that it will lead to extreme public panic that may be disproportionate to the actual casualties. The public responds emotionally to remote but terrifying threats, and this leads us to make choices about security that are not always rational.

After the 9/11 attacks, for example, officials at Orlando International Airport began testing a new security device. Let's call it the Naked Machine, for that's more or less what it is. A kind of electronic strip search, the Naked Machine bounces a low-energy X-ray beam off the human body. In addition to exposing any metal, ceramic or plastic objects that are concealed by clothing, the Naked Machine also produces an anatomically correct naked image of everyone it scrutinizes. The Naked Machine promises a high degree of security, but it demands a high sacrifice of privacy. With a simple programming shift, however, researchers at the Pacific Northwest National Laboratory in Richland, Wash., have built a prototype of a redesigned Naked Machine that extracts the images of concealed objects and projects them onto a sexless mannequin, turning the naked body into an unrecognizable and nondescript blob. This redesigned version of the Naked Machine—let's call it the Blob Machine—guarantees exactly the same amount of security while also protecting privacy.

The choice between the Blob Machine and the Naked Machine might seem to be easy. But in presenting the choice hypothetically to groups of students and adults since 9/11, I've been struck by a surprising pattern: there are always some people who say they would prefer to go through the Naked Machine rather than the Blob Machine. Some say they are already searched so thoroughly at airports that they have abandoned all hope of privacy. Others say those who have nothing to hide should have nothing to fear. But in each group, there are some who say they are so anxious about the possibility of terrorism that they would do anything possible to make themselves feel better. They don't care, in other words, whether or not the Naked Machine makes them safer than the Blob Machine, because they are more concerned about *feeling* safe than being safe.

In their willingness to choose laws and technologies that threaten privacy without bringing more security, the people who prefer the Naked Machine to the Blob Machine are representative of an important strain in public opinion as a whole. When presented with images of terrifying events, people tend to miscalculate their probability. A single memorable image—of the World Trade Center collapsing, for example—will crowd out less visually dramatic risks in the public mind. This explains why people overestimate the frequency of deaths from disasters like floods and fire and underestimate the frequency of deaths from more mundane threats like diabetes and strokes.

How can we protect ourselves from our psychological vulnerabilities? First, we can turn off the TV. A study of psychological responses to the 9/11 found that, two months after the attacks, 17 percent of the American population outside New York City reported symptoms of post-traumatic stress related to 9/11. High levels of stress were especially notable in those who watched a lot of television. This anxiety is only heightened by cable networks, which have converted themselves into 24-hour purveyors of alarm.

But cable TV isn't the only institution of democracy that has an incentive to exaggerate risks. We've seen the temptations for politicians to pass along vague and unconfirmed threats of future violence in order to protect themselves from criticism in the event that another attack materializes. Ultimately, our success in overcoming fear will depend on political leadership that challenges us to live with our uncertainties rather than catering to them. After 9/11, for example, Mayor Rudolph Giuliani understood that the greatest leaders of democracies in earlier wars did not pander to public fears; instead, they challenged citizens to transcend their self-involved anxieties, embracing ideals of liberty and justice larger than themselves. It is hard to imagine Franklin D. Roosevelt instituting a color-coded system of terrorist alerts.

The vicious cycle at this point should be clear. The public fixates on low-probability but vivid risks because of images we absorb from television and from politicians. This cycle fuels the public's demand for draconian and poorly designed laws and technologies to eliminate the risks that are, by their nature, difficult to reduce. We have the ability to resist this dangerous cycle by choosing leaders who will insist on laws and technologies that strike a reasonable balance between freedom and security. What we need now is the will.

Examining the Reading

Finding Meaning

1. Why do people make choices about security that are not always rational?
2. What is the purpose of the Naked Machine?
3. What improvements did researchers at the Pacific Northwest National Laboratory make to the Naked Machine to create the Blob Machine?
4. Why do some people say they would prefer to go through the Naked Machine than the Blob Machine?
5. Why do people overestimate the frequency of deaths from disasters and underestimate the frequency of deaths from more mundane threats?
6. What effect can television watching have on our psychological vulnerabilities?
7. What does the author recommend that Americans do to break the vicious cycle of exaggerating risks?

Understanding Technique

1. Highlight the author's thesis statement.
2. Why does the author introduce the Naked Machine and the Blob Machine? What effect does this information have on the essay?
3. Why does the author provide the results of the study of psychological responses to September 11?
4. Does the author approve of the Bush administration's handling of freedom and security concerns after September 11? Identify sentences or paragraphs that support your answer.
5. Why does the author mention Mayor Rudolph Giuliani and Franklin D. Roosevelt?

Thinking Critically

1. Describe the tone of the article.
2. Identify several national disasters or health problems that pose a continuing threat to U.S. citizens' well-being.
3. What does the author mean when he writes, "The greatest leaders of democracies in earlier wars did not pander to public fears; instead, they challenged citizens to transcend their self-involved anxieties, embracing ideals of liberty and justice larger than themselves"?
4. Give some examples from history of poorly designed laws, technologies, or policies that were adopted.

Writing About the Reading

A Paragraph

1. Write a paragraph describing a situation in which you feel your privacy was violated.
2. Would you prefer to go through the Naked Machine or the Blob Machine? Write a paragraph explaining your reasons.

An Essay

1. Write an essay about a major event in your life. What changes did the event prompt you to make?
2. Describe some changes you would like to see made in American society that would improve our safety and maintain our privacy.
3. Write an essay about one or more effects of the September 11, 2001, terrorist attacks that you have observed or experienced.

A Creative Activity

Imagine a new technology that greatly reduces security risk. Write a short essay describing how the technology works and describing what improvements it will make.

Breaking Glass

▸ Jonathan Rosen

This essay, which was originally published in the New York
Times Magazine *in 1996, explains what a Jewish wedding custom came to mean to the author. He also describes how his wedding anniversary has become linked with his father's past.*

Journal Writing

Write a journal entry about an event in your life or your family's history that you would like people to remember.

Reading Strategy

The writer of this essay switches back and forth in time. After
you read the essay, construct a time line, list, or diagram of the
events in the order in which they occurred.

Vocabulary Preview

pulverizing (2) crushing
symbolic (2) standing for or representing something else
euphoniously euphemistic (3) more pleasant sounding than
                          a more blunt or offensive term
ran amok (3) savagely attacked everyone in their path
eerie (5) weird; strange
perverse (5) odd; offbeat; intentionally in error
pogrom (6) organized massacre or persecution of a minority
          group
obliterating (6) wiping out
commemoration (6) act of honoring the memory of an event
grandiose (8) extremely impressive
naïve (8) innocent; simple

$\mathcal{T}$he morning of my wedding, my father gave me a piece of unexpected   1
advice. "When you step on the glass," he said, "why don't you imagine
that all the doubts and fears of childhood are inside and that you're
smashing them too?"

He was referring to one of the more mysterious customs at a Jew-   2
ish wedding, in which the bridegroom stamps on a glass, marking the

end of the ceremony. I liked my father's suggestion, though I was so afraid that the wineglass, wrapped in a white handkerchief, would shoot out unbroken (as I had once seen happen) that I forgot everything in my pulverizing zeal. But I was touched by his words, particularly because breaking the glass had already assumed a symbolic place in my mind—though one connected not to my own childhood but to his.

I was married on November 10, the anniversary of Kristallnacht. The German name, which means "the night of broken glass," is too euphoniously euphemistic to describe accurately what really happened in 1938, beginning on the night of November 9 and running into the next day. Mobs, urged on by the Nazi Government, ran amok throughout Germany and Austria, murdering, looting, smashing Jewish shop windows and burning synagogues. Thirty thousand Jews were arrested—including my grandfather, my father's father. 3

My father was 14, and Kristallnacht shattered his world. One month later he left Vienna on a children's transport, finding refuge first in Scotland and later in the United States. He never saw his parents again. Strange then, that I chose the anniversary of this terrible day for my wedding five years ago. 4

I cannot claim this was strictly by design. I'd wanted to get married in winter and my wife-to-be had inched the date forward until we settled on November 10. It was my father who pointed out the eerie accident. He did not ask me to change the date, but we easily could have. We had planned a small wedding in my parents' house. But after initial discomfort the coincidence had a distinct, if perverse, appeal. 5

More than 50 years had passed since the pogrom of 1938. The world could not be counted on to remember forever—hadn't I myself forgotten the date? Here was a way to graft my father's story onto my own. Soon the year 2000, with its obliterating zeros, would roll the terrible events of the twentieth century deeper into the past. My wedding would at least guarantee a kind of private commemoration. I would lash a piece of history to my back and carry it with me into the future. 6

But by mingling Kristallnacht with my own wedding, was I preserving it or erasing it further? Perhaps I did not wish to mark the date so much as unmark it—a typical childhood fantasy. I wanted to make whole my father's broken past, to offer up my own wedding as the joyful answer to tragic times.

Both impulses, of course, are equally grandiose and impossibly naïve. My own life can never contain or summarize the suffering of earlier generations, any more than it can answer or redeem those losses. My father understood this when he spoke to me on the morning of my wedding. For all he knew of the world, he could still have for me a father's wish—that I would banish the fears of childhood, even 7 though the fears of *his* childhood were fully founded in real events. Every generation is born innocent, and if that is bad for history, it is nevertheless necessary for life.

And yet how can I stop trying to connect myself in some way to the past? Which brings me back to my wedding and the ritual of the broken glass, which forms the final moment of the traditional Jewish ceremony. There are several explanations for this practice. The one I like is that it is a reminder of the destruction of the temple in Jerusalem— an event that happened some 1,900 years ago—and in a larger sense, a reminder that the world itself is broken and imperfect. Smashing the glass recalls this fact and introduces a fleeting note of sadness into an otherwise festive occasion.   8

It is in this spirit that I celebrate my wedding anniversary today. I think about my grandparents who were murdered and their son—my father—who escaped to America and married my mother. I think about my own lucky American life and joyful marriage and how little, and how much, separates the past from the present, sorrow from celebration. I hear my father's kind advice, the cheerful cries of friends and family and the distant echo of breaking glass.   9

Examining the Reading

Finding Meaning

1. What happened in Germany and Austria, on November 9–10, 1938?
2. What happened to Jonathan Rosen's father and grandparents after Kristallnacht?
3. Why does the bridegroom break a glass at traditional Jewish weddings?
4. What did the author's father want him to think about when he broke the glass?
5. Why didn't the author change his wedding date?

Understanding Technique

1. Discuss the effect of using dialogue to open this essay.
2. Evaluate how Rosen's use of questions helps to develop the essay.

Thinking Critically

1. Why did the author want to remember such a sad event at a happy occasion?
2. What are the different meanings of "breaking glass" in this essay?
3. What does the author think will happen to memories of twentieth-century events, after the year 2000, "with its obliterating zeros"?

4. What does the author mean by "every generation is born innocent, and if that is bad for history, it is nevertheless necessary
   for life"?

Writing About the Reading

A Paragraph

1. If you were the author, would you have chosen a different wedding
   date? Why or why not?
2. Why is it important for people to remember what happened during
   the Holocaust?

An Essay

1. Write an essay about how your childhood was different from your
   parents'. In what ways do you think yours was better; in what ways
   was theirs better?
2. Write an essay about some of your family's traditions and what they
   mean to you.

A Creative Activity

What do you think the author will tell his children about their grandparents' and great-grandparents' experiences?

Blind to Faith

▶ Karl Taro Greenfeld

Erik Weihenmayer, blind since age thirteen, climbed to the summit of Mount Everest—a feat most sighted people can't ever hope to undertake. His amazing story first appeared in Time *magazine in 2001.*

Journal Writing

Write a journal entry about a time when you achieved a difficult or challenging goal.

Reading Strategy

As you read, highlight the many dangers faced by the climbers.

Vocabulary Preview

misgivings (1) doubts; feelings of uncertainty
crevasse (1) deep crack, as in the ice
hereditary (3) passed down genetically
banal (3) commonplace
deprivation (3) not having enough; being denied something
diabolically (6) devilishly; with evil
treacherously (6) dangerously
seracs (6) large chunks of ice broken off from a glacier
nubbins (8) small pieces
insurmountable (9) impossible to conquer or overcome
rapport (9) relationship
preserve (14) something restricted to one group
slog (16) an exhausting hike
shale (17) fine, crumbly rock
contemporary (21) modern day
jubilant (22) very happy

When he saw Erik Weihenmayer arrive that afternoon, Pasquale   1
Scaturro began to have misgivings about the expedition he was leading. Here they were on the first floor of Mount Everest, and Erik—the reason for the whole trip—was stumbling into Camp 1 bloody, sick and dehydrated. "He was literally green," says fellow climber and team-

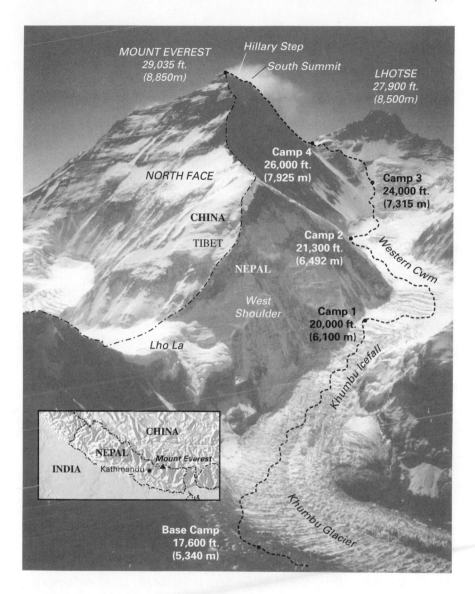

MOUNT EVEREST
29,035 ft.
(8,850m)

Hillary Step

South Summit

LHOTSE
27,900 ft.
(8,500m)

NORTH FACE

Camp 4
26,000 ft.
(7,925 m)

Camp 3
24,000 ft.
(7,315 m)

CHINA

TIBET

Camp 2
21,300 ft.
(6,492 m)

NEPAL

Western Cwm

West
Shoulder

Camp 1
20,000 ft.
(6,100 m)

Lho La

Khumbu Icefall

CHINA

NEPAL   Mount Everest

INDIA   Kathmandu

Khumbu Glacier

Base Camp
17,600 ft.
(5,340 m)

mate Michael O'Donnell. "He looked like George Foreman had beat the crap out of him for two hours." The beating had actually been administered by Erik's climbing partner, Luis Benitez. Erik had slipped into a crevasse, and as Benitez reached down to catch him, his climbing pole raked Erik across the nose and chin. Wounds heal slowly at that altitude because of the thin air.

As Erik passed out in his tent, the rest of the team gathered in a worried huddle. "I was thinking maybe this is not a good idea," says

Scaturro. "Two years of planning, a documentary movie, and this blind guy barely makes it to Camp 1?"

This blind guy. Erik Weihenmayer, 33, wasn't just another yuppie   3
trekker who'd lost a few rounds to the mountain. Blind since he was 13, the victim of a rare hereditary disease of the retina, he began attacking mountains in his early 20s. But he had been having the same doubts as the rest of the team. On that arduous climb to camp through the Khumbu Icefall, Erik wondered for the first time if his attempt to become the first sightless person to summit Mount Everest was a colossal mistake, an act of Daedalian hubris[1] for which he would be punished. There are so many ways to die on that mountain, spanning the spectacular (fall through an ice shelf into a crevasse, get waylaid by an avalanche, develop cerebral edema from lack of oxygen and have your brain literally swell out of your skull) and the banal (become disoriented because of oxygen deprivation and decide you'll take a little nap, right here, in the snow, which becomes a forever nap).

Erik, as he stumbled through the icefall, was so far out of his com-   4
fort zone that he began to speculate on which of those fates might await him. For a moment he flashed on all those clichés about what blind people are supposed to do—become piano tuners or pencil salesmen— and thought maybe they were stereotypes for good reason. Blind people certainly shouldn't be out here, wandering through an ever changing ice field, measuring the distance over a 1,000-ft.-deep crevasse with climbing poles and then leaping, literally, over and into the unknown.

The blind thrive on patterns: stairs are all the same height, city blocks   5
roughly the same length, curbs approximately the same depth. They learn to identify the patterns in their environment much more than the sighted population do, and to rely on them to plot their way through the world.

But in the Khumbu Icefall, the trail through the Himalayan glacier   6
is patternless, a diabolically cruel obstacle course for a blind person. It changes every year as the river of ice shifts, but it's always made up of treacherously crumbly stretches of ice, ladders roped together over wide crevasses, slightly narrower crevasses that must be jumped, huge seracs, avalanches and—most frustrating for a blind person, who naturally seeks to identify patterns in his terrain—a totally random icescape.

In the icefall there is no system, no repetition, no rhyme or reason to   7
the lay of the frozen land. On the other hand, "it is so specific in terms of where you can step," Erik recalls. "Sometimes you're walking along and then boom, a crevasse is right there, and three more steps and another one, and then a snow bridge. And vertical up, then a ladder and then a

---

[1]Excessive pride. Daedalus was the father of Icarus, in Greek mythology. Icarus wore wings made by his father, but flew too close to the sun, fell into the sea, and drowned.

jumbly section." It took Erik 13 hrs. to make it from Base Camp through the icefall to Camp 1, at 20,000 ft. Scaturro had allotted seven. . . .

Watching Erik scramble up a rock face is a little like watching a   8
spider make its way up a wall. His hands are like antennae, gathering information as they flick outward, surveying the rock for cracks, grooves, bowls, nubbins, knobs, edges, and ledges, converting all of it into a road map etched into his mind. "It's like instead of wrestling with a person, I am moving and working with a rock," he explains. "It's a beautiful process of solving a puzzle." He is an accomplished rock climber, rated 5.10 (5.14 being the highest), and has led teams up sections of Yosemite's notorious El Capitan. On ice, where one wrong strike with an ice ax can bring down an avalanche, Erik has learned to listen to the ice as he pings it gently with his ax. If it clinks, he avoids it. If it makes a thunk like a spoon hitting butter, he knows it's solid ice.

Despite being an accomplished mountaineer—summiting Denali,[2]   9
Kilimanjaro in Africa and Aconcagua in Argentina, among other peaks, and, in the words of his friends, "running up 14ers" (14,000-ft. peaks)—Erik viewed Everest as insurmountable until he ran into Scaturro at a sportswear trade show in Salt Lake City, Utah. Scaturro, who had already summited Everest, had heard of the blind climber, and when they met the two struck an easy rapport. A geophysicist who often put together energy-company expeditions to remote areas in search of petroleum, Scaturro began wondering if he could put together a team that could help Erik get to the summit of Everest.

"Dude," Scaturro asked, "have you ever climbed Everest?"   10
"No."   11
"Dude, you wanna?"   12

Climbing with Erik isn't that different from climbing with a   13
sighted mountaineer. You wear a bell on your pack, and he follows the sound, scuttling along using his custom-made climbing poles to feel his way along the trail. His climbing partners shout out helpful descriptions: "Death fall 2 ft. to your right!" "Emergency helicopter-evacuation pad to your left!" He is fast, often running up the back of less experienced climbers. His partners all have scars from being jabbed by Erik's climbing poles when they slowed down.

For the Everest climb, Scaturro and Erik assembled a team that   14
combined veteran Everest climbers and trusted friends of Erik's. Scaturro wrote up a Braille proposal for the Everest attempt and submitted it to Marc Maurer, president of the National Federation of the Blind [N.F.B.]. Maurer immediately pledged $250,000 to sponsor the climb. (Aventis Pharmaceuticals agreed to sponsor a documentary on

---

[2]Native American name for Mount McKinley in Alaska.

the climb to promote Allegra, its allergy medication; Erik suffers from seasonal allergies.) For Erik, who already had numerous gear and clothing sponsors, this was the greatest challenge of his life. If he failed, he would be letting down not just himself but all the blind, confirming that certain activities remained the preserve of the sighted. . . .

When Erik and the team began the final ascent from Camp 4—the camp he describes as Dante's Inferno[3] with ice and wind—they had been on the mountain for two months, climbing up and down and then up from Base Camp to Camps 1, 2, and 3, getting used to the altitude and socking away enough equipment—especially oxygen canisters—to make a summit push. They had tried for the summit once but had turned back because of weather. At 29,000 ft., the Everest peak is in the jet stream,[4] which means that winds can exceed 100 m.p.h. and that what looks from sea level like a cottony wisp of cloud is actually a killer storm at the summit. Bad weather played a fatal role in the 1996 climbing season documented in *Into Thin Air*.[5]   15

On May 24, with only seven days left in the climbing season, most of the N.F.B. expedition members knew this was their last shot at the peak. That's why when Erik and Chris Morris reached the Balcony, the beginning of the Southeast Ridge, at 27,500 ft., after a hard slog up the South Face, they were terribly disappointed when the sky lit up with lightning, driving snow, and fierce winds. "We thought we were done," Erik says. "We would have been spanked if we made a push in those conditions." A few teammates gambled and went for it, and Jeff Evans and Brad Bull heroically pulled out fixed guidelines that had been frozen in the ice. By the time Base Camp radioed that the storm was passing, Erik and the entire team were coated in 2 in. of snow. Inspired by the possibility of a break in the weather, the team pushed on up the exposed Southeast Ridge, an additional 1,200 vertical feet to the South Summit. At that point the climbers looked like astronauts walking on some kind of Arctic moon. They moved slowly because of fatigue from their huge, puffy down suits, backpacks with oxygen canisters and regulators and goggles.   16

With a 10,000-ft. vertical fall into Tibet on one side and a 7,000-ft. fall into Nepal on the other, the South Summit, at 28,750 ft., is where many climbers finally turn back. The 656-ft.-long knife-edge ridge leading to the Hillary Step consists of ice, snow, and fragmented shale, and the only way to cross it is to take baby steps and anchor your way with an ice ax. "You can feel the rock chip off," says Erik. "And you can hear it falling down into the void."   17

---

[3]Hell.
[4]High-speed wind high up in the atmosphere.
[5]An account of a disastrous climb up Mount Everest in May 1996 that resulted in five deaths.

The weather was finally clearing as they reached the Hillary Step,   18
the 39-ft. rock face that is the last major obstacle before the true summit. Erik clambered up the cliff, belly flopping over the top. "I cele-
brated with the dry heaves," he jokes. And then it was 45 minutes of
walking up a sharply angled snow slope to the summit.

"Look around, dude," Evans told the blind man when they were   19
standing on top of the world. "Just take a second and look around."

It could be called the most successful Everest expedition ever, and   20
not just because of Erik's participation. A record 19 climbers from the
N.F.B. team summited, including the oldest man ever to climb Everest—64-year-old Sherman Bull—and the second father-and-son team
ever to do so—Bull and his son Brad.

What Erik achieved is hard for a sighted person to comprehend.   21
What do we compare it with? How do we relate to it? Do we put on a
blindfold and go hiking? That's silly, Erik maintains, because when a
sighted person loses his vision, he is terrified and disoriented. And Erik
is clearly neither of those things. Perhaps the point is really that there
is no way to put what Erik has done in perspective because no one has
ever done anything like it. It is a unique achievement, one that in the
truest sense pushes the limits of what man is capable of. Maurer of the
N.F.B. compares Erik to Helen Keller.[6] "Erik can be a contemporary
symbol for blindness," he explains. "Helen Keller lived 100 years ago.
She should not be our most potent symbol for blindness today."

Erik, sitting in the Kathmandu international airport, waiting for the   22
flight out of Nepal that will eventually return him to Golden, Colo., is sur-
rounded by his teammates and the expedition's 75 pieces of luggage. Success has made the group jubilant. This airport lounge has become the
mountaineering equivalent of a winning Super Bowl locker room. As
they sit amid their luggage, holding Carlsberg beers, they frequently raise
a toast. "*Shez! Shez!*" shouts a climber. That's Nepali for drink! drink! "No
epics," a climber chimes in, citing what really matters: no one died.

In between posing for photos and signing other passengers' board-   23
ing passes, Erik talks about how eager he is to get back home. He says
summiting Everest was great, probably the greatest experience of his
life. But then he thinks about a moment a few months ago, before
Everest, when he was walking down the street in Colorado with daughter Emma in a front pack. They were on their way to buy some banana
bread for his wife, and Emma was pulling on his hand, her little fingers
curled around his index finger. That was a summit too, he says. There
are summits everywhere. You just have to know where to look.

---

[6]Helen Keller, blind and deaf since infancy, learned to read and write. She became an advocate for sightless people.

Examining the Reading

Finding Meaning

1. Why did Scaturro have misgivings at the beginning of the expedition?
2. How did Erik lose his sight?
3. Name some ways climbers are injured or die on Mount Everest.
4. What problems did Erik encounter in the Khumbu Icefall?
5. What special gear does Erik use when climbing?
6. How did Scaturro and Erik raise the money for the climb?
7. What kinds of weather may prevent climbers from reaching the summit?
8. Why do some climbers turn back after they reach the South Summit?

Understanding Technique

1. The opening paragraphs do not paint a positive picture of Erik. Why does the author begin the article this way?
2. The author is writing about a remarkable event. How does he convey the greatness of Erik Weihenmayer's climb?
3. Examine the last paragraph. What is its purpose?

Thinking Critically

1. Who are the "yuppie trekkers" mentioned by the author?
2. Why would blind people be thought of as piano tuners and pencil salesmen?
3. Why is Erik like a spider when he climbs?
4. Erik thought of Everest as insurmountable. What changed his mind?
5. Do you agree that Erik would have let down all the blind if he had failed to reach the summit? Explain your answer.
6. What did Evans mean when he told the blind climber to look around at the summit?
7. Why can't we comprehend Erik's accomplishment?
8. Why does the blind community need a symbol other than Helen Keller? Can Erik be that symbol?
9. Explain the phrase, "there are summits everywhere."

Writing About the Reading

A Paragraph

1. Write a definition of a hero. Then write a paragraph evaluating whether Erik fits your definition of a hero.

2. Mountain climbing is a challenging activity. Write a paragraph about a difficult pursuit or challenging activity you have undertaken.
3. The climbers worked together as a team. Write a paragraph describing the most important aspect of teamwork.

An Essay

1. Erik and his team succeeded in their climb, but many climbers do not, often at great risk and expense to their rescuers. Write an essay exploring the issue of whether limitations, qualifications, restrictions, or bans are appropriate in high-risk sports.
2. At the end of the article, the author states, "There are summits everywhere. You just have to know where to look." Write an essay defining "summits" and discuss where you personally look for them.
3. Write an essay giving reasons why people engage in high-risk sports.

A Creative Activity

Imagine that you lost your sight. How would you have to change your daily routine? Another suggestion for this activity is to pick a sport at which you would like to excel. What sport would you pick and why?

Desert Storm and Shield

▶ **Scott Stopa**
Student Essay

*Scott Stopa, a college student, wrote this essay explaining how a
phone call from his platoon sergeant changed his life. His essay
describes how his experiences in the Persian Gulf became a turning point in his life.*

*T*here are many events that have been major turning points in my   1
life. Some of these are my marriage, the birth of my children, my divorce, going back to school, and joining the Marine Corps. The biggest
turning point in my life, however, was going off to war in the Persian
Gulf (Operations Desert Shield and Desert Storm). It was November
1990 when the 8th Tank Battalion, of which I was a part, was activated.
I was 20 years old and just out of boot camp. I had only been home for
two weeks when we were sent overseas.

When Iraq invaded Kuwait, there was a lot of talk of the United   2
States going to war, but of course I never thought in a million years
that I would be sent off to war. I thought, no, I'd never be sent. After all,
I'm only in the reserves. Boy, was I wrong. The news came by phone. I
was living at my parents' house at the time. My mother answered the
phone. It was my platoon sergeant. When my mother handed me the
phone, I could see the tears in her eyes. Then he gave me the news. My
heart dropped. I was speechless when I got off the phone. All I could do
when I looked at my mother was tell her I'm sorry.

I remember that night like it was yesterday. I got in my car and   3
drove, with nowhere special in mind. I ended up down by the falls,
where I walked around and did a lot of thinking. What would we be in
for, and how would I react if certain situations arose? At that point I
made up my mind that no matter what, I was coming home. I was
scared, and if anybody says they weren't, they're lying. This was going
to be life as I never knew it, and it was.

Other than the ground war, the first month was probably the most   4
difficult. A lot of thinking about home and being there for Christmas
didn't make matters any better. After a while I got used to it. A situation
like that makes you grow up quickly and appreciate the basic things in

life, like running water, hot showers, hot meals, a bed—just things like that. You don't realize how much you take these things for granted until you're forced to be without them. I can remember countless nights of walking guard duty in the pouring rain, being soaked all day, going to sleep wet and freezing, and being totally miserable because of these discomforts. But now I realize that it has made me a very strong person.

The night before the ground war started, our company was briefed on what was expected and what exactly our mission was after we breached the minefield and got into Kuwait. During the briefing, they told us we were expected to take at least 70 percent casualties. You could have heard a pin drop. We knew it wasn't going to be easy because we were a tank battalion and we'd be right on the front line with the tanks. If ever at one instant I felt like I "grew up overnight," that was it, definitely.   5

The morning came, and we went in. We took incoming fire going through the minefield. Fortunately, we made it through. The ground war only lasted three days, but it was the most intense three days of my life. Explosions, blown-up tanks and vehicles everywhere, fires, lots of smoke, planes and helicopters flying overhead—it was like a movie. But it was reality, definitely reality, and when I encountered sights of death, more and more I realized this is war. I guess you could say reality set in. Seeing things like that really makes you cherish your life a little more. Unfortunately, I lost a very good friend over there, but his memory will never be forgotten—Thomas Scholand, from Semper, Florida.   6

Although these experiences may all seem bad, nothing can ever take away the feeling of pride, rolling through Kuwait City and seeing people lining the streets waving and calling out in appreciation of the fact that we had just liberated their country. Seeing the faces of the men, women, and especially the children was a feeling that no words can explain.   7

In summary, of all the events that unfolded for me as well as for others who served in Operations Desert Shield and Desert Storm, this was a major turning point in my life. I learned a lot about myself and life in general. I now look at things in a positive perspective. I've grown up a lot overseas, and now I take nothing for granted anymore. Life's short; appreciate all it has to offer, and live it to the fullest. I will!   8

Examining the Essay

1. Evaluate Stopa's thesis statement.
2. Stopa uses details to make his experiences seem real and vivid. In which parts of the essay was his use of detail particularly effective?

Writing an Essay

1. Write an essay describing your response to receiving surprising or important news. Describe how you reacted and how the news affected you.
2. Stopa says he felt as if he grew up overnight. Write an essay discussing a situation in which you were forced to grow up or accept responsibility. Explain how the situation affected you.
3. Stopa's experiences made him value his life and appreciate basic things in life. Write an essay recounting an experience that helped you see life in a new or different way.

Making Connections

1. Salinas's "The Scholarship Jacket" and White's "Ragtime, My Time" both deal with racism. Compare the experiences, reactions, and lasting effects described in these readings.

2. Compare the once-in-a-lifetime experiences from Greenfeld's "Blind to Faith" and Stopa's "Desert Storm and Shield."

Internet Connections

1. The American Civil Liberties Union has launched a campaign to end racial profiling. Read about highlights of this campaign at **http://www.aclu.org/RacialEquality/RacialE-qualitylist.cfm?c=133.** Write a summary of their activities. Do you think their actions will be effective? Why or why not?

2. Speeches at ceremonies often mark important events in our lives. Visit the following sites, which give advice about and examples of speeches for special occasions:

   http://www.foreverwed.com/speeches/examples.htm

   http://www.toastmasters.org/pdfs/top10.pdf

   http://www.uiowa.edu/~c100298/anxiety.html

   Write a paragraph discussing whether the quality of a speech can affect your attitude toward and perception of an event. Use examples from the web sites you just visited and from your own experience.

3. Every year around December 31, we look back at the major events of that year. Here is a site where you can look back on every year since 1990. Go to **http://www.info-please.com/yearbyear.html** and examine the information there. Try a quiz or look over a few of the lists. Write an essay examining the ways in which one of the events listed at this web site affected your life.

(If any of these web sites are unavailable, use a search engine to locate another appropriate site.)

Chapter 3

Work That Shapes Our Lives

Work is a complex, important part of our lives. Jobs, of course, provide needed income to purchase life's necessities. Some jobs offer an outlet for creative expression or help develop skills such as problem-solving. Other jobs can simply be repetitive and dull. Even those jobs, however, can be a source of personal satisfaction, a means of demonstrating that we are competent, self-sufficient individuals. By contrast, work can also make leisure time valuable and meaningful. Work can open new doors, as well as lead to new friends, new experiences, and new realizations.

The readings in this chapter provide several different perspectives on work and the workplace. You will read about a new trend among families with young children—stay-at-home fathers ("Mr. Mom's World"). You will also learn important career preparatory skills: how to search for a job ("Seven Easy Ways to Become an Unhappy Job Seeker"), how to use the Internet to search for a job ("Job Search 2.OH!"), and how to prepare for a job interview ("Preparing for a Job Interview"). The differences in communication between men and women as they affect workplace relationships are considered in "Cross Talk." The issue of pre-employment drug and personality testing is addressed by a well-known journalist who posed as an applicant for low-paying jobs ("What Are They Probing For?"). A student offers a humorous perspective on his part-time job at a fish market ("A Seafood Survey").

Brainstorming About Work

Class Activity: Have students in groups of three or four discuss and attempt to define the ideal or perfect job. Identify its characteristics and try to think of examples. Also try to take into account individual differences. Why may a job be ideal for one person and unappealing to another?

Mr. Mom's World

▸ David Case

More and more fathers are staying home to raise their children while mothers work. This article, which first appeared in an online magazine called Salon **(www.salon.com),** *profiles several of these families.*

Journal Writing

Write a journal entry exploring whether fathers make good caregivers for infants and toddlers. What are the advantages and disadvantages of male caregivers?

Reading Strategy

Many details, including names, ages, and occupations, of several different families are included in this article. As you read, focus on the issues and trends these families illustrate.

Vocabulary Preview

scenario (1) string of events
progressive (1) forward thinking; broad-minded; interested in new ideas
conjure (2) call to mind
regime (2) system or pattern
vulnerability (4) exposure; openness to attack
transpired (5) happened; occurred
progeny (8) children
deft (12) skilled at; clever at
stigma (12) a mark of disgrace
pundits (14) teachers; authorities
vociferous (14) loud and noisy
oratory (14) speech; public speaking
parity (16) equality
kudos (16) praise

When we imagine what it takes to raise a happy, healthy child, most   1
of us picture fresh air, a green yard with a blow-up wading pool, and maybe even a golden retriever standing guard. Most important, we

---

imagine a nurturing, attentive caregiver willing to dedicate endless days to encouragement, discipline, and guidance. In this perfect parenting scenario, most of us probably visualize ideal moms like Carol Brady or June Cleaver, no matter how progressive we may be.

Most of us probably wouldn't conjure up someone like my old friend Tal Birdsey. Here's a guy who, when we met during college, could go for months without washing his hair, a guy who bragged about laundering his sheets only once a semester. The closest he came to taking care of another human was nurturing his gut, a jiggly beast widely known as Joe, which he kept healthy on a strict regime of barley and hops. And now he's molding in his image not one, but two tiny lives? Simultaneously? With no help?   2

"It's like this," he says. "When I was first taking care of the kids, my wife Blair had to come home every three hours to breast-feed the baby. One day she's real late. The baby starts wailing hysterically—I worry he's gonna drop. So I fix him a bottle, which he's never had before. I'm trying to convince him the plastic nipple works just as well as his mom's, then nature calls—urgently. I don't know, maybe the stress loosened my bowels.   3

"Next thing, I'm sitting on the loo, cradling the baby, balancing his bottle under my chin. After a few moments repose, 'brrrrrrnng, brrrrrrnng.' It must be Blair calling from a pay phone. I've got to get it before the voice mail picks up. So with my trousers around my ankles, the baby in my arms, I scurry, bent at the waist, across the living room. I pick it up—a man's voice. The bank calling about our mortgage application. From behind, the 3-year-old senses my momentary vulnerability, and attacks. Giggling like a madman, he starts spanking me. Funniest thing he's ever seen—his daddy bare-assed in the living room cradling the baby and talking on the phone."   4

This certainly isn't a scene that could have transpired under my mother's roost. But a growing number of men in their 30s find themselves at home full time, changing diapers, hunting down lost socks, playing daddy rides the hay wagon. . . .   5

"When I was a child," remembers Tom Funk, 33, who shares the parenting and income-generating more or less equally with his wife, Liz, "I remember a neighbor's father, during a rare bout with solo parenting, being confronted with a dangerously dirty diaper. He packed the crying child in the back of the car and drove 45 minutes to find a woman who could change it for him. That doesn't cut it anymore."   6

Well, men, we've got something to thump our chests about. More and more of us are pulling our weight at home. In the late '90s, men in dual-earner couples take on 60 percent more child care than did our fathers. And we do an impressive 2.5 times more housework, according to Scott Coltrane, a professor of sociology at the University of California at Riverside and author of the book *Family Man: Brotherhood,*   7

Housework and Gender Equity. Sadly, that brings us to a mere 28 percent of the housework and 33 percent of child care. The emerging class of stay-at-home dads, or SAHDs, are no doubt helping our stats.

So who are these domesticated dads, and what are they thinking? Some are the disillusioned progeny of workaholic fathers—stockbrokers, lawyers, and executives—sons who seek a closer bond with their kin. For others, office politics out-repulse even the most colicky child. "This is a lot better than most of the jobs I could get," points out Yale Lewis, a journalist and, for now, stay-at-home dad. Many, like Lewis and Birdsey, have advanced degrees, though these days they're more apt to cite "Mike Mulligan and the Steam Shovel" than Milton. Along with their wives, SAHDs feel strongly that even the best day care can't replace an attentive parent. When both Birdseys were working, Tal says, "The only time I ever felt comfortable, the only time I stopped thinking about the baby was when he was napping. Then I knew he was all right."

The SAHDs may be the first significant group of men with little lingering notion of male superiority. While they may remain haunted by societal biases, some readily admit that their wives are more clever, more energetic, and better able to cope in society—or at least that they had played their cards more effectively.

Andrew Stockwood has great admiration for his partner, Shirley Netten, a lawyer and political advisor. "Shirley has the education, experience, and talent to make lots of money," says Stockwood, who recently passed up a job as a roving photojournalist in the South Pacific. Having relished two years with his first child, he prefers to stay home in anticipation of "oogling" his soon-to-arrive second. "I love the fact that this lets us live an alternative lifestyle and still be very comfortable. Her skills are extremely valuable and sought after. Succeeding as a professional still feels like a triumph for women," Stockwood muses. "I was always expected to be a successful professional, so that route seemed boring and constraining to me. And given the choice, I would rather bake the bread than buy the flour." . . .

For the time being, some SAHDs say they feel isolated. Away from the workaday adult world, they're often alone in their convictions, and are outcasts among the generally more traditional moms they see during the day. "Yesterday at the playground there was a little boy who got along so well with Emily," says Andy Murray, referring to his 2-year-old, an adorable firecracker with an Einsteinian flop of white hair. "I wanted the kids to get together again, but there's this whole thing about me, a man alone with a child, giving out my phone number to a woman."

The flip side is the sandbox-as-pickup joint, a throwback to the parents' own schoolyard days. Some moms admit to going gooey at the site of a man with a stroller, a male counterpart deft at caring for a child in a way that perhaps their spouses aren't. The dads, however, contend that they're family types, and are not apt to notice this feminine yearning. Instead, they're preoccupied with the "Mr. Mom" stigma—the hairy eyeball from older relatives and neighbors who still believe that it takes three men to handle a baby.

"You should see the stares I get at the playground," says Walter   13
Garschagen, a photographer whose wife is an actress. "It's like, Why isn't he working, and why does he make his wife toil 80 hours a week to support him? I love taking care of Emma (another 2-year-old), but I'd feel better about myself if I were out moving rocks. At least I'd be sweating." . . .

While relatively little research has been done on the impact of   14
father-reared families, so far the pundits say that generally, everyone wins. When men participate in routine child care, women enjoy a higher public status and share political authority with men, says UC-Riverside professor Coltrane. "Men who do more parenting report they are more in touch with their emotions, are more compassionate, and can relate better to their wives. [They] are unlikely to celebrate their manhood through combative contests, vociferous oratory, and violent rituals."

And growing up with dad around benefits kids in unique ways.   15
"Compared to mothers, men spend more of their child-care time in games or rough-and-tumble play. We know the children learn important skills in this kind of interaction, such as how to regulate their emotions," says Coltrane. Joseph Pleck of the University of Illinois adds, "Children with involved fathers tend to do better socially and academically, they generally have better self-control, confidence, and self-esteem and they avoid gender stereotyping." . . .

But don't let all this mushy man-speak fool you into believing that   16
America is finally achieving domestic parity. Women, it seems, are still routinely overburdened. While the SAHDs deserve kudos for their efforts, even they tend to kick back when mom gets home. Whether it's guilt or higher standards that drive them, even some women who are the sole wage earners put in an extra effort at home. As Birdsey's wife, Blair, an ad copywriter, puts it, "Tal is a typical guy. He's never cleaned the toilet, he doesn't even notice the hair balls gathering dust on the staircase, or the musty towels in a ball on the bathroom floor. I still have to do all the housework and cook." But, she adds, "I guess it's fair, because I like to do it."

Funk admits late one evening while his wife washes the dishes, "I'd   17
like to think that we do half and half, but in reality it's probably more like 30–70." Men, he says, justify this by comparing themselves to other men who do even less. Like most guys, Funk finds child care much harder than office work. "On the days when I have the baby, we're more apt to just get a pizza for dinner."

Women, he concedes, are just more capable of working long hours.   18

Examining the Reading

Finding Meaning

1. Summarize the ideal parenting situation that the author describes in paragraph 1.
2. What was the author's old friend, Tal Birdsey, like in college? What is he like now?
3. Why did the author include the funny experience Birdsey had one day while watching his children?
4. According to Scott Coltrane's figures, what percentage of men are helping with housework and child care? How much higher is this percentage compared to that of their fathers' generation?
5. List some of the reasons men become stay-at-home dads.
6. Why do some SAHDs feel isolated?
7. Who makes the SAHDs feel like outcasts?
8. What are the benefits of a father-reared family?
9. How do many SAHDs act when their wives come home from work?

Understanding Technique

1. The author profiles several different families. How do these personal accounts add to Case's article? Would the article be effective if he had interviewed only one family in depth?
2. How does Case use humor in this story? What does humor contribute to the article?
3. How does the author show the positive and negative aspects of a SAHD's life?

Thinking Critically

1. Why is it not progressive to think of television moms as ideal parents?
2. Tom Funk's neighbor drove a long way to get his child's diaper changed. Why doesn't this "cut it anymore"? What has changed?
3. Why would the son of a workaholic father feel the need to stay at home with his own children?
4. Why does Andrew Stockton consider his family to be living an "alternative lifestyle"?
5. Why does Andy Murray feel he cannot give his phone number to women at the playground?
6. Why does Walter Garschagen say that he would feel better about himself if he were "out moving rocks"?
7. Why do you think children whose fathers spend more time with them do better in school?

Writing About the Reading

A Paragraph

1. Write a paragraph about the most important quality a mother or father should possess.
2. Write a paragraph describing a time when you took on someone else's responsibilities. What were the outcomes?
3. Housework never ends. Write a paragraph about how you either accomplish or avoid household chores.

An Essay

1. Write an essay describing the ways in which men and women are still not equal in the workplace.
2. Mothers and fathers often differ in their approaches to raising children. Write an essay comparing and contrasting male and female childrearing practices that you have observed or experienced.
3. Not all families have mothers and fathers. Write an essay about a nontraditional family that you have observed or experienced and describe its effect on the children.

Creative Activities

1. If you could reverse roles with someone for a day, who would it be and why?
2. What stereotypes exist for male and female parents? Brainstorm a list of stereotypes that exist for each.

Cross Talk

▶ Deborah Tannen

Deborah Tannen is a professor who has become a well-recognized expert on communication between men and women. This essay, excerpted from Tannen's book You Just Don't Understand, *describes gender differences that affect how people communicate with each other on the job.*

Journal Writing

Have you experienced or observed miscommunication between men and women? Describe the situation.

Reading Strategy

As you read, note differences between the way men and women communicate.

Vocabulary Preview

literally (5) in the simplest, most obvious sense; word for word
insubordination (6) disobedience to authority
opaque (7) unclear, difficult to understand or explain, impenetrable by light; unintelligible
manifestations (8) demonstrations
rapport (8) relationship marked by harmony or ability to get along
hierarchical (8) organized into ranks or orders
egalitarian (10) affirming, promoting, or characterized by belief in human equality
countenanced (10) approved of or tolerated
ostracized (10) excluded from the group
imperious (14) commanding or domineering
curtness (19) rudeness or brusqueness

A woman who owns a bookstore needed to have a talk with the store   1
manager. She had told him to help the bookkeeper with billing, he had agreed, and now, days later, he still hadn't done it. Thinking how much she disliked this part of her work, she sat down with the manager to clear things up. They traced the problem to a breakdown in communication.

She had said, "Sarah needs help with the bills. What do you think 2 about helping her out?" He had responded, "OK," by which he meant, "OK, I'll think about whether or not I want to help her." During the next day, he thought about it and concluded that he'd rather not.

This wasn't just an ordinary communication breakdown that could 3 happen between any two people. It was a particular sort of breakdown that tends to occur between women and men.

Most women avoid giving orders. More comfortable with decision- 4 making by consensus, they tend to phrase requests as questions, to give others the feeling they have some say in the matter and are not be- ing bossed around. But this doesn't mean they aren't making their wishes clear. Most women would have understood the bookstore owner's question, "What do you think about helping her out?" as as- signing a task in a considerate way.

The manager, however, took the owner's words literally. She had 5 asked him what he thought; she hadn't told him to *do* anything. So he felt within his rights when he took her at her word, thought about it and decided not to help Sarah.

Women in positions of authority are likely to regard such re- 6 sponses as insubordination: "He knows I am in charge, and he knows what I want; if he doesn't do it, he is resisting my authority."

There may be a kernel of truth in this view—most men are inclined 7 to resist authority if they can because being in a subordinate position makes them intensely uncomfortable. But indirect requests that are transparent to women may be genuinely opaque to men. They assume that people in authority will give orders if they really want some- thing done.

These differences in management styles are one of many manifes- 8 tations of gender differences in how we talk to one another. Women use language to create connection and rapport; men use it to negotiate their status in a hierarchical order. It isn't that women are unaware of status or that men don't build rapport, but that *the genders tend to fo- cus on different goals.*

The Source of Gender Differences

These differences stem from the way boys and girls learn to use lan- 9 guage while growing up. Girls tend to play indoors, either in small groups or with one other girl. The center of a girl's social life is her best friend, with whom she spends a great deal of time sitting, talking and exchanging secrets. It is the telling of secrets that makes them best friends. Boys tend to play outdoors, in larger groups, usually in com- petitive games. It's doing things together that makes them friends.

Anthropologist Marjorie Harness Goodwin compared boys and 10 girls at play in a black innercity neighborhood in Philadelphia. Her findings, which have been supported by researchers in other settings, show that the boys' groups are hierarchical: high-status boys give orders, and low-status boys have to follow them, so they end up being told what to do. Girls' groups tend to be egalitarian: girls who appeared "better" than others or gave orders were not countenanced and in some cases were ostracized.

So while boys are learning to fear being "put down" and pushed   11 around, girls are learning to fear being "locked out." Whereas high-status boys establish and reinforce their authority by giving orders and resisting doing what others want, girls tend to make suggestions, which are likely to be taken up by the group.

Cross-Gender Communication in the Workplace

The implications of these different conversational habits and concerns   12 in terms of office interactions are staggering. Men are inclined to continue to jockey for position, trying to resist following orders as much as possible within the constraints of their jobs.

Women, on the other hand, are inclined to do what they sense their   13 bosses want, whether or not they are ordered to. By the same token, women in positions of authority are inclined to phrase their requests as suggestions and to assume they will be respected because of their authority. These assumptions are likely to hold up as long as both parties are women, but they may well break down in cross-gender communication.

When a woman is in the position of authority, such as the book-   14 store owner, she may find her requests are systematically misunderstood by men. And when a woman is working for a male boss, she may find that her boss gives bald commands that seem unnecessarily imperious because most women would prefer to be asked rather than ordered. One woman who worked at an all-male radio station commented that the way the men she worked for told her what to do made her feel as if she should salute and say, "Yes, boss."

Many men complain that a woman who is indirect in making re-   15 quests is manipulative: she's trying to get them to do what she wants without telling them to do it. Another common accusation is that she is insecure: she doesn't know what she wants. But if a woman gives direct orders, the same men might complain that she is aggressive, unfeminine or worse.

Women are in a double bind: *If we talk like women, we are not re-*   16 *spected. If we talk like men, we are not liked.*

We have to walk a fine line, finding ways to be more direct without   17 appearing bossy. The bookstore owner may never be comfortable by directly saying, "Help Sarah with the billing today," but she might find some compromise such as, "Sarah needs help with the billing. I'd appreciate it if you would make some time to help her out in the next day or two." This request is clear, while still reflecting women's preferences for giving reasons and options.

What if you're the subordinate and your boss is a man who's of- 18
fending you daily by giving you orders? If you know him well enough, one potential solution is "metacommunication"—that is, talk about communication. Point out the differences between women and men, and discuss how you could accommodate to each other's styles. (You may want to give him a copy of this article or my book.)

But if you don't have the kind of relationship that makes meta- 19
communication possible, you could casually, even jokingly, suggest he give orders another way. Or just try to remind yourself it's a cross-cultural difference and try not to take his curtness personally.

A Starting Point

Simply knowing about gender differences in conversational style pro- 20
vides a starting point for improving relations with the women and men who are above and below you in a hierarchy.

The key is *flexibility;* a way of talking that works beautifully with 21
one person may be a disaster with another. If one way of talking isn't working, try another, rather than trying harder to do more of the same.

Once you know what the parameters are, you can become an ob-server of your own interactions, and a style-switcher when you choose.

Examining the Reading

Finding Meaning

1. According to the author, how do most women give orders? Why was this method of communication confusing for the bookstore's male manager?
2. What is the goal of communication for women? What is the goal for men?
3. What are the differences in how boys and girls play? What types of shared experiences establish friendships for each gender?
4. How do men and women see indirect requests differently?
5. What is "metacommunication"?

Understanding Technique

1. How does the author begin the essay? Is the introduction effective?
2. Identify the author's thesis statement.
3. How does the author use the original example throughout the article?
4. How does the author conclude the essay?
5. Describe the tone of the essay.

Thinking Critically

1. Do you agree that men are more inclined than women to resist authority?
2. Are most work situations hierarchical or egalitarian? Support your answer with examples.
3. Think of an example from your experience that illuminates the "double bind" that women face.
4. Evaluate the author's advice for improving communication in the workplace. How easy or difficult is it to become a "style switcher"?
5. In discussing gender differences in communication at work, does the author seem to take sides with either gender? If you hadn't seen the author's name, would you know she was a woman?

Writing About the Reading

A Paragraph

1. The author says the key to improving relations with the men and women above and below you in a hierarchy is flexibility. In what ways can flexibility help you on the job and in life in general? Choose a situation in which your flexibility improved a difficult situation. Write a paragraph describing the situation.
2. How might the gender differences described in the article affect communication in friendships and romantic relationships? Choose a situation and write a paragraph describing the role communication played in your relationship.

An Essay

1. Choose a job you hold or have held, or observe a workplace that employs both men and women. Observe or recall how men and women communicate. Write an essay describing your observations, noting whether they are consistent or inconsistent with Tannen's findings.
2. What makes an effective supervisor? Write an essay describing the major traits you think either gender should have to be a good boss.

A Creative Activity

1. Create a game for children or adults that would teach them how to become more effective communicators.
2. Write a short scene that highlights a communication breakdown between men and women.
3. Create a list of examples that illustrate the differences in the way men and women communicate.

What Are They Probing For?

▶ **Barbara Ehrenreich**

Barbara Ehrenreich, a well-known journalist, analyzes the drug and personality tests given by companies to potential employees. Her essay first appeared in Time *magazine in 2001.*

Journal Writing

Write a journal entry describing your worst experiences with testing, either in the workplace or in the classroom.

Reading Strategy

As you read, highlight statements that reveal the author's attitude toward pre-employment testing.

Vocabulary Preview

simulation (1) imitation; copy
proclivities (1) tendencies
trumped (2) outdone; surpassed
discernible (4) recognizable
vagrant (5) drifter; roamer; homeless person
propositions (6) statements; suggestions
blatantly (6) obviously
innocuous (7) harmless; unlikely to offend

*O*ne of the great things about a job, as opposed to a position as a serf or slave, is that a job is supposed to have definite boundaries. You show up in the morning, do your level best or some reasonable simulation thereof for eight to 10 hours, then you're free to go home and indulge your neurotic proclivities: gorging on Doritos, tormenting small animals, practicing Satanism, whatever. At least that's how things worked before the invention of pre-employment testing.   1

Now that the boss has the tools to get at them, he wants your weekends, your secret self-doubts and—to the extent that you still possess one after trying to fake your way through the tests—your soul. First there's the pre-employment drug test, now routine at more than 80% of large companies—and not just for the person who will be piloting the   2

Source: Barbara Ehrenreich, "What Are They Probing For?" *TIME Magazine,* June 4, 2001. © 2001 TIME Inc. Reprinted by permission.

executive jet or loading plutonium rods into the reactor. Winn-Dixie tests the people who stack Triscuit boxes; Wal-Mart tests its people greeters. What a preference for weed over Bud as a Saturday-night relaxation aid says about your work habits has never been established, but this in no way dulls management's eagerness to pry into your personal recreational choices. You may have a brilliant résumé and a unique set of skills, but all these can be trumped by your pee.

And now, arising in just the past decade or so, there's the pre-employment "personality test." This practice is at an all-time high, according to *The New York Times*, with 2,500 tests on the market supplied by the $400 million-a-year "personality-assessment" industry. In the past three years, I have taken five of these tests in the course of applying for a series of jobs: as a cleaning person, a supermarket clerk, and as an "associate" at various big-box stores. No, I hadn't given up on writing; I was doing research for a book on the low-wage life. I was expecting to toil and sweat, even wear unflattering uniforms. But I wasn't expecting to have to share my innermost thoughts.

Some of the standard questions on these personality tests are, I suppose, justifiable. Management probably has a right to ask, for example, what you would do if you caught a fellow worker stealing, or whether you have ever gone postal[1] on the job. But other questions bore no discernible relevance to the task at hand: Do you consider yourself a loner? Do you often think other people are talking about you behind your back? And my personal favorite, this from a test for a housecleaning job paying $6.63 an hour: Do you suffer from "moods of self-pity"?

Fortunately, the tests are easy to ace. Take the common question "In the past year, I have stolen (check dollar amount below) from my employers." If you can't guess that the answer is zero, proceed directly to the nearest park bench and begin your career as a vagrant. Or: "I tend to get into fistfights more than other people?" (Not!) and "It's easier to work when you're a little bit high." (Not, again!)

True, some of the test propositions are confusingly worded, like "Marijuana is the same as a drink." (The same? How?) But the only way I ever screwed up was by being too clever. My strategy had been to give the "right" answers, but not so blatantly right that it would look as if I was faking out the test. Then, at a Wal-Mart in Minnesota, the personnel manager informed me I had got a couple of answers "wrong," apparently forgetting that she had introduced the test by telling me there were "no right or wrong answers, just whatever you think." In one case, I had agreed that "rules have to be followed to the letter at all times" only "strongly" rather than "totally," in the hope of not appearing to be too much of a suck-up. But no, she told me, the

[1]The term *postal* alludes to recent violence committed by frustrated post-office employees.

correct answer was "totally." You can never be too much of a suck-up in low-wage America.

The mystery is why employers are so addicted to these pre- 7 employment tests. Drug tests seldom detect anything but the most innocuous of illegal drugs, usually marijuana; and personality tests only measure some combination of literacy and hypocrisy, not your ability to get the job done. Maybe the real function of the tests is not to convey information to the employer but to the potential employee, and the information being conveyed is, You will have no secrets from us. We don't just want your time and your effort, we want your entire self.

Examining the Reading

Finding Meaning

1. According to the author, what do today's bosses want from their employees?
2. For whom are drug tests now routine?
3. Why has the author been applying for so many jobs in recent years?
4. What personality test question is Ehrenreich's "personal favorite"?
5. How did the author "screw up" on one of the personality tests?
6. What does Ehrenreich feel is the true purpose of pre-employment testing?

Understanding Technique

1. What is the author's thesis? How does she support it?
2. How does the author's inclusion of her personal experiences contribute to the story?
3. Tone is the author's attitude toward his or her subject. Describe the tone of this article.

Thinking Critically

1. What does Ehrenreich mean when she says that we do a "reasonable simulation" of our best at work?
2. Why are companies so eager to test their employees?
3. Why are some of the questions on the personality tests "justifiable"?
4. Why would the author be asked about "moods of self-pity" for a housecleaning job?
5. Do you think the author would be "faking out the test" by giving all the right answers?
6. What effect do you think pre-employment tests have on potential employees?

7. Why do you think employers continue to ask questions to which the "right" answer is very obvious?

Writing About the Reading

A Paragraph

1. Employers often have difficulty finding and keeping quality workers. Write a paragraph about the most important characteristics a good employee should have.
2. Write a paragraph about a job interview that you have had. Describe what questions you were asked, and explain whether or not you feel your privacy was violated.
3. Many people are worried about their personal privacy. Based on the article and your own experiences, write a paragraph explaining whether you feel pre-employment testing violates peoples' right to privacy.
4. Write a paragraph identifying jobs or positions for which you feel drug and personality tests are necessary.

An Essay

1. Write an essay describing a low-wage job you have held and how you were treated. Did your employer want "your entire self"?
2. Write an essay giving reasons why you think pre-employment testing is or is not appropriate.

A Creative Activity

Imagine that you are the boss of a company of your choice. What questions would you ask potential employees before hiring them?

Seven Easy Ways to Become an Unhappy Job Seeker

▶ Mary Ellen Slayter

This article describes seven of the most common mistakes people make when seeking a job. The article first appeared in the Washington Post *on September 14, 2003.*

Journal Writing

Write a list of the activities you enjoy. Next to each activity, list a job that would allow you to be paid for being involved with that activity.

Reading Strategy

As you read this article, try to determine the audience for whom it is written.

Vocabulary Preview

temperament (2) disposition; personality characteristics of an individual
criterion (2) standard for comparison or judgment
secretive (3) not open or outgoing in speech or activity
plethora (3) an excess
stigma (3) a mark of disgrace
detrimental (3) obviously harmful
proverbial (4) commonly spoken of
mangling (5) spoiling or injuring
cull (7) to select from a group
dysfunctional (9) impaired or abnormal

*H*appy families are all alike; every unhappy family is unhappy in its   1
own way," wrote Leo Tolstoy. The same could probably be said of unhappy job seekers, if the questions and stories that you have shared with me through the online chat and by e-mail are any indication. Every step of the process between you and a better job (or, in the case

of recent grads, any job at all) can seem filled with chances to screw up in new ways. And while a few of you have certainly impressed me with your unique ability to offend potential employers, some mistakes seem to occur more often than others. Here are a few of the most common ones:

Chasing "Hot" Jobs

You are more likely to be successful, including financially, if you do   2
work that you enjoy and that suits your temperament. One of the scariest questions I ever got from a reader was from a man who was trying to decide whether to study nursing or engineering, and his main criterion was which one was hotter—that is, which would pay better. What would be more disturbing: driving over a bridge designed by the guy who should have been a nurse or being cared for by a nurse who should have been an engineer?

Being Too Secretive

Your teachers, friends, family and professional peers can't help you   3
find a job if they don't know you're looking. The plethora of jobs advertised on the Internet did not change the one fundamental truth of job hunting: Contacts matter. Other people are a crucial part of your job search. So, what stops people from including people in their social and professional networks in their job searches? Are we afraid to burden them with our request for help? Perhaps it's plain old-fashioned shame, especially if we're jobless. Even though most of us will be unemployed at some point in our lives, being out of work carries quite a stigma in our culture—one that can be extremely detrimental to our careers if it keeps us from asking for help when we need it.

Advertising the Quest for a New Job to the Wrong People

That wrong person, nine times out of 10, includes your current boss as   4
well as most of your co-workers. If it's too obvious that you're itching to leave, you will be treated differently—and not in a good way. Looking for a job is no guarantee that you'll find one any time soon, and if you start loudly counting those proverbial chickens, you might find yourself clucking out the door with a pink slip and no nest egg.

Not Proofreading Resumes and Cover Letters

This should be a no-brainer, but typos and misspellings on these   5
documents remain a top complaint of hiring managers in industry surveys year after year. Your enthusiasm for working at "Northrup Grumman" is very charming, but it won't make up for mangling the company's name. (It's spelled Northrop.) Your best bet is to have sev-

eral other people edit your work before submitting it. Spell-check is not enough.

Not Taking Entry-Level Jobs Seriously

Every job is a "real" job, including temp jobs. We almost all start off 6 working poorly paid, low-skilled, not-very-fun jobs. The way you get a better job is by doing the one you have really well, not by whining about how bored you are or how you don't make enough money. Do you really think your boss will give you a raise and a promotion just to shut you up?

Underdressing for an Interview

I know a suit feels uncomfortable after four or five years in tank tops, 7 baggy skirts and sandals. But your college uniform is simply not the uniform of the working world. It is especially inappropriate for job interviews. Hiring managers are looking for reasons to cull applicants; don't give them such an easy one to drop you.

Not Following Up

After an interview, send a thank-you note to everyone you spoke with. 8 It doesn't have to be handwritten on fancy stationery; e-mail is often fine. Basically, you just need to thank them for taking the time to meet with you and to say that you are still interested in the job. This helps keep communication lines open. It's best to do this within two days. Hiring managers shouldn't have to guess if you are still interested in the job.

Don't worry if you see yourself in this list — that just makes you a 9 member of one big, mildly dysfunctional but still mostly employable, happy family.

Examining the Reading

Finding Meaning

1. What is meant by the term "'hot' job"?
2. Why should job seekers let their friends, family, and professional peers know that they are looking for jobs?
3. What are some of the reasons that people are afraid to ask others to help them find a job?
4. Why should a person be careful about letting her supervisor and coworkers know that she is dissatisfied with a current job?
5. Explain why "Spellcheck is not enough."
6. How does the author define a "real job"?
7. According to the author, what is the only way to get a better job?

8. Why is it important to send a thank-you note to the people you spoke with during an interview?
9. What advice does the author give to people that have made some of the errors described in the article?

Understanding Technique

1. Why do you think the author chose to call the article "Seven Easy Ways to Become an Unhappy Job Seeker"? Is the title effective in inspiring your interest?
2. The author begins the article with the quote "Happy families are all alike; every unhappy family is unhappy in its own way." What does this quote by Leo Tolstoy mean? Why does the author choose to start the article with this metaphor? Does the metaphor continue to work well in the conclusion?
3. Find examples in the article where the author uses sarcasm and slang. Why does the author use these devices? Are they effective?
4. In paragraph 5, the author plays on the common phrase "Don't count your chickens before they are hatched." Does the author's use of this phrase work effectively in the article? Why or why not?

Thinking Critically

1. Why are people more likely to be successful in a job that they enjoy?
2. Why does being out of work carry a stigma in our culture?
3. Why do typos and misspellings on résumés and cover letters remain a top complaint of hiring managers?
4. Why are hiring managers looking for reasons to cull applicants?
5. The author takes a reverse approach: She tells her readers what not to do to find a job instead of telling the readers what *to* do to find one. Evaluate the effectiveness of this reverse approach.

Writing About the Reading

A Paragraph

1. Imagine that you have just completed an interview for your dream job. Write a paragraph to include in a thank-you letter to the interviewer assuring him or her of your interest in the job.
2. Explain the advantages and disadvantages of getting a job through your friends, teachers, family, or professional peers.

An Essay

1. The author asserts that interviewees should be careful to dress professionally. Others may argue that attire should not matter when a

person is being interviewed. Choose one of these positions to support in an essay.
2. Can you think of other mistakes that people typically make when seeking a job? Write an essay explaining the additional mistakes you have identified.
3. Select a job that you would like to have in the future. Write a cover letter to the employer explaining why you are uniquely qualified for that job.

A Creative Activity

Create several scenarios portraying people making mistakes during interviews. Exchange your scenarios with a peer and attempt to identify the mistake in each scenario.

Job Search 2.OH!: There Are Some New Rules of the Road for Searching the Web for Work

▶ Jill Rachlin Marbaix

Journal Writing

Write a journal entry about the risks of sharing personal information online.

Reading Strategy

This article provides advice and guidelines for job seekers who are using the Web to search for employment. As you read, highlight the main points the author makes about searching for work online. The article first appeared in *U.S. News & World Report* in 2004.

Vocabulary Preview

niche (2) a special area of demand for a product or service
fads (6) trends
leverage (6) use to your advantage
downsides (8) disadvantages
avid (9) enthusiastic, devoted
comped (10) complimentary, free

Are you one of the millions of people searching for a job online? Be- 1
fore you send another resume out into cyberspace, there are some important things you need to know about how and where to find a job on the Web.

Despite fewer job openings and more job seekers, real opportuni- 2
ties exist. Employers say that one third of all new hires last year came through the Internet. However, only about 15 percent of those hires applied through the big job boards such as Monster.com, Career Builder.com, and Hotjobs.com, according to a new study by Career-Xroads, a recruiting technology group in Kendall Park, N.J. Industry-

focused niche sites were slightly more effective; 17.6 percent of new online hires came from sites like Medzilla.com, a pharmaceutical industry site, and IEEE.org, the electrical engineering association's Web site.

3   The best place to find work on the Web: a company's own site. Employers say that a whopping 67.9 percent of Internet hires came from their own backyards last year. "So, what they're saying," explains Gerry Crispin, who coauthored the study by CareerXroads, "is that no matter where you find the lead about us, we want you to apply through the company Web site."

4   Why do companies prefer their own Web sites by such a wide margin? "It saves them money, brands them with candidates, and builds a good pool of candidates," says Kevin Marasco, director of marketing for Recruitmax, which makes workforce management software for Fortune 500 firms.

Name Dropping

5   Simply sending your resume directly to the company's Web site is not enough, however. Experts say you need to include a referral from an employee of the target company in your application if you want your résumé to shoot to the top of the pile. The person referring you doesn't have to be your best friend, just someone in the company willing to let you use his or her name. "I'd never apply to a company today without getting an employee to refer me," says Crispin. "I believe that the advantage is 100 to 1. I'd even stand outside and offer an employee $5 to refer me because it means that much to me."

6   Ironically, the tried-and-true technique of networking is one of the latest fads in Internet job hunting. Social networking sites like LinkedIn.com, ZeroDegrees.com, Spoke.com, Tribe.net, and Ryze.com have begun hooking up professionals in formal and informal ways. In fact, LinkedIn.com, which lets a member leverage his E-mail address book into a huge web of professional contacts, has taken referral-based job hunting to the next level. It has just announced a partnership with the Direct Employers Association, a job board whose 200,000 listings link directly to corporate Web sites. When LinkedIn members go to a listing, they'll not only get the job description but also find out whom they know who could introduce them to a person already working at that company. Even the largest job site of them all, Monster.com, is getting into the act. It is introducing a networking feature that lets users enter their own professional profiles, search for someone else's profile, or try to find people with similar professional experience. "We match people who wouldn't otherwise meet," says Monster's senior vice president of consumer products, Michael Schutzler.

Through the Grapevine

This trend doesn't surprise career-counseling veterans like Dick Bolles,   7
author of *What Color Is Your Parachute?* "Personal contacts are the
best way," says Bolles, who runs his own Web site. "Employers never
liked resumes. When an employer has a vacancy, where do they advertise? Well, 80 percent of the time they don't. They have a grapevine."

One important job-hunting rule to remember: Be careful about   8
giving out your personal information. Many searchers don't realize
that if they post a resume or hire a firm to "blast" it to hundreds of
companies, their personal information could be circling cyberspace
for years to come—and possibly fall into the hands of an identity thief.
"At this point in time, I don't recommend posting a resume online anymore," says Pam Dixon, executive director of the World Privacy Forum. "The risks outweigh the benefit." Even when you answer an
Internet ad, Dixon suggests caution. Use only your first initial, not your
name, on your resume, use a post office box, not a permanent address,
and create a disposable E-mail address exclusively for job hunting.
Never include your Social Security number or the names and phone
numbers of your references on your resume, either. "If you never look
online, you'll miss opportunities," says Dixon, "but there are some serious downsides to it if you do not know what you're doing."

Julianna Firtel, a 26-year-old administration manager from San   9
Diego, is one job hunter who made the Internet work for her. After

---

Career Clicks

It's no longer wise to splatter your résumé across the Net. Better
bets are corporate, industry-specific, and so-called networking
sites:

- Medzilla.com: The place to go for jobs in the pharmaceutical
  industry.

- LinkedIn.com: You can network here with like-minded professionals and follow links to corporate Web sites.

- Malakye.com: "Action" sports fanatics might find a dream job
  here.

- Monster.com: Still the 800-pound gorilla but now with a networking feature that allows job seekers to meet up with others of similar career interests.

- IEEE.org: Here's where an electrical engineer might find job
  leads.

2½ months of answering ads on both large and small job boards with no results, the avid snowboarder started networking and was told about Malakye.com, a job site for the "action" sport industry.

Firtel applied to several companies before getting a call from Pen-   10
tagon Distribution, a maker of snowboards and accessories. During the phone interview, she discovered that she and the interviewer had a former colleague in common. Both sought him out for references, and a week and a half later, she was hired to manage Pentagon's office and work on its Web site. "It's my ideal job!" she says happily. "We even get comped lift tickets. When you enjoy what you do, it's not work."

Examining the Reading

Finding Meaning

1. According to employers, what percentage of new employees were hired through the Internet last year?
2. What is the best place to find work on the Web?
3. Describe two networking trends that assist job seekers on the Internet.
4. What are the risks of disclosing personal information online? List at least four "job-hunting rules" for giving out personal information online.
5. Why do companies prefer that applicants use their own web site to apply for jobs?

Understanding Technique

1. Why is the title appropriate for the content of this article?
2. Evaluate the effectiveness of opening the article with a question. Does the author succeed in capturing the reader's interest?
3. Highlight the author's thesis statement.
4. What types of evidence does the author use to support her thesis?

Thinking Critically

1. Describe the tone of this article. Underline examples of words and phrases that establish the tone.
2. Explain the term "name dropping" (paragraph 5). How effective do you think such referral-based job hunting is?
3. Explain the phrase "through the grapevine" (paragraph 7). What informal networks (or grapevines) are you a part of?
4. How do the expert opinions included in the article support the author's thesis?
5. Who is the intended audience for this article?

Writing About the Reading

A Paragraph

1. Visit one of the job search sites mentioned in the essay. Write a paragraph describing how the site works, what you learned, and whether you would consider using it.
2. Write a paragraph describing how you or someone you know found a job. Explain how you learned about the job, how you applied, and whether you were hired.

An Essay

1. Think about the statement by job seeker/snowboarder Julianna Firtel: "When you enjoy what you do, it's not work" (paragraph 10). Write an essay describing your ideal job and how you would go about finding it.
2. What other aspects of life involve networking and going through the grapevine? Write an essay exploring the ways that our connections to family, friends, colleagues, and community affect our lives. (Hint: finding someone to date, trying new restaurants, shopping, etc.)

A Creative Activity

Visit all of the sites listed in the article. Compare the sites and then write about the things you liked or disliked about each site. Which sites were most (and least) helpful to you, considering your interests and your chosen field?

Preparing for a Job Interview

▶ **Courtland L. Bovée, John V. Thill, and Barbara E. Schatzman**

This article, originally published in Business Communication Today, *offers useful advice for preparing for a job interview.*

Journal Writing

Write a journal entry about an experience in which you found yourself completely unprepared. What did the experience teach you?

Reading Strategy

As you read this article, highlight the key steps you should follow in preparing for a job interview.

Vocabulary Preview

mandatory (1) required, essential
bolster (1) reinforce
collaborate (4) work together
elicit (8) bring out
adept (11) skillful
inarticulate (13) unable to express ideas clearly
frivolous (18) lacking in seriousness or substance

*F*or a successful interview, preparation is mandatory. The best way to   1
prepare for a job interview is to think about the job itself and prepare. It's perfectly normal to feel a little anxious before an interview. But good preparation will help you perform well. Be sure to consider any cultural differences when preparing for interviews, and base your approach on what your audience expects. Before the interview, learn about the organization, think ahead about questions, bolster your confidence, polish your interview style, plan to look good, and be ready when you arrive.

Source: Bovee/Thill/Schatzman, *Business Communication Today,* 7th Edition, © 2003. Reprinted by permission of Pearson Education, Inc., Upper Saddle River, NJ.

Learn About the Organization

When planning your employment search, you probably already re-   2
searched the companies you sent your résumé to. But now that you've
been invited for an interview, you'll want to fine-tune your research
and brush up on the facts you've collected.

Today's companies expect serious candidates to demonstrate an   3
understanding of the company's operations, its market, and its strategic and tactical problems. Learning about the organization and the job
enables you to show the interviewer just how you will meet the organization's particular needs. With a little research, for instance, you would
discover that Microsoft plans on investing heavily in the technical and
marketing support of software developers as well as making things
simpler for all users and system administrators. Knowing these facts
might help you pinpoint aspects of your background (such as the ability to simplify processes) that would appeal to Microsoft's recruiters.

Plan for the Employer's Questions

Employers usually gear their interview questions to specific organiza-   4
tional needs. You can expect to be asked about your skills, achievements, and goals, as well as about your attitude toward work and
school, your relationships with others (work supervisors, colleagues,
and fellow students), and occasionally your hobbies and interests.
Candidates might be asked to collaborate on a decision or to develop a
group presentation. Trained observers evaluate the candidates' performance using predetermined criteria and then advise management on
how well each person is likely to handle the challenges normally faced
on the job.

For a look at the types of questions often asked, see Table A. Jot   5
down a brief answer to each one. Then read over the answers until you
feel comfortable with each of them. Although practicing your answers
will help you feel prepared and confident, you don't want to memorize
responses or sound overrehearsed. You might also give a list of interview questions to a friend or relative and have that person ask you various questions at random. This method helps you learn to articulate
answers and to look at the person as you answer.

Plan Questions of Your Own

The questions you ask in an interview are just as important as the an-   6
swers you provide. By asking intelligent questions, you demonstrate
your understanding of the organization, and you can steer the discussion into those areas that allow you to present your qualifications to
best advantage. Before the interview, prepare a list of about a dozen
questions you need answered in order to evaluate the organization and
the job.

Table A Twenty-Five Common Interview Questions

Questions About College

1. What courses in college did you like most? Least? Why?
2. Do you think your extracurricular activities in college were worth the time you spent on them? Why or why not?
3. When did you choose your college major? Did you ever change your major? If so, why?
4. Do you feel you did the best scholastic work you are capable of?
5. Which of your college years was the toughest? Why?

Questions About Employers and Jobs

6. What jobs have you held? Why did you leave?
7. What percentage of your college expenses did you earn? How?
8. Why did you choose your particular field of work?
9. What are the disadvantages of your chosen field?
10. Have you served in the military? What rank did you achieve? What jobs did you perform?
11. What do you think about how this industry operates today?
12. Why do you think you would like this particular type of job?

Questions About Personal Attitudes and Preferences

13. Do you prefer to work in any specific geographic location? If so, why?
14. How much money do you hope to be earning in 5 years? In 10 years?
15. What do you think determines a person's progress in a good organization?
16. What personal characteristics do you feel are necessary for success in your chosen field?
17. Tell me a story.
18. Do you like to travel?
19. Do you think grades should be considered by employers? Why or why not?

Questions About Work Habits

20. Do you prefer working with others or by yourself?
21. What type of boss do you prefer?
22. Have you ever had any difficulty getting along with colleagues or supervisors? With instructors? With other students?
23. Would you prefer to work in a large or a small organization? Why?
24. How do you feel about overtime work?
25. What have you done that shows initiative and willingness to work?

Don't limit your questions to those you think will impress the in- 7
terviewer, or you won't get the information you'll need to make a wise
decision if and when you're offered the job. Here's a list of some things
you might want to find out:

- **Are these my kind of people?** Observe the interviewer, and if
  you can, arrange to talk with other employees.
- **Can I do this work?** Compare your qualifications with the requirements described by the interviewer.
- **Will I enjoy the work?** Know yourself and what's important to
  you. Will you find the work challenging? Will it give you feelings
  of accomplishment, of satisfaction, and of making a real contribution?
- **Is the job what I want?** You may never find a job that fulfills all
  your wants, but the position you accept should satisfy at least
  your primary ones. Will it make use of your best capabilities?
  Does it offer a career path to the long-term goals you've set?
- **Does the job pay what I'm worth?** By comparing jobs and
  salaries before you're interviewed, you'll know what's reasonable
  for someone with your skills in your industry.
- **What kind of person would I be working for?** If the interviewer is your prospective boss, watch how others interact with
  that person, tactfully query other employees, or pose a careful
  question or two during the interview. If your prospective boss is
  someone else, ask for that person's name, job title, and responsibilities. Try to learn all you can.
- **What sort of future can I expect with this organization?** How
  healthy is the organization? Can you look forward to advancement? Does the organization offer insurance, pension, vacation,
  or other benefits?

Rather than bombarding the interviewer with these questions the 8
minute you walk in the room, use a mix of formats to elicit this information. Start with a warm-up question to help break the ice. You
might ask a Microsoft recruiter, "What departments usually hire new
graduates?" After that, you might build rapport by asking an open-
ended question that draws out the interviewer's opinion ("How do you
think Internet sales will affect Microsoft's continued growth?"). Indirect questions can elicit useful information and show that you've prepared for the interview ("I'd really like to know more about Microsoft's
plans for expanding its corporate presence on the web" or "That recent
Business Week article about the company was very interesting"). Any
questions you ask should be in your own words so that you don't sound
like every other candidate. For a list of other good questions you might
use as a starting point, see Table B.

Table B Fifteen Questions to Ask the Interviewer	
Questions About the Job	**Questions About the Organization**
What are the job's major responsibilities?	What are the organization's major strengths? Weaknesses?
What qualities do you want in the person who fills this position?	Who are the organization's major competitors, and what are their strengths and weaknesses?
Do you want to know more about my related training?	What makes your organization different from others in the industry?
What is the first problem that needs the attention of the person you hire?	What are your organization's major markets?
Would relocation be required now or in the future?	Does the organization have any plans for new products? Acquisitions?
Why is this job now vacant?	How would you define your organization's managerial philosophy?
What can you tell me about the person I would report to?	What additional training does your organization provide?
	Do employees have an opportunity to continue their education with help from the organization?

Write your list of questions on a notepad and take it to the interview. If you need to, jot down brief notes during the meeting, and be sure to record answers in more detail afterward. Having a list of questions should impress the interviewer with your organization and thoroughness. It will also show that you're there to evaluate the organization and the job as well as to sell yourself.

Polish Your Interview Style
Confidence helps you walk into an interview, but once you're there, you want to give the interviewer an impression of poise, good manners,

and good judgment. Some job seekers hire professional coaches and image consultants to create just the right impression. Charging any-where from $125 to $500 an hour, these professionals spend a majority of their time teaching clients how to assess communication styles, and to do so they use role-playing, videotaping, and audiotaping. You can use these techniques too.

You can develop an adept style by staging mock interviews with a   11 friend. After each practice session, try to identify opportunities for im-provement. Have your friend critique your performance. You can tape-record or videotape these mock interviews and then evaluate them yourself. The taping process can be intimidating, but it helps you work out any problems before you begin actual job interviews.

As you stage your mock interviews, pay particular attention to   12 your nonverbal behavior. In the United States, you are more likely to have a successful interview if you maintain eye contact, smile fre-quently, sit in an attentive position, and use frequent hand gestures. These nonverbal signals convince the interviewer that you're alert, as-sertive, dependable, confident, responsible, and energetic. Some com-panies based in the United States are owned and managed by people from other cultures, so during your research, find out about the company's cultural background and preferences regarding nonverbal behavior.

The sound of your voice can also have a major impact on your suc-   13 cess in a job interview. You can work with a tape recorder to overcome voice problems. If you tend to speak too rapidly, practice speaking more slowly. If your voice sounds too loud or too soft, practice adjust-ing it. Work on eliminating speech mannerisms such as *you know, like,* and *um,* which might make you sound inarticulate.

Plan to Look Good

Physical appearance is important because clothing and grooming re-   14 veal something about a candidate's personality and professionalism. When it comes to clothing, the best policy is to dress conservatively. Wear the best-quality businesslike clothing you can, preferably in a dark, solid color. Avoid flamboyant styles, colors, and prints. Even in companies where interviewers may dress casually, it's important to show good judgment by dressing (and acting) in a professional man-ner. Some candidates are asking interviewers ahead of time what they should wear. One human resources executive tells job seekers to dress business casual because dressing in a suit, for example, looks awkward at his company.

Good grooming makes any style of clothing look better. Make sure   15 your clothes are clean and unwrinkled, your shoes unscuffed and well shined, your hair neatly styled and combed, your fingernails clean, and your breath fresh. If possible, check your appearance in a mirror before entering the room for the interview. Finally, remember that one of the best ways to look good is to smile at appropriate moments.

Be Ready When You Arrive

Plan to take a small notebook, a pen, a list of the questions you want to ask, two copies of your résumé (protected in a folder), an outline of what you have learned about the organization, and any past correspondence about the position. You may also want to take a small calendar, a transcript of your college grades, a list of references, and a portfolio containing samples of your work, performance reviews, and certificates of achievement. In an era when many people exaggerate their qualifications, visible proof of your abilities carries a lot of weight. 16

Be sure you know when and where the interview will be held. The worst way to start any interview is to be late. Check the route you will take, even if it means phoning the interviewer's secretary to ask. Find out how much time it takes to get there; then plan to arrive early. Allow a little extra time in case you run into a problem on the way. 17

Once you arrive, relax. You may have to wait a little while, so bring along something to read (the less frivolous or controversial, the better). If company literature is available, read it while you wait. In any case, be polite to the interviewer's assistant. If the opportunity presents itself, ask a few questions about the organization or express enthusiasm for the job. Refrain from smoking before the interview (nonsmokers can smell smoke on the clothing of interviewees), and avoid chewing gum in the waiting room. Anything you do or say while you wait may well get back to the interviewer, so make sure your best qualities show from the moment you enter the premises. That way you'll be ready for the interview itself once it actually begins. 18

Examining the Reading

Finding Meaning

1. According to the author, a candidate should be able to demonstrate an understanding of certain aspects of a company. What are these aspects?
2. Name at least five things that a candidate should expect to be asked about during an interview.
3. In addition to gaining information about the job, why is it important for a candidate to ask questions during an interview?
4. How do professional coaches and image consultants teach their clients about communication styles?

5. Describe four nonverbal signals that contribute to a successful interview in the United States.
6. What should a candidate bring to an interview?
7. Why does the author recommend that candidates bring "visible proof" of their abilities?

Understanding Technique

1. What is the writer's thesis? Evaluate how well it is supported.
2. Describe the essay's organization.
3. What do the headings and bulleted lists contribute to the essay?
4. Evaluate the essay's introduction. Because this article first appeared within a textbook chapter, it does not have a strong conclusion. What should a stronger conclusion contain?

Thinking Critically

1. Why should candidates consider cultural differences when preparing for an interview?
2. Evaluate the list of questions in Table A. What questions would you add to the list?
3. What do clothing and grooming reveal about a job candidate? Do you agree with the author that the best policy is to dress conservatively? Explain why or why not.
4. What visible proof of your abilities could you present at a job interview?

Writing About the Reading

A Paragraph

1. Choose one of the questions from Table A and write a paragraph answering it. Write as though you were answering an interviewer.
2. Suppose you are applying for a job as a high school teacher (a job of your choice). Write a paragraph describing how you would dress for the interview.

An Essay

1. Write an essay describing your first job interview or an experience in which you met someone in authority for the first time. Describe whether the interview went well or poorly, and explain why you think so. Did you prepare for the interview in any of the ways de-

scribed in the article? If the interview did not go well, discuss how it might have gone better if you had followed some of the suggestions in the article.

2. Question 17 in Table A is "Tell me a story." What story would you choose to tell an interviewer? Write an essay in which you tell that story, and explain why you think it is appropriate for a job interview.

3. Suppose you are interviewing a candidate for a job. Choose a job that you have held or are familiar with. Create a short list of questions and write an essay explaining what you would learn about the candidate from each question.

Creative Activities

1. In paragraph 7, the author simply lists questions you might want answered during an interview. Read the list and consider how you would rank the questions in order of importance. For example, is salary or the potential for advancement more important to you? Rewrite the list in the order of your priorities, and then justify your rankings.

2. Imagine that you are preparing for a job interview. Take the author's advice about using a tape recorder to practice answering interview questions. Evaluate the sound of your voice and make adjustments to the speed of your speech and the volume level of your voice as necessary. Identify and work on eliminating any undesirable speech mannerisms you may have.

A Seafood Survey

▶ **Robert Wood**
Student Essay

*Robert Wood, a student at Niagara County Community College,
humorously describes his work experiences at the fish department of a local supermarket. You will be surprised by the questions his customers ask him and how he responds.*

*O*verall, I would have to say I have a very unique part-time job. I   1
work in the seafood department at Wegmans supermarket, and since I
deal with customers all day long, I get a wide range of questions and
requests from people of all ages. Sometimes the questions come so fast
that it feels like I am responding to a seafood survey!

When I first started at Wegmans I really didn't know very much   2
about seafood, only what I had tried in the past. At first I was kind of
nervous when customers would ask me question after question about
seafood and I didn't have the answers. Now, after two years on the job,
I think I know a great deal about seafood, and more than I want to
know about customers and how to handle them.

Most of the time, customers' questions are just the routine ones.   3
They might want to know how long the fish should be cooked or what
recipes are best for a particular type of fish. Routine, polite answers are
all that are required. But once in a great while I get some really out of the
ordinary questions or requests and they require diplomatic handling.

Once a customer asked me for a lobster. We have those live in a big   4
tank, so you have to go in with these special tongs and get them out.
But they had just brought in a lot of lobsters that day, and they were all
packed on top of each other. So, the lady picked out the one she wanted
which, of course, was on the bottom of the pile. The tongs kept slip-
ping, and each time I would go to grab the lobster she wanted, he'd get
away. Finally, I got a good hold on him and dragged him up to the top,
and he was struggling. I didn't think anything of it because they always
do that, but the lady was watching him the whole time and I guess she
felt sorry for him or something because she told me to put him back!
Naturally, I asked her why, and she said that after seeing him fight for
his life, she couldn't take him home and cook him. It was as if she
thought he would be on her conscience. She went over to the meat department instead and bought a steak.

Another thing about lobsters is that once people see them crawling around alive in that tank, they think all the other fish on the ice is frozen and maybe not really fish. One customer asked me once, "How fresh are those fish—really?" He stressed the word *really* like he didn't believe they were all that fresh. I told him they were, and he tried to tell me that to be really fresh, they should be swimming around in a tank of their own! I explained to him, politely of course, that if Wegmans had a tank for each fish, there wouldn't be room for anything else. He said he thought he'd rather go down to the river and catch his own. That way he'd know it was fresh.

One of the weirdest requests I ever had was made when we handled "whole fish" at my store, and we would scale, clean, and fillet each fish to order. One day, an old lady wanted to purchase some whole yellow pike. She selected her fish and I weighed it up and asked what she would like done to it. She said that she would like it scaled, gutted, and the head and fins removed—so far a normal order. But then she said she wanted me to dig out the eyes for her and wrap them separately. I thought to myself, "What does she want with a yellow pike's eyes?" I finished processing the fish and marked the package with the eyes in it so she could find it when she got home. After I handed her order to her, I had to ask her why she needed the eyes. She replied that she used the eyes in a recipe for a delicious soup! I didn't ask her what it tastes like.

Every once in a while you get those questions or customers that make your day. There was a young boy who came to the seafood department every Saturday when I would be working, to look at the fish on display. He was about eight years old, was very bright, and was interested in fish. He always asked questions about where particular fish came from and what they ate. One time, he asked me if he could have a clam for his aquarium at home. Of course I gave him one to take home. The next Saturday, he came back and asked me what clams eat for food because he thought his clam was hungry. I was surprised that the clam was still alive. When I told him this, he said he thought it was still alive, but it never moved or opened up. He said he had taken good care of it. He had even cleaned it up and removed some meat that was stuck in its shell. I tried not to laugh as I explained to him that the meat part was the clam's body and that was why it wasn't moving. He replied, "Well, it tasted pretty good, anyway."

One of the funniest things that ever happened, though, was when a girl about my age came up to me with a shopping cart that had about 10 cans of tuna fish in it. She told me she wanted to impress her new boyfriend by cooking outdoors for him, and he didn't eat meat. She asked me what was the easiest way to grill tuna. I thought she was pulling my leg, so I told her she could open all those cans and empty them onto the barbecue or she could just buy one big one. That's how I said it, "one big one." And she looked at me like I was crazy! Then she looked at all the cans of tuna fish in her cart and said, "You mean I can buy, like, one really, really big can of tuna fish?" Then I realized she didn't have a clue, so I pointed to the whole tuna lying there on the ice next to the flounder, and she got really wide-eyed and said, "Oh, you mean there's an actual fish called a tuna? I thought they only came in a can." I couldn't help laughing. Fortunately, she laughed too, or I could've lost my job.

During the time I worked at Wegmans, I have learned many im-   9 portant skills. In addition to the skills required for processing and selling seafood, this job has taught me important "people" skills. I have learned that if you keep an open mind and maintain your sense of humor, you can succeed not only at the seafood market but also at anything in your life.

Examining the Essay

1. Evaluate the essay's title.
2. Wood relates stories about customers to support his thesis. What other types of details might he have used?
3. Evaluate Wood's use of transitions to connect his ideas.

Writing an Essay

1. Write an essay describing strange or peculiar people you have met, tasks that you have been asked to perform, or questions or requests that you have encountered on the job.
2. Wood asserts that he has learned a great deal about customers and how to handle them. Write an essay discussing what you have learned from a job that you hold now or have held.
3. Write an essay describing your best or worst employment experience.

 ## Making Connections

1. Both "Job Search 2.OH!: There Are Some New Rules of the Road for Searching the Web for Work" and "Seven Easy Ways to Become an Unhappy Job Seeker" offer advice for those looking for a job. Compare the two articles. What information is practical and useful to you? Write an essay identifying the more useful article, giving reasons for your choice.

2. Both "Preparing for a Job Interview" and "What Are They Probing For?" focus on assessment in the workplace.

Write an essay explaining the role and importance of assessment in the workplace.

3. Both "Cross Talk" and "A Seafood Survey" focus on communication in the workplace. Whereas Tannen focuses on communication between men and women employees, Wood focuses on communication between employee and customers. Do you think differences between men's and women's communication styles affect relationships between customers and employees? Observe a variety of employee–customer interactions (male customer–male employee, female customer–male employee, etc.). Note the similarities and differences and write an essay reporting your findings.

Internet Connections

1. Every year the Great Place to Work Institute produces the "100 Best Companies to Work for in America." This list is published in *Fortune* magazine and appears on the web site (**http://www.greatplacetowork.com/best/list-bestusa .htm**). Look over this list. Examine the nomination process (**http://www.greatplacetowork.com/best/nominations/ nominations.php?thelist=100best**). Write a summary and evaluation of the steps followed in creating this list.

2. Visit several of the career planning sites listed below. Then write an essay explaining what you learned about the career planning process.

   http://www.employmentguide.com/ careeradvice/index.html

   http://www.medaille.edu/careerplanning/ whatcanIdo.html

   http://www.careerexplorer.net/features/ career_assessment.asp

3. The U.S. government publishes a guide to careers called the *Occupational Outlook Handbook*. Browse some of the job types listed in the online version at **http://stats.bls. gov/search/ooh.asp?ct=OOH.** Write a paragraph contrasting two of the jobs listed at the site—one you would like to have and one you would not like to have.

   (If any of these web sites are unavailable, use a search engine to locate another appropriate site.)

Chapter 4

Cultures That Shape Our Lives

People in the United States represent a wide variety of cultural backgrounds. "Culture" refers to the values and ways of doing things that a group of people share. Except for the Native Americans, our ancestors all came from somewhere else—Africa, China, Eastern or Western Europe, South America, Vietnam, and so on. Although Americans are an ethnically diverse bunch, we share some common concerns, goals, and values. Regardless of our cultural heritage, we all value our families; we value our friendships; we seek self-worth and self-esteem; we seek freedom, opportunity, and knowledge.

Subcultures exist within a culture. They are groups that share some common identity. From the shared identity, shared customs and behaviors develop. A good example is the college student subculture. All members of this group attend college (their shared identity), and many act and dress in similar ways (many carry backpacks, wear jeans, etc.). Other subcultures include religious sects, sports players, and musicians.

Learning about others' cultures and subcultures can give life and meaning to our shared concerns and values. As we discover how different cultures celebrate a holiday, for example, the significance of our own celebrations becomes more important and more clear. Or as we study birth and death rituals of various groups, our own traditions become more meaningful, and feelings toward those experiences surface, making us richer, more self-aware people. Cultural awareness shapes our lives by expanding our self-awareness.

The readings in this chapter are about subcultures, ethnic and otherwise, and how they define who we are. For example, you will read a description of Kurdish sisters who escaped from Iraq and immigrated to the United States ("The Beautiful Laughing Sisters—An Arrival Story"). But many times, these cultural "definitions" are limiting and lead to divisions between cultures. This is the topic of "Fifth Chinese Daughter," in which a young woman attempts to break away from cultural traditions; "Cultural Education in America," in which a college student experiences differences between his American college friends and the cultural tradition of his native Hong Kong; "Primary Colors," which describes how an interracial child fits in society; and "Black *and* Latino," which relates a young man's experience of being both black and Puerto Rican. Subcultures do not always have to be racial or ethnic divisions, as you will see in a homeless man's account of how he searches for food ("Dumpster Diving") and how some deaf people wish to maintain a separate subculture ("Silenced Voices: Deaf Cultures and 'Hearing' Families").

Brainstorming About Culture

Class Activity: Each group of students should brainstorm to create lists of all the cultures and subcultures of which any group member has any inside knowledge or experience.

Primary Colors

▸ **Kim McLarin**

In this essay from the New York Times Magazine, *a mother writes about how society has trouble seeing the connection between her and her lighter-skinned daughter.*

Journal Writing

Write a journal entry about an event or situation in which you felt that you stood out from other people around you.

Reading Strategy

As you read, highlight words and phrases that reveal the author's attitude toward her daughter.

Vocabulary Preview

retrospect (5) looking back
eccentricities (6) oddities; exceptions
umber (6) brownish
abduction (9) kidnapping
disconcerting (10) unsettling; upsetting
condemnation (13) strong criticism or disapproval
allegiances (13) loyalties
denounce (13) condemn; criticize openly
align (14) join; line up

A few weeks after my daughter was born, I took her to a new pedia-   1
trician for an exam. The doctor took one look at Samantha and exclaimed: "Wow! She's so light!" I explained that my husband is white,
but it didn't seem to help. The doctor commented on Sam's skin color
so often that I finally asked what was on her mind.

"I'm thinking albino," she said.   2

The doctor, who is white, claimed she had seen the offspring of   3
many interracial couples, but never a child this fair. "They're usually a
darker, coffee-with-cream color. Some of them are this light at birth,
but by 72 hours you can tell they have a black parent."

To prove her point, she held her arm next to Samantha's stomach.   4
"I mean, this could be my child!"

It's funny now, in retrospect. But at the time, with my hormones 5 still raging from childbirth, the incident sent me into a panic. Any fool could see that Samantha wasn't an albino—she had black hair and dark blue eyes. It must be a trick. The doctor, who had left the room, probably suspected me of kidnapping this "white" child and was outside calling the police. By the time she returned I was ready to fight.

Fortunately, her partner dismissed the albino theory, and we escaped and found a new pediatrician, one who knows a little more about genetic eccentricities. But the incident stayed with me because, in the months since, other white people have assumed Samantha is not my child. This is curious to me, this inability to connect across skin tones, especially since Samantha has my full lips and broad nose. I'll admit that I myself didn't expect Sam to be quite so pale, so much closer to her father's Nordic coloring than my own umber tones. My husband is a blue-eyed strawberry blond; I figured that my genes would take his genes in the first round. 6

Wrong. 7

Needless to say, I love Sam just as she is. She is amazingly, heart- 8 breakingly beautiful to me in the way that babies are to their parents. She sweeps me away with her mischievous grin and her belly laugh, with the coy way she tilts her head after flinging the cup from her high chair. When we are alone and I look at Samantha, I see Samantha, not the color of her skin.

And yet, I admit that I wouldn't mind if she were darker, dark 9 enough so that white people would know she was mine and black people wouldn't give her a hard time. I know a black guy who, while crossing into Canada, was suspected of having kidnapped his fair-skinned son. So far no one has accused me of child abduction, but I have been mistaken for Samantha's nanny. It has happened so often that I've considered going into business as a nanny spy. I could sit in the park and take notes on your child-care worker. Better than hiding a video camera in the living room.

In a way it's disconcerting, my being mistaken for a nanny. Be- 10 cause, to be blunt, I don't like seeing black women caring for white children. It may be because I grew up in the South, where black women once had no choice but to leave their own children and suckle the offspring of others. The weight of that past, the whiff of a power imbalance, still stains such pairings for me. That's unfair, I know, to the professional, hard-working (mostly Caribbean) black nannies of New York. But there you are.

On the flip side, I think being darker wouldn't hurt Samantha with 11 black people, either. A few weeks ago, in my beauty shop, I overheard a woman trashing a friend for "slathering" his light-skinned children with sunscreen during the summer.

"Maybe he doesn't want them getting skin cancer," suggested the   12
listener. But my girl was having none of that.

"He doesn't want them getting black!" she said, as full of righteous   13
condemnation as only a black woman in a beauty shop can be. Now,
maybe the woman was right about her friend's motivation. Or maybe
she was 100 percent wrong. Maybe because she herself is the color of
butterscotch she felt she had to declare her allegiances loudly, had to
place herself prominently high on the unofficial black scale and denounce anyone caught not doing the same. Either way, I know it
means grief for Sam.

I think that as time goes on my daughter will probably align with   14
black people anyway, regardless of the relative fairness of her skin. My
husband is fine with that, as long as it doesn't mean denying him or his
family.

The bottom line is that society has a deep need to categorize   15
people, to classify and, yes, to stereotype. Race is still the easiest, most
convenient way of doing so. That race tells you, in the end, little or
nothing about a person is beside the point. We still feel safer believing
that we can sum up one another at a glance.

Examining the Reading

Finding Meaning

1. When McLarin took Samantha to her pediatrician, how did the
   doctor respond?
2. Why did this incident cause the author to "panic"?
3. Why did McLarin find a new pediatrician?
4. What does the author's husband look like?
5. How does the author feel about black women caring for white children who are not their own?

Understanding Technique

1. Identify McLarin's thesis and evaluate its placement.
2. How does McLarin reveal the attitude of various groups within our
   society toward her daughter?

Thinking Critically

1. What does the author mean by an "inability to connect across skin
   tones" (paragraph 6)?
2. Describe the tone of this essay.
3. What do you think was the author's purpose in writing this essay?

4. Why does the author say, "I think being darker wouldn't hurt Samantha."
5. What does the author most worry about for her daughter?

Writing About the Reading

A Paragraph

1. Write a paragraph explaining what you notice first when you meet a person for the first time.
2. Write a paragraph about how it feels to be different in any sense of the word.

An Essay

1. Do you agree with the author that society needs to categorize, classify, and stereotype people? Write an essay defending or rejecting this idea.
2. Write an essay explaining how your first impression of another person proved to be incorrect.

Creative Activities

1. Imagine yourself in the author's situation. If you were part of an interracial couple, what concerns might you have for your child? What could you do to protect your child?
2. Compose a letter to the author's light-skinned child explaining the challenges she will face and suggesting how she might confront them.

Black *and* Latino

▶ Roberto Santiago

Am I black or am I Latino? This is the question that troubled Santiago throughout his childhood as a member of two ethnic groups. Read this essay, first published in Essence *magazine, to discover how he resolved this issue.*

Journal Writing

Write a journal entry describing what you know about your ethnic origins. Are they important to you?

Reading Strategy

To strengthen your comprehension of this essay, highlight statements by Santiago that reveal his attitude toward his biracial heritage.

Vocabulary Preview

perplexes (1) confuses
heritages (1) inherited backgrounds
parody (4) ridiculous imitation
eons (6) long periods of time
conquests (6) subjugations; forced colonizations
predominant (6) most important
determinant (6) deciding
slur (8) disrespectful remark
solace (9) comfort
pegged (11) marked; identified
iconoclast (11) someone who overthrows a traditional idea
                    or image

"*T*here is no way that you can be black and Puerto Rican at the same   1
time." What? Despite the many times I've heard this over the years,
that statement still perplexes me. I *am* both and always have been. My
color is a blend of my mother's rich, dark skin tone and my father's
white complexion. As they were both Puerto Rican, I spoke Spanish
before English, but I am totally bilingual. My life has been shaped by
my black and Latino heritages, and despite other people's confusion, I

don't feel I have to choose one or the other. To do so would be to deny a part of myself.

There has not been a moment in my life when I did not know that   2
I looked black—and I never thought that others did not see it, too. But growing up in East Harlem, I was also aware that I did not "act black," according to the African-American boys on the block.

My lighter-skinned Puerto Rican friends were less of a help in this   3
department. "You're not black," they would whine, shaking their heads. "You're a *boriqua* [slang for Puerto Rican], you ain't no *moreno* [black]." If that was true, why did my mirror defy the rules of logic? And most of all, why did I feel that there was some serious unknown force trying to make me choose sides?

Acting black. Looking black. Being a real black. This debate among   4
us is almost a parody. The fact is that I am black, so why do I need to prove it?

The island of Puerto Rico is only a stone's throw away from Haiti,   5
and, no fooling, if you climb a palm tree, you can see Jamaica bobbing on the Atlantic. The slave trade ran through the Caribbean basin, and virtually all Puerto Rican citizens have some African blood in their veins. My grandparents on my mother's side were the classic *negro como carbón* (black as carbon) people, but despite the fact that they were as dark as can be, they are officially not considered black.

There is an explanation for this, but not one that makes much   6
sense, or difference, to a working-class kid from Harlem. Puerto Ricans identify themselves as Hispanics—part of a worldwide race that originated from eons of white Spanish conquests—a mixture of white, African, and *Indio* blood, which, categorically, is apart from black. In other words, the culture is the predominant and determinant factor. But there are frustrations in being caught in a duo-culture, where your skin color does not necessarily dictate what you are. When I read Piri Thomas's searing autobiography, *Down These Mean Streets*, in my early teens, I saw that he couldn't figure out other people's attitudes toward his blackness, either.

My first encounter with this attitude about the race thing rode on   7
horseback. I had just turned six years old and ran toward the bridle path in Central Park as I saw two horses about to trot past. "Yea! Horsie! Yea!" I yelled. Then I noticed one figure on horseback. She was white, and she shouted, "Shut up, you f—g nigger! Shut up!" She pulled back on the reins and twisted the horse in my direction. I can still feel the spray of gravel that the horse kicked at my chest. And suddenly she was gone. I looked back, and, in the distance, saw my parents playing Whiffle Ball with my sister. They seemed miles away.

They still don't know about this incident. But I told my Aunt Aure-   8
lia almost immediately. She explained what the words meant and why

they were said. Ever since then I have been able to express my anger appropriately through words or action in similar situations. Self-preservation, ego, and pride forbid men from ever ignoring, much less forgetting, a slur.

Aunt Aurelia became, unintentionally, my source for answers I   9
needed about color and race. I never sought her out. She just seemed to appear at my home during the points in my childhood when I most needed her for solace. "Puerto Ricans are different from American blacks," she told me once. "There is no racism between what you call white and black. Nobody even considers the marriages interracial." She then pointed out the difference in color between my father and mother. "You never noticed that," she said, "because you were not raised with that hang-up."

Aunt Aurelia passed away before I could follow up on her observa-   10
tion. But she had made an important point. It's why I never liked the attitude that says I should be exclusive to one race.

My behavior toward this race thing pegged me as an iconoclast of   11
sorts. Children from mixed marriages, from my experience, also share this attitude. If I have to bear the label of iconoclast because the world wants people to be in set categories and I don't want to, then I will.

A month before Aunt Aurelia died, she saw I was a little down   12
about the whole race thing, and she said, "Roberto, don't worry. Even if—no matter what you do—black people in this country don't, you can always depend on white people to treat you like a black."

Examining the Reading

Finding Meaning

1. What problems did Santiago face during childhood?
2. According to the author, what other race (besides white and African) do all Puerto Rican citizens have in their blood?
3. What explanation does the author give for his maternal grandparents being "black as carbon" and yet being "officially not considered black"?
4. Describe the author's first encounter with prejudice.
5. According to his aunt, why had the author never noticed the difference in color between his mother and his father?

Understanding Technique

Santiago opens his essay with a question. Discuss the effectiveness of this strategy as a means of starting the essay.

Thinking Critically

1. Is there a tendency in our society to label or compartmentalize people? Why do you think people do this, and what are its positive and negative effects?
2. When the author had his first encounter with prejudice, why do you think he chose to tell his aunt but not his parents?
3. What part did the author's aunt play in shaping his life—particularly with regard to ideas about race?
4. What does the last sentence of the reading reveal about discrimination in our country?

Writing About the Reading

A Paragraph

1. Santiago experiences conflict about his ethnic origins. Write a paragraph describing a conflict, ethnic or otherwise, that you have experienced. Explain how you resolved it.
2. Santiago read an autobiography of a man who shared his confusion about race. Have you ever read a book or watched a movie or television program that dealt with a problem you were experiencing? Write a paragraph explaining whether seeing others deal with a problem helps you cope with it.

An Essay

1. Santiago felt that people wanted him to be either black or Puerto Rican; they wanted him to choose sides. Many times in our lives, we are asked or forced to take sides. Write an essay discussing a situation in which you were asked or forced to take sides or to take a stand on an issue.
2. Santiago asks, "I am black, so why do I need to prove it?" Often, in our culture, we are called upon to prove who or what we are. Write an essay describing a situation in which you were called upon to prove yourself.
3. Imagine that you are black raised in a white family or white raised in a black family. Write an essay discussing the problems you would face.

A Creative Activity

Suppose Santiago, in adulthood, were to meet the woman on the horse. What do you think he would say to her? Role-play your answers to this question in class.

Fifth Chinese Daughter

▶ Jade Snow Wong

Traditional Chinese families hold to a culture in which children must obey their parents and seek permission for what they do. In this essay, the author describes her breaking from this cultural tradition. This essay was taken from a book titled The Immigrant Experience.

Journal Writing

Write a journal entry on how you feel after having a heated argument with a family member or close friend.

Reading Strategy

Highlight words, phrases, and descriptions that reveal how Wong's parents felt about her actions.

Vocabulary Preview

impulsively (1) without thinking or planning
incredulous (5) not believing
unfilial (5) against family
revered (5) admired and respected
denounced (5) spoke out against
ingrate (5) ungrateful person
whims (5) sudden, fanciful ideas
proclamation (6) announcement
innuendoes (7) subtle or indirect usually negative comments
underscored (7) emphasized
devastated (8) stunned; overwhelmed
conceding (9) acknowledging; admitting

*O*ne afternoon on a Saturday, which was normally occupied with my   1
housework job, I was unexpectedly released by my employer, who was departing for a country weekend. It was a rare joy to have free time and I wanted to enjoy myself for a change. There had been a Chinese-American boy who shared some classes with me. Sometimes we had

---

Source: Jade Snow Wong, "The Fifth Chinese Daughter," from *The Immigrant Experience* by Thomas C. Wheeler. Copyright © 1971 by Doubleday, a division of Bantam Doubleday Dell Publishing Group, Inc. Used by permission of Doubleday, a division of Random House, Inc.

found each other walking to the same 8:00 A.M. class. He was not a special boyfriend, but I had enjoyed talking to him and had confided in him some of my problems. Impulsively, I telephoned him. I knew I must be breaking rules, and I felt shy and scared. At the same time, I was excited at this newly found forwardness, with nothing more purposeful than to suggest another walk together.

He understood my awkwardness and shared my anticipation. He   2
asked me to "dress up" for my first movie date. My clothes were limited but I changed to look more graceful in silk stockings and found a bright ribbon for my long black hair. Daddy watched, catching my mood, observing the dashing preparations. He asked me where I was going without his permission and with whom.

I refused to answer him. I thought of my rights! I thought he surely   3
would not try to understand. Thereupon Daddy thundered his displeasure and forbade my departure.

I found a new courage as I heard my voice announce calmly that I   4
was no longer a child, and if I could work my way through college, I would choose my own friends. It was my right as a person.

My mother heard the commotion and joined my father to face me;   5
both appeared shocked and incredulous. Daddy at once demanded the source of this unfilial, non-Chinese theory. And when I quoted my college professor, reminding him that he had always felt teachers should be revered, my father denounced that professor as a foreigner who was disregarding the superiority of our Chinese culture, with its sound family strength. My father did not spare me; I was condemned as an ingrate for echoing dishonorable opinions which should only be temporary whims, yet nonetheless inexcusable.

The scene was not yet over. I completed my proclamation to my father,   6
who had never allowed me to learn how to dance, by adding that I was attending a movie, unchaperoned, with a boy I met at college.

My startled father was sure that my reputation would be subject to   7
whispered innuendoes. I must be bent on disgracing the family name; I was ruining my future, for surely I would yield to temptation. My mother underscored him by saying that I hadn't any notion of the problems endured by parents of a young girl.

I would not give in. I reminded them that they and I were not in   8
China, that I wasn't going out with just anybody but someone I trusted! Daddy gave a roar that no man could be trusted, but I devastated them in declaring that I wished the freedom to find my own answers.

Both parents were thoroughly angered, scolded me for being   9
shameless, and predicted that I would some day tell them I was wrong. But I dimly perceived that they were conceding defeat and were perplexed at this breakdown of their training. I was too old to beat and too bold to intimidate.

Examining the Reading

Finding Meaning

1. How did Wong's father respond when she refused to tell him where she was going and with whom?
2. What was the argument between father and daughter really about?
3. What rules was Wong breaking?
4. Summarize the father's argument.
5. What was Wong's mother's reaction when she heard the argument between her husband and her daughter?
6. In the end, how did Wong win the argument?

Understanding Technique

1. Although Wong recounts a family dispute, she does not include dialogue. How would her essay have been changed by including it? Suggest places where dialogue could be added.
2. Describe how the essay is organized.
3. Wong's sentence structure is varied and therefore interesting. Cite several examples.

Thinking Critically

1. Why did the author assume that her father would not understand even before she attempted to explain the situation?
2. Why do you think the author's parents were so upset by her need for privacy and independence?
3. In what way was this incident a turning point in the author's life?
4. To what extent and in what ways do you think this incident shaped Wong's future actions in going against cultural traditions?

Writing About the Reading

A Paragraph

1. Write a paragraph explaining a conflict between you and your parents or an incident in which you disagreed with them about "the way to do things" (cultural traditions).
2. Sometimes it's necessary to do the opposite of what you know your family or friends want you to do. Write a paragraph describing a time when you felt that way or when you observed someone else doing so.

An Essay

At some point, we have all decided to act against a cultural tradition. Write an essay describing a situation in which you acted against tradition. Explain how other people responded to your decision and how you attempted to resolve any conflicts.

A Creative Activity

Write a paragraph describing what you think happened between Wong and her parents the day after her movie date.

The Beautiful Laughing Sisters—An Arrival Story

▶ Mary Pipher

This essay describes the story of a courageous Kurdish family who fled one life in search of another. The essay is excerpted from Pipher's book The Middle of Everywhere.

Journal Writing

Write a journal entry exploring the problems immigrants from the Middle East might face in the United States.

Reading Strategy

The author of this story writes that she is struck by the resilience of the sisters that she has met. As you read, note the instances when the sisters recover from misfortune.

Vocabulary Preview

array (1) arrangement
amendment (3) correction or alteration
sporadically (12) in irregular intervals
incredulously (15) unwilling to accept as true; skeptically
defiantly (17) boldly; in a challenging manner
sacred (24) entitled to reverence and respect
resilience (27) an ability to recover from misfortune or
               change
tactfully (31) with a keen sense of what to do to maintain
               good relationships with others

One of the best ways to understand the refugee experience is to be- 1
friend a family of new arrivals and observe their experiences in our country for the first year. That first year is the hardest. Everything is new and strange, and obstacles appear like the stars appear at dusk, in an uncountable array. This story is about a family I met during their first month in our country. I became their friend and cultural broker[1]

---

[1]Someone who helps people from other countries learn the customs of the new country.

and in the process learned a great deal about the refugee experience, and about us Americans.

On a fall day I met Shireen and Meena, who had come to this country from Pakistan. The Kurdish sisters were slender young women with alert expressions. They wore blue jeans and clunky high-heeled shoes. Shireen was taller and bolder, Meena was smaller and more soft-spoken. Their English was limited and heavily accented. (I later learned it was their sixth language after Kurdish, Arabic, Farsi, Urdu, and Hindi.)[2] They communicated with each other via small quick gestures and eye movements. Although they laughed easily, they watched to see that the other was okay at all times.   2

Shireen was the youngest and the only one of the six sisters who was eligible for high school. Meena, who was twenty-one, had walked the ten blocks from their apartment to meet Shireen at school on a bitterly cold day. Shireen told the family story. Meena occasionally interrupted her answers with a reminder, an amendment, or laughter.   3

Shireen was born in Baghdad in 1979, the last of ten children. Their mother, Zeenat, had been a village girl who entered an arranged marriage at fourteen. Although their family had been well educated, Zeenat couldn't read or write in any language. The family was prosperous and "Europeanized," as Shireen put it. She said, "Before our father was in trouble, we lived just like you. Baghdad was a big city. In our group of friends, men and women were treated as equals. Our older sisters went to movies and read foreign newspapers. Our father went to cocktail parties at the embassies."   4

However, their father had opposed Saddam Hussein, and from the time of Shireen's birth, his life was in danger. After Hussein came to power, terrible things happened to families like theirs. One family of eleven was taken to jail by his security forces and tortured to death. Prisoners were often fed rice mixed with glass so that they would quietly bleed to death in their cells. Girls were raped and impregnated by the security police. Afterward, they were murdered or killed themselves.   5

It was a hideous time. Schoolteachers tried to get children to betray their parents. One night the police broke into the family's house. They tore up the beds, bookcases, and the kitchen, and they took their Western clothes and tapes. After that night, all of the family except for one married sister made a daring escape into Iran.   6

Meena said, "It was a long time ago but I can see everything today." There was no legal way to go north, so they walked through Kurdistan at night and slept under bushes in the day. They found a guide who   7

---

[2]These languages, in addition to many others, are spoken in the Middle Eastern countries of Iran, Iraq, India, and Palestine.

made his living escorting Kurds[3] over the mountains. Twice they crossed rivers near flood stage. Entire families had been swept away by the waters and one of the sisters almost drowned when she fell off her horse. The trails were steep and narrow and another sister fell and broke her leg. Meena was in a bag slung over the guide's horse for three days. She remembered how stiff she felt in the bag, and Shireen remembered screaming, "I want my mama."

This was in the 1980s. While this was happening I was a psychologist building my private practice and a young mother taking my kids to *Sesame Street Live* and Vacation Village on Lake Okoboji.[4] I was dancing to the music of my husband's band, Sour Mash, listening to Van Morrison and Jackson Browne and reading P. D. James and Anne Tyler. Could my life have been happening on the same planet?

The family made it to a refugee camp in Iran. It was a miserable place with smelly tents and almost no supplies. Shireen said this was rough on her older siblings who had led lives of luxury. She and Meena adjusted more quickly. The sisters studied in an Iranian school for refugees.

They endured this makeshift camp for one very bad year. The Iranians insisted that all the women in the camp wear heavy scarves and robes and conform to strict rules. The soldiers in the camp shouted at them if they wore even a little lipstick. Shireen once saw a young girl wearing makeup stopped by a guard who rubbed it off her face. He had put ground glass in the tissue so that her cheeks bled afterward.

They decided to get out of Iran and traveled the only direction they could, east into Pakistan. They walked all the way with nothing to drink except salty water that made them even thirstier. I asked how long the trip took and Shireen said three days. Meena quickly corrected her: "Ten years."

Once in Pakistan they were settled by a relief agency in a border town called Quetta, where strangers were not welcome. The family lived in a small house with electricity that worked only sporadically. The stress of all the moves broke the family apart. The men left the women and the family has never reunited.

Single women in Quetta couldn't leave home unescorted and the sisters had no men to escort them. Only their mother, Zeenat, dared go out to look for food. As Meena put it, "She took good care of us and now we will take care of her."

The sisters almost never left the hut, but when they did, they wore robes as thick and heavy as black carpets. Meena demonstrated how

8

9

10

11

12

13

14

---

[3]A people of the Middle East whose homelands is in the mountainous regions of Iraq, Iran, and Turkey.
[4]A family resort in northwestern Iowa.

hard it was to walk in these clothes and how she often fell down. Even properly dressed, they were chased by local men. When they rode the bus to buy vegetables, they were harassed.

Without their heroic mother, they couldn't have survived. For   15 weeks at a time, the family was trapped inside the hut. At night the locals would break their windows with stones and taunt the sisters with threats of rape. Meena interrupted to say that every house in the village but theirs had weapons. Shireen said incredulously, "There were no laws in that place. Guns were laws."

One night some men broke into their hut and took what little   16 money and jewelry they had left. They had been sleeping and woke to see guns flashing around them. The next day they reported the break-in to the police. Shireen said, "The police told us to get our own guns." Meena said, "We were nothing to them. The police slapped and pushed us. We were afraid to provoke them."

During the time they were there, the Pakistanis tested a nuclear   17 bomb nearby and they all got sick. An older sister had seizures from the stress of their lives. Shireen said defiantly, "It was hard, but we got used to hard."

Still, the young women laughed as they told me about the black   18 robes and the men with guns. Their laughter was a complicated mixture of anxiety, embarrassment, and relief that it was over. It was perhaps also an attempt to distance themselves from that time and place.

They'd studied English in the hut and made plans for their future   19 in America or Europe. Shireen said, "I always knew that we would escape that place."

In Quetta the family waited ten years for papers that would allow   20 them to immigrate. Shireen looked at me and said, "I lost my teenage years there—all my teenage years."

Finally, in frustration, the family went on a hunger strike. They   21 told the relief workers they would not eat until they were allowed to leave Quetta. After a few days, the agency paperwork was delivered and the family was permitted to board a train for Islamabad.

In Islamabad they lived in a small apartment with no air condi-   22 tioning. Every morning they would soak their curtains in water to try to cool their rooms. It was dusty and polluted and they got typhoid fever and heat sickness. They had a year of interviews and waiting before papers arrived that allowed them to leave for America. Still, it was a year of hope. Zeenat picked up cans along the roads to make money. One sister ran a beauty parlor from their home. They all watched American television, studied English, and dreamed of a good future.

Finally they flew to America—Islamabad to Karachi to Amsterdam   23 to New York to St. Louis to Lincoln. Shireen said, "We came in at night. There were lights spread out over the dark land. Lincoln looked beautiful."

We talked about their adjustment to Lincoln. Five of the sisters had found work. They didn't have enough money though, and they didn't like the cold. Meena needed three root canals and Zeenat had many missing teeth and needed bridgework, false teeth, everything really. Still, they were enjoying the sense of possibilities unfolding. Shireen put it this way, "In America, we have rights." She pronounced "rights" as if it were a sacred word. 24

Meena mentioned the traffic here was more orderly and less dangerous than in Pakistan. The girls loved American clothes and makeup. Two of their sisters wanted to design clothes. Another was already learning to do American hairstyles so that she could work in a beauty shop. Meena wanted to be a nurse and Shireen a model or flight attendant. She said, "I have traveled so much against my will. Now I would like to see the world in a good way." 25

Shireen said that it was scary to go to the high school. Fortunately, her study of English in Pakistan made it easy for her to learn Nebraska English. She liked her teachers but said the American students mostly ignored her, especially when they heard her thick accent. 26

I was struck by the resilience of these sisters. In all the awful places they had been, they'd found ways to survive and even joke about their troubles. These young women used their intelligence to survive. Had they lived different lives, they would probably have been doctors and astrophysicists. Since they'd been in Lincoln, they'd been happy. Shireen said, "Of course we have problems, but they are easy problems." 27

I gave the sisters a ride home in my old Honda. They invited me in for tea, but I didn't have time. Instead I wrote out my phone number and told them to call if I could help them in any way. 28

When I said good-bye, I had no idea how soon and how intensely I would become involved in the lives of this family. Two weeks later Shireen called to ask about an art course advertised on a book of matches. It promised a college degree for thirty-five dollars. I said, "Don't do it." A couple of weeks later she called me again. This time she had seen an ad for models. She wondered if she should pay and enter the modeling contest. Again I advised, "Don't do it." I was embarrassed to tell her that we Americans lie to people to make money. Before I hung up, we chatted for a while. 29

I wanted to make sure they learned about the good things in our city. Advertisers would direct them to the bars, the malls, and anything that cost money. I told them about what I loved: the parks and prairies, the lakes and sunsets, the sculpture garden, and the free concerts. I lent them books with Georgia O'Keefe paintings and pictures of our national parks. 30

For a while I was so involved with the lives of the sisters that   31
Zeenat told me that her daughters were now my daughters. I was
touched that she was willing to give her daughters away so that they
could advance. I tactfully suggested we could share her daughters, but
that she would always be the real mother.

Examining the Reading

Finding Meaning

1. Compare and contrast the sisters that the author meets.
2. What does the author mean when she writes that the family was
   "Europeanized"?
3. How did Shireen's and Meena's lives change after Saddam Hussein
   came to power?
4. Why was the Iranian refugee camp more difficult to adjust to for
   Shireen and Meena's older sisters?
5. Describe the mistreatment Shireen and Meena's family experienced
   in Pakistan.
6. How did the family's life change when they arrived in Islamabad?
7. Describe the family's life in Lincoln.

Understanding Technique

1. Why do you think the author chose to name the essay, "The Beautiful Laughing Sisters—An Arrival Story"?
2. Reread paragraphs 4 and 5. How does the author use contrast to
   make her point?
3. The author uses graphic details to describe the family's experiences.
   What is the effect of these details? How would the essay be different
   without them?
4. The author provides quotations from the sisters as she tells their
   story. How does this enhance the essay?
5. Is the last paragraph effective as a conclusion? Why or why not?

Thinking Critically

1. What does Meena mean when she corrects Shireen's description of
   their walk into Pakistan by saying, "Ten years"?
2. Why does the author include information about what she was doing
   in the 1980s?
3. Why does Shireen pronounce the word "rights" as if it were a sacred
   word?
4. Why do the sisters describe their troubles in Lincoln as "easy
   problems"?

Writing About the Reading

A Paragraph

1. Why do you think the American students mostly ignored Shireen? What advice would you have for Shireen to help her deal with this situation?
2. Describe the treatment of women in each country the sisters lived in. Compare this treatment to the lives of women in the United States.
3. Write a paragraph on the issue of immigration. Offer reasons why immigration to the United States should or should not be permitted.

An Essay

1. Compare and contrast American culture with the Middle Eastern cultures described in the story.
2. Imagine that you are a "cultural broker" for new immigrants in your city or town. Write an essay describing the things you love in your city and the experiences people on a limited budget might enjoy.
3. Brainstorm a list of aspects of American life or culture that may have been unfamiliar to the sisters. (Pipher provides such a list later in her book, and includes such things as what tissue is, how to eat an ice cream cone, what seat belts are, and how many weeks are in a year.) Write an essay identifying several of these aspects and indicating how you would explain them to the sisters.

A Creative Activity

How do you think the sisters' lives might have been different if the men had not left the family in Pakistan? Describe how Shireen and Meena's lives might have played out.

Dumpster Diving

▶ **Lars Eighner**

In this essay, the author, at the time homeless, describes how he and others survived by scavenging for food and possessions in Dumpsters. Through the essay you learn about Eighner's values and attitudes toward others, as well as his survival techniques. This essay first appeared in The Threepenny Review.

Journal Writing

Think of a homeless person you've seen and write a journal entry describing him or her and what thoughts or feelings you had at the time.

Reading Strategy

Highlight factual information that Eighner provides about Dumpster diving. Annotate your responses to these facts.

Vocabulary Preview

niche (3) suited to one
pristine (6) pure; unspoiled
utility (7) usefulness
bohemian (8) unconventional, usually with an interest in the arts
dilettanti (9) amateurs; dabblers
contaminants (10) dirt; germs; unhealthy material
dysentery (12) a temporary intestinal disorder; extreme diarrhea
transience (14) briefness
envisioning (15) picturing in one's mind
gaudy (16) flashy; showy
bauble (16) small ornament; piece of jewelry
sated (16) satisfied
confounded (16) mixed up; confused

I began Dumpster diving about a year before I became homeless.   1

I prefer the term "scavenging." I have heard people, evidently meaning to be polite, use the word "foraging," but I prefer to reserve that word for gathering nuts and berries and such, which I also do, according to the season and opportunity.   2

I like the frankness of the word "scavenging." I live from the refuse 3
of others. I am a scavenger. I think it a sound and honorable niche, although if I could I would naturally prefer to live the comfortable consumer life, perhaps—and only perhaps—as a slightly less wasteful
consumer owing to what I have learned as a scavenger.

Except for jeans, all my clothes come from Dumpsters. Boom 4
boxes, candles, bedding, toilet paper, medicine, books, a typewriter, a
virgin male love doll, coins sometimes amounting to many dollars: all
came from Dumpsters. And, yes, I eat from Dumpsters, too.

There is a predictable series of stages that a person goes through in 5
learning to scavenge. At first the new scavenger is filled with disgust
and self-loathing. He is ashamed of being seen.

This stage passes with experience. The scavenger finds a pair of 6
running shoes that fit and look and smell brand-new. He finds a pocket
calculator in perfect working order. He finds pristine ice cream, still
frozen, more than he can eat or keep. He begins to understand: people
do throw away perfectly good stuff, a lot of perfectly good stuff.

At this stage he may become lost and never recover. All the Dump- 7
ster divers I have known come to the point of trying to acquire everything they touch. Why not take it, they reason, it is all free. This is, of
course, hopeless, and most divers come to realize that they must restrict themselves to items of relatively immediate utility.

The finding of objects is becoming something of an urban art. 8
Even respectable, employed people will sometimes find something
tempting sticking out of a Dumpster or standing beside one. Quite a
number of people, not all of them of the bohemian type, are willing to
brag that they found this or that piece in the trash.

But eating from Dumpsters is the thing that separates the dilet- 9
tanti from the professionals. Eating safely involves three principles: using the senses and common sense to evaluate the condition of the
found materials; knowing the Dumpsters of a given area and checking
them regularly; and seeking always to answer the question "Why was
this discarded?"

Yet perfectly good food can be found in Dumpsters. Canned goods, 10
for example, turn up fairly often in the Dumpsters I frequent. I also
have few qualms about dry foods such as crackers, cookies, cereal,
chips, and pasta if they are free of visible contaminants and still dry
and crisp. Raw fruits and vegetables with intact skins seem perfectly
safe to me, excluding, of course, the obviously rotten. Many are discarded for minor imperfections that can be pared away.

A typical discard is a half jar of peanut butter—though nonorganic 11
peanut butter does not require refrigeration and is unlikely to spoil in
any reasonable time. One of my favorite finds is yogurt—often discarded, still sealed, when the expiration date has passed—because it
will keep for several days, even in warm weather.

No matter how careful I am I still get dysentery at least once 12
a month, oftener in warm weather. I do not want to paint too romantic a
picture. Dumpster diving has serious drawbacks as a way of life.

I find from the experience of scavenging two rather deep lessons. 13
The first is to take what I can use and let the rest go. I have come to
think that there is no value in the abstract. A thing I cannot use or make
useful, perhaps by trading, has no value, however fine or rare it may be.

The second lesson is the transience of material being. I do not sup- 14
pose that ideas are immortal, but certainly they are longer-lived than
material objects.

The things I find in Dumpsters, the love letters and rag dolls of so 15
many lives, remind me of this lesson. Now I hardly pick up a thing
without envisioning the time I will cast it away. This, I think, is a
healthy state of mind. Almost everything I have now has already been
cast out at least once, proving that what I own is valueless to someone.

I find that my desire to grab for the gaudy bauble has been largely 16
sated. I think this is an attitude I share with the very wealthy—we both
know there is plenty more where whatever we have came from. Between us are the rat-race millions who have confounded their selves
with the objects they grasp and who nightly scavenge the cable channels for they know not what.

I am sorry for them. 17

Examining the Reading

Finding Meaning

1. What is Dumpster diving?
2. Why does the author prefer the word "scavenging"?
3. What does the author say is the primary disadvantage of eating out
   of Dumpsters?
4. Summarize the three stages that Dumpster divers go through.
5. What two lessons has the author learned through Dumpster diving?

Understanding Technique

1. Eighner uses topic sentences to structure his paragraphs and help
   identify the main point in his paragraphs. Identify several topic sentences and note their placement.
2. Describe Eighner's tone (his attitude toward his subject).
3. Evaluate the title and its meaning.

Thinking Critically

1. How do you think the average person looks upon a Dumpster
   diver? Why?

2. Can you imagine yourself eating out of a Dumpster? Why or why not?
3. Do you think Lars Eighner would continue to acquire things from Dumpsters if he didn't need to? What in the reading might indicate that he would or would not?
4. What does the author mean by the statement: "I do not suppose that ideas are immortal"?
5. The author says he feels sorry for people who "scavenge the cable channels." Why do you think he feels this way?

Writing About the Reading

A Paragraph

1. Eighner places little value on personal possessions. As he picks something up, he imagines throwing it out. Think of a personal possession that you could easily do without or one that you could never do without. Write a paragraph explaining why the object is or is not important to you.
2. Imagine that some people in your neighborhood that you didn't know were moving and left their unwanted, but useful belongings on the sidewalk. Write a paragraph describing the kinds of "treasures" you might expect to find.

An Essay

1. The author believes that the usefulness of material possessions is short-lived. He also describes this belief as a "healthy state of mind." Write an essay discussing whether you agree or disagree and why.
2. The number and variety of perfectly good items the author has found in Dumpsters emphasizes the amount of waste in our society. Write an essay explaining how this waste affects us and suggesting alternatives to just throwing out unwanted items.

A Creative Activity

Imagine that you were the author of this essay, finding "love letters and rag dolls of so many lives," as he does. Recall an object or letter and write an essay that re-creates the life of the person who threw it away.

Silenced Voices: Deaf Cultures and "Hearing" Families

▶ **Richard Appelbaum and William J. Chambliss**

This textbook excerpt, taken from Sociology, *describes one of many groups that have formed their own subculture. These authors take the position that deaf people prefer to share experiences with others who are deaf.*

Journal Writing

Write a journal entry discussing the problems deaf people experience in day-to-day life.

Reading Strategy

Highlight the topic sentence of each paragraph and the key details that support each topic sentence.

Vocabulary Preview

heritage (2) inherited background
simulated (4) imitated
virtually (4) practically
fraught (4) filled
wary (5) cautious; worried
confront (5) face; challenge
daunting (5) intimidating
confer (6) give; bestow
mainstream (6) integrate
fundamental (7) basic

*T*here are as many as 450,000 Americans who are completely unable   1
to hear; about 250,000 were born deaf. For them, family life poses
unique challenges. As a consequence, many deaf people prefer to practice endogamy, marrying others who are deaf and therefore share a
common experience.

There is a growing movement within the deaf community to   2
redefine the meaning of deafness not as a form of disability, but rather

as a positive culture. A growing number of deaf people see themselves as similar to any ethnic group, sharing a common language (American Sign Language, or ASL), possessing a strong sense of cultural identity, and taking pride in their heritage. One survey reported that the overwhelming majority would not even elect to have a free surgical implant that would enable them to hear.

Roslyn Rosen is an example of a person who takes great pride in   3
being deaf. Born of deaf parents and the mother of deaf children, Rosen is the president of the National Association of the Deaf:

> *I'm happy with who I am, and I don't want to be "fixed." Would an Italian-American rather be a WASP [White Anglo-Saxon Protestant]? In our society everybody agrees that whites have an easier time than blacks. But do you think that a black person would undergo operations to be a white?*

The desire for a deaf identity reflects the near impossibility of deaf   4
people ever learning to communicate with "hearing" people (people who are not deaf) through lipreading and simulated speech. People who have never heard a sound find it virtually impossible to utter sounds that most "hearing" people can recognize as words. Lipreading is equally problematic and is fraught with error. Reading, which depends on an understanding of the meaning of spoken words, can prove to be a frustrating experience. Yet for those who "hear" and "speak" ASL, a rich form of communication is possible, and with it comes a strong sense of shared identity.

Many deaf parents are wary when their deaf children get involved   5
in relationships with "hearing" people, preferring that they remain within their own community. Among those who marry, 90 percent choose spouses who are also deaf. Although many deaf people have succeeded in the "hearing" world, the problems that confront them can be daunting. Most will never be able to speak in a way that is likely to be understood by "hearing" people, and most of the "hearing" people they encounter will not know ASL. It is not surprising that when it comes to intimate relations, most deaf people choose to marry others who share their own language and culture.

Although families ordinarily confer their own ethnic status on   6
their children, this is not true for the nine out of ten deaf children who are born to "hearing" parents. Their parents are of one culture; they are of another. This can pose difficult choices for their families. On the one hand, "hearing" parents want the same sorts of things for their deaf children as do any parents: happiness, fulfillment, and successful lives as adults. Many would like their children to mainstream into the "hearing" world as best as possible. Yet they know that this will prove extremely difficult.

On the other hand, the deaf community argues that the deaf chil- 7
dren of "hearing" parents can never fully belong to the "hearing"
world, or, for that matter, even to their own "hearing" parents. Many
leaders in the deaf community urge "hearing" parents to send their
deaf children to residential schools for the deaf, where they will be
fully accepted, learn deaf culture, and be with their own people. Fundamental questions about the meaning of "family" arise when the children and parents largely live in two different cultures.

Examining the Reading

Finding Meaning

1. What is endogamy?
2. According to the article, how do many deaf people wish to define
   themselves?
3. Why are deaf parents of deaf children wary when their children become involved with hearing people?
4. Why is it almost impossible for people who are deaf to speak?
5. Name one problem with lipreading.

Understanding Technique

1. Identify the authors' tone.
2. What type of evidence do the authors provide to support their thesis?

Thinking Critically

1. Explain what is meant by deaf people desiring a "deaf identity."
2. Discuss the advantages and disadvantages of deaf people learning
   American Sign Language.
3. Discuss the problems that confront deaf people when they mainstream into a hearing society.
4. What other groups of people have formed their own subculture?

Writing About the Reading

A Paragraph

1. Suppose you had become deaf through illness or injury. Would you
   elect to read lips or learn American Sign Language? Write a paragraph explaining your choice.
2. Write a paragraph identifying what you think would be the major
   challenges in a relationship between a hearing person and a deaf
   person.

An Essay

1. If you had a child who was born deaf, would you choose a residential school for the deaf or a traditional school? Write an essay explaining your choice.
2. Deaf people develop their own language, which builds group identity. In a sense, groups of hearing people also develop language that establishes their identity. For example, teenagers use slang; medical doctors speak in medical jargon. Choose a group of people and describe the language that identifies them. (*Hint:* You might write about football fans, salespeople, computer hackers, car enthusiasts.)

A Creative Activity

Some deaf people have formed their own culture. Do you think other groups of people with physical illnesses and disabilities (blindness, cancer, muscular dystrophy, etc.) also have a separate culture? Write a paragraph describing the shared problems and concerns of a particular group.

Cultural Education in America

▸ **Jonathan Wong**
  Student Essay

A college student from Hong Kong writes about his adjustment to life in America.

*A*fter merely a month of college in Oregon coming from Hong Kong, I could not endure the uninspiring cafeteria style cooking any longer. I longed for some good old-fashioned Chinese food. Therefore, I convinced my roommate to venture out with me to the lone, local Asian restaurant in the rural town of McMinnville. Without any preconceived notions or expectations regarding the authenticity of the cooking, my taste buds even so were quick to protest this imposter Chinese food—at the first bite! Then came dessert, the fortune cookie, and while the tradition did not originate in China, but rather in America, it foretold the fortune of excellent food and great company. Alas, it was only half true—the great company part. Deep within the secret recesses of my self-indulgent, hungry heart, lay the temptation to bargain my friend's company for the fortune of some tasty, genuine Chinese food! So that was how my cultural education had its humble beginning . . . with this first Chinese dinner and with this tiny piece of an after-meal dessert. It was the food that was not Chinese and the fortune cookie that was American that seemed to predetermine a certain discovery and a certain destiny.

If food adjustment were the only discovery, life would have been simple. There are many more. For example, 5 feet 8 inches tall is an admirable height for men back home but relatively short when compared with most American men. This "shortness" becomes even more painfully evident on the volleyball court each time I attempt to spike the ball above the towering wall of blocking hands. I find solace, however, on the soccer field. Unknowingly gifted in agility due to my small stature in the United States, I easily dribble the ball around and outrun those taller, but sluggish, husky soccer opponents, just like a seasoned fighter pilot who skillfully dodges around the charging missiles without getting hit.

Hitting the overweight category is another unpleasant surprise. 3
One can blame this on the American diet as well as the sedentary
lifestyle or alternatively perhaps, on the prevalent indulgent attitude
here which often overrides my self-discipline and an upbringing that
would prompt me to say "no" to dessert. Consequently, my sparkling
commercial quality white teeth have fallen victim to the cavity filled
teeth of a sweets lover. This is costly in terms of dental health and personal finance. Furthermore, I have transformed myself from a traditional, lean Asian to a typical, obese American. No self-respecting lover
would want to handle these "love handles" of mine. Celibacy is not exactly what I have in mind! Was coming to the States a mistake of Titanic
proportions? This is a question I have found myself asking repeatedly.

Regardless of the negatives thus far, one of the biggest advantages 4
of living here is freedom of choice. Coupled with clever word manipu-
lation, one can choose to elevate oneself from an unglamorous state of
existence to a grandiose state, and there is no shame. For instance,
housewife is analogous to household executive, while custodian becomes an environmental service engineer. Today, I can proudly pro-
claim (that which I dare not assert back home) that I am a bionic
toothed, financially unique, and physically challenged (both height
and width) American. Moreover, I am proud of it! Isn't life in the English language grand here?

Another interesting, positive discovery is the eating etiquette—it is 5
proper to eat with lips closed and to converse after the food is swal-
lowed. In Hong Kong, it is customarily acceptable to eat with the lips
open while talking with the mouth full. Although I have adjusted to
this new custom quite well, environment still dictates behavior. Quite
unconsciously and predictably, Miss Manner's advice on table manners
is inevitably left behind every time I visit China. My natural form of in-
gestion instinctively takes control. Yet, I would instantly notice my
overseas relatives' vulgar table manners here. Embarrassment is an
understatement, especially when I have American guests at the dining
table. I watch in horror but am too polite to correct my overseas guests
as the food particles fly across the table between bites, and they glee-
fully engage in their lively conversation in absolute oblivion.

Bite by bite and little by little, I have gradually assimilated this cul- 6
ture while retaining my own, or so it seems. Nevertheless, my friends
here, on occasion, still tease me about my writing skills and my accent—
a constant reminder of my foreign past. My relatives and Chinese
friends, on the other hand, never fail to point out my American way
of thinking as well as lifestyle—a personification of a yellow-skinned,
white-cored "banana" they struggle to accept.

Struggling for acceptance by both cultures is apparently a com- 7
mon challenge shared by all new immigrants, and most of us somehow

are able to resolve these (outer and inner) conflicts eventually. Many even gain invaluable insights about life in general and specific multicultural skills. I personally feel the formal education attained in America is literally pale in comparison to the colorful cultural experiences acquired here. Such experiences have become the cultural education I will treasure for the rest of my life.

Examining the Essay

1. Highlight and evaluate Wong's thesis statement.
2. Wong begins his essay by telling a story. Why is this an effective introduction? How clearly does it illustrate his thesis?
3. Evaluate Wong's use of humor. Is it effective? Did the humor help you understand the author's main points?
4. Examine the author's use of descriptive language. Highlight several particularly effective examples.
5. What is Wong's conclusion? How does he reach it?

Writing an Essay

1. Write an essay on manners. You might discuss whether there is too much emphasis on manners among people or groups of people you know. Or you might discuss which rules of etiquette are the most important and which violations are most offensive.
2. Write an essay explaining the importance of food in our culture.
3. Many people are judged by their height and weight. Write an essay describing this problem and some possible solutions.

 ## Making Connections

1. Compare the ways that Santiago in "Black *and* Latino" and Wong in "Cultural Education in America" deal with being in the middle of two cultures.

2. Both "Silenced Voices: Deaf Cultures and 'Hearing' Families" and "Dumpster Diving" deal with subcultures, groups with their own identity that create customs and behaviors. Write an essay comparing the two subcultures.

3. Every culture and subculture has its own set of customs, rituals, and behaviors. As a college student, you belong to a subculture. Identify the customs, rituals, and behaviors that characterize college students. Write an essay explaining these to an immigrant student planning to attend college.

Internet Connections ————————————

1. When people travel to other countries for business, they often seek advice on local customs. Visit this site: **http://www.globalrealestategateway.com/pages/global-buset.aspx.** Read the general tips and then choose one country link to follow. Write a paragraph that compares one aspect of that country's business culture with that of the United States.

2. Summarize the activities carried out by Creative Connections, as listed on their web site at **http://www.creativeconnections.org/.** How effective do you think these programs are in promoting cultural awareness and understanding?

3. Browse this fruitarianism site: **http://www.fruitarian.com/ao/WhatIsFruitarianism.htm.** Write an essay evaluating the site and its content. How convincing are the arguments for eating fruit only? Do you think fruitarians are a type of subculture? Why?

   (If any of these web sites are unavailable, use a search engine to locate another appropriate site.)

Chapter 5

Others Who Shape Our Lives

Our lives are shaped by those around us, particularly our family and friends. We have vivid memories of fun-filled days spent with a close friend; we recall someone we could confide in; we treasure intimate moments with a mate or spouse; and we remember close, comforting times with a parent.

As important as friends and family may be, our lives are also shaped by those we do not know personally—a radio disk jockey who wakes us up each morning, a sports star we cheer for at each game, or a character we admire in a novel. Local, state, and national figures—presidents, senators, talk show hosts—may shape our lives through the issues they raise and the actions they take. And then there are the unsung heroes—people who may shape our lives without our directly knowing it or them. A local businessperson who donates food for a community fair, a medical researcher who develops a new vaccine or antibiotic, and people who selflessly volunteer their time by working in a local homeless shelter are examples.

In this chapter, the readings focus on people who have shaped the lives of others. You will read about how people—both friends and strangers, in the family and at work—influence one another, and the positive experiences that result from such influence. Examples can be found in the story of a woman who tries to offer advice to an uncle suffering from heart disease ("Our Wounded Hearts"), how gay marriages affect families ("Gay Marriages Unite, and Divide, Families"), and how Bill Cosby's parents shaped their lives so that they "fit" each other ("The Promised Land"). You will also read about people whose actions affect hundreds, even thousands, of other people, such as the group of teenagers who begin their own company in "Food from the 'Hood" and Bill Gates, the world's richest man, who started his own computer empire ("Bill Gates: Computer Wizard"). In addition, you will read about how others make shopping a difficult task for a blind woman ("Shopping Can Be a Challenge") and consider whether sports heroes should follow the golden rule ("Do unto Others").

Brainstorming About Others

Class Activity: Form groups of three to four students. Each group member should brainstorm a list of at least ten influential or important people in the news over the past week. Group members should compare lists and prepare a final list that includes names that appeared on two or more individual lists. Groups then can compare lists and, again, identify recurring names.

Shopping Can Be a Challenge

▶ **Carol Fleischman**

This essay, published in the Buffalo News, *provides a fresh viewpoint of a common experience—shopping. The writer, who is blind,
focuses on how her experience is shaped by those around her.*

Journal Writing

Write a journal entry describing a time in your life when you
were unable to carry out everyday activities without help from
others. How did you feel about this situation?

Reading Strategy

In this essay, Fleischman reveals her attitude toward the
sighted people around her in several different ways. As you
read, highlight words, phrases, and sentences that reveal how
the writer feels.

Vocabulary Preview

ritual (2) habit; routine
beeline (4) direct route; straight line
imposing (5) impressive; mildly threatening
chastised (19) scolded; criticized
composing (21) calming; controlling
preoccupied (23) engrossed; distracted
retrieve (23) get and bring back
reminiscent (24) reminding one of
foiled (24) prevented

*H*ave you ever tried to buy a dress when you can't see? I have, be-   1
cause I'm blind.

At one time, I would shop with friends. This ritual ended after the   2
time I happily brought home a dress a friend had helped me choose,
and my husband, Don, offered a surprising observation: "The fit is
great, but do you like all those huge fish?" The dress went back.

Now I rely on Don and my guide dog, Misty, as my shopping partners.   3

We enter the store and make a beeline for the dress department.   4
Don usually sees two or three salespeople scatter. The aisles empty as
if a bomber had come on the scene.

Then I realize I'm holding the "live wire." But I'm not judgmental—   5
once I, too, was uneasy around large dogs. Although Misty is better
behaved than most children, I know a 65-pound German shepherd is
imposing.

On one recent shopping trip, a brave saleswoman finally ap-   6
proached us. "Can I help you?" she said to my husband.

"Yes, I'm looking for a dress," I replied. (After all, I'm the one who   7
will be wearing it.) "Maybe something in red or white."

"RED OR WHITE," she said, speaking very slowly and loudly even   8
though my hearing is fine. I managed not to fall as Misty jumped back
on my feet, frightened by the woman's booming voice.

Don was distracted too. I heard him rustling through hangers on a   9
nearby rack. I called his name softly to get his attention, and another
man answered my call. Bad luck. What were the chances of two Dons
being in earshot?

"This is great!" Don said, holding up a treasure.   10

I swept my hand over the dress to examine it. It had a neckline that   11
plunged to the hemline. "Hmmm," I said. I walk three miles daily with
Misty and stay current with fashion, but I'm positive this costume
would look best on one of the Spice Girls.

Finally, I chose three dresses to try on.   12

Another shopper distracted Misty, even though the harness sign   13
reads: "Please do not pet. I'm working." She said, "Your dog reminds
me of my Max, who I recently put to sleep," so I am sympathetic. We
discussed her loss for 15 minutes. Some therapists don't spend that
much time with grieving clients.

Don was back. He told me the route to travel to the dressing room.   14
I commanded Misty: right, left, right and straight ahead. We wove our
way past several small voices.

"Mom, why is that dog in the store?"   15

"Mom, is that a dog or a wolf?"   16

And my personal favorite: "But that lady's eyes are open."   17

I trust parents to explain: "The lady is giving her guide dog com-   18
mands. Her dog is a helping dog. They're partners." I questioned
whether this positive message had been communicated though, when
I heard an adult say: "Oh, there's one of those blind dogs."

Other people, though well-intentioned, can interfere with my ef-   19
fective use of Misty. Guide dogs are highly trained and very dependable
but occasionally make potentially dangerous mistakes. On my way
through the aisles, Misty bumped me into a pointed rack, requiring my
quick action. I used a firm tone to correct her, and she dived to the

ground like a dying actress. Witnessing this performance, another shopper chastised me for being cruel.

I was shocked. Misty's pride was hurt, but I needed to point out the   20
error in order to avoid future mistakes. If I did not discipline her, what would prevent Misty from walking me off the curb into traffic?

Composing myself, I was delighted by the saleswoman's sugges-   21
tion: "Can I take you to your dressing room?" I was less delighted when she grabbed me and pushed me ahead while Misty trailed us on a leash. I wriggled out of the woman's hold. Gently pushing her ahead, I lightly held her elbow in sighted-guide technique (called so because the person who sees goes first).

"This is better. Please put my hand on the door knob. I'll take it   22
from here," I said.

In the room, Misty plopped down and sighed with boredom. I   23
sighed with relief that she was still with me. On one shopping trip, I was so preoccupied with trying on clothes that Misty sneaked out beneath the dressing room's doors. I heard her tags jingling as she left but was half-dressed and couldn't retrieve her. Fortunately, Don was outside the door and snagged her leash.

I modeled the dresses for Don and, feeling numb, bought all three.   24
As we left the store, Misty's magnetism, reminiscent of the Pied Piper's, attracted a toddler who draped himself over her. She remained calm, as he tried to ride her. The boy's fun was soon foiled by his frantic mother.

When we returned to our car, I gave Misty a treat and lots of praise.   25
A good day's work deserves a good day's pay for both of us.

"Shop till you drop" or "retail therapy" could never be my motto.   26
To me, "charge" means going into battle.

Examining the Reading

Finding Meaning

1. Summarize Fleischman's attitude toward shopping.
2. Why did the author stop shopping with friends?
3. According to Fleischman, what types of problems do blind people face?
4. What did the author do when Misty bumped her into a pointed display rack? Why?
5. Describe Fleischman's attitude toward those around her. Where in the essay are these attitudes revealed?

Understanding Technique

1. Evaluate the effectiveness of opening this essay by asking and answering a question.

2. Fleischman makes extensive use of dialogue and description to express her ideas. Identify several particularly effective examples of each.
3. How does Fleischman establish a humorous tone?

Thinking Critically

1. Why do you think the saleswoman spoke loudly to the author?
2. Why might some people find the writer's guide dog threatening?
3. According to the article, what can you infer is meant by "sighted-guide technique"?
4. What did the author mean when she said, "To me, 'charge' means going into battle"?
5. From this article, can you conclude that most people understand the partnership between blind people and their dogs? Why?

Writing About the Reading

A Paragraph

1. Write a paragraph explaining what a parent should teach a child about guide dogs.
2. Write a paragraph describing the disability of a family member, friend, or acquaintance.

An Essay

1. Write an essay explaining a situation in which you felt frustrated by those around you.
2. Write a letter to the salesclerk who assisted Fleischman, informing her about the needs and sensitivities of blind customers and suggesting how she might change her approach.

A Creative Activity

Imagine that Fleischman is deaf rather than blind, and that she has a hearing guide dog. What problems might she experience while shopping or elsewhere?

The Promised Land

▶ **Bill Cosby**

In this reading, actor and humorist Bill Cosby tells of the stage of ultimate marital bliss his parents have reached. This essay is taken from his book titled Love and Marriage.

Journal Writing

Write a journal entry about longlasting marriages. Why do some marriages last while others do not?

Reading Strategy

This essay is intended to be light and entertaining. As you read it, highlight or annotate sections that contribute to Cosby's light, humorous tone.

Vocabulary Preview

residing (1) living
mellowness (1) the state of being toned down (by passage of years)
Dalai Lama (1) religious and political Tibetan leader, known for being wise and calm
ascended (2) gone up; risen
plane (2) level
rapport (9) relationship marked by mutual trust
literal (9) actual
planetarium (16) a building for viewing a model of the solar system
lotus land (18) a place of extreme contentment
follies (24) silly actions; foolish decisions

> *Grow old along with me!*
> *The best is yet to be.*

When Browning wrote these lines, he wasn't thinking of my mother and father or anyone else in North Philadelphia; but whenever I see my mother and father together, I know they're residing in a state where I   1 want to live with Camille, a state of such blessed mellowness that they make the Dalai Lama seem like a Type A personality.

I will never forget my first awareness that my mother and father had ascended to a matrimonial plane where only God knew what they were doing—perhaps. We were driving to Philadelphia from Atlantic City, with my father at the wheel, my mother beside him, and me in the back. 2

"Oh, there's a car from Pittsburgh," said my mother, looking at a license plate in the next lane. 3

"How do you know it's from Pittsburgh?" said my father. 4

"Because I couldn't think of Pennsylvania," she replied. 5

And I waited for my father to respond to this Einsteinian leap into another dimension, but he didn't speak. He simply continued to drive, a supremely contented man. 6

Because he had understood. 7

He had understood that my mother's Pittsburgh was a mythical place, located where the Monongahela entered the twilight zone. My mother also had not been able to think of Afghanistan, but she didn't say that the car was from Kabul. However, *had* she said that the car was from Kabul, my father would have understood it bore Afghans moving to Allentown. 8

For the next twenty minutes, I thought about fifty-three years of marriage and how they had bonded my parents in this remarkable Zen rapport; but then I was suddenly aware that my father had just driven past the exit for Philadelphia. Not the exit for Pennsylvania or for North America, but for Philadelphia, the literal city. 9

"Mom," I said, "didn't Dad just pass the exit we want?" 10

"Yes, he did," she replied. 11

"Well, why don't you *say* something?" 12

"Your father knows what he's doing." 13

Had *I* driven past the proper exit, my wife would have said, *Please pull over and let me out. I'd like to finish this trip by hitching a ride on a chicken truck.* 14

But if Camille and I can just stay together another twenty-five years, then we also will have reached the Twilight Zone, where one of us will do something idiotic and the other one not only will understand it but admire it as well. 15

You turned out the light where I'm reading, I will tell her. *Thank you for the surprise trip to the planetarium.* 16

You left your shoes in the bathtub, she will tell me. *Thank you for giving me two more boats.* 17

One morning a few days after that memorably roundabout trip to Philadelphia, I got another glimpse of the lotus land where my parents 18 dwelled. My father came into the house, took off his hat, put it on a chair, gave some money to my children, and then went back and sat on his hat.

"You just sat on your hat," my mother told him.   19

"Of course I did," he replied, and then neither one of them said an-   20
other word about hat reduction. When the time came to leave, my
father picked up the crushed hat and put it on his head, where it sat
like a piece of Pop Art. My mother glanced at it, as if to make sure that
it would not fall off, and then she took his arm and they walked out the
door, ready to be the sweethearts of the Mummers Parade.

However, if *I* ever sat on my hat, Camille would say, *Can't you feel*   21
that you're sitting on your hat?

And I would reply, *It's a tradition in my family for a man to sit on his*   22
hat. It's one of the little things that my father did for my mother.

Yes, twenty-five years, happy as they have been, are still not   23
enough to have given Camille and me that Ringling Brothers rhythm
my mother and father enjoy. But we can hear the circus calling to us.

Love, what follies are committed in thy name, said Francis Bacon.   24

So far, most of marriage has been the Ziegfeld Follies for Camille   25
and me. And now we're getting ready to send in the clowns.

Examining the Reading

Finding Meaning

1. What is it about his parents' marriage that Cosby finds so endearing?
2. How did Cosby's father respond when his mother said the car was from Pittsburgh?
3. Why didn't Cosby's mother stop his father from driving past the correct exit?
4. How did Cosby's father respond when his mother informed him that he was sitting on his hat?

Understanding Technique

1. Evaluate the effectiveness of opening the essay with a quotation.
2. Describe the essay's organization.

Thinking Critically

1. How has Cosby's parents' marriage shaped the expectations Cosby now has in his own marriage?
2. Explain what Cosby means when he refers to his parents' marriage as having "that Ringling Brothers rhythm."
3. Discuss how Cosby views his own twenty-five years of marriage.

4. Explain Bacon's statement, "Love, what follies are committed in thy name."

Writing About the Reading

A Paragraph

1. Our lives are constantly being shaped by others' experiences. Write a paragraph on how a couple you know has influenced a relationship you have had.
2. Every individual has different "requirements" for a spouse. Write a paragraph identifying the requirements you have found essential—or would look for—in a spouse or potential spouse.

An Essay

1. Cosby's parents seemed to have reached a state of complete compatibility and understanding of each other. Have you ever reached that state in a relationship? Write an essay explaining why you have or have not reached it with another person.
2. Write an essay describing a couple you know. Explain the type of relationship they have. Use specific instances, events, or conversations to illustrate your points.
3. Cosby's parents readily accept each other's idiosyncrasies. Think of a person with whom you are close. Write an essay describing how you respond to that person's idiosyncrasies and how he or she reacts to yours.

Creative Activities

1. What other crazy, zany, or inconsistent exchanges can you imagine might have occurred between Cosby's parents? Describe several in paragraph form.
2. Role-play incidents that have occurred in your parents' marriage that reveal the nature of their relationship.

Our Wounded Hearts

▶ **Allison Bernard**

What could you do about a relative whose personal habits are killing him or her? In this reading from Health *magazine, the author relates her experience with an uncle who suffered from heart disease.*

Journal Writing

Write a journal entry describing your lifestyle. How do you think it affects your health?

Reading Strategy

As you read, highlight the details that describe the uncle's original condition and those that reveal a change in his lifestyle following his second heart attack.

Vocabulary Preview

malice (3) ill will; evil intent
bypass (4) heart surgery that replaces clogged arteries
  with clear ones
squelched (10) put down; crushed
momentous (11) eventful; important
abundance (12) large amount
bullied (12) forced; pushed
deteriorate (16) worsen

*I*t didn't take a rocket scientist to see the problem. My uncle ate too   1
much, never exercised, threw few but awesome temper tantrums, and
was an on-again, off-again smoker. In fact, more than a decade before,
at the age of 40, he'd had a minor heart attack. After that there was a
lot of talk and activity: This cheese is fat-free, that omelette was made
with egg whites only. Always turkey breast, never lasagna. A new treadmill in front of the television—but little change in his habits.

It drove me nuts. Not necessarily him or his health, but the entire   2
situation. Everyone ate so much at my aunt and uncle's home in Con-
necticut. No one ever left the house, and the television was always on.
When I first came to the East Coast for college, I would visit them on

holidays and realize only on the way home, two or three days later, that I hadn't gone outdoors the entire time. I found myself suggesting walks and tentatively volunteering recipes for brown rice. I pointed out articles on nutrition, cooking, starting exercise programs. I wanted to help; I was aching to help.

"We eat fat-free," my aunt would tell me impatiently. I got the message, though I felt like a bystander watching an accident in slow motion. During these visits my uncle didn't talk much. He watched sports on TV with my male cousins. He was always friendly if distant, not particularly interested in a young woman who didn't understand football. One day when I was visiting him and my aunt at the beach, a friend I'd brought along commented, "Your uncle is a very large person." It was said without malice, and I was about to point out that he was just tall and big-boned when I realized that, yes, he was fat.

So it wasn't a major shock when I heard he'd had a second heart attack. Initially everyone was calm. He seemed fine, was in the hospital, resting. Then tests showed that as much as 70 percent of his heart was dead. A bypass would be useless, and the alternatives narrowed to a transplant. Before he could get on the list for a new heart, however, he would have to lose 75 pounds.

I was visiting when the doctor gave him the news. My cousin asked about a possible genetic basis for his condition, but the doctor politely dismissed the idea. "Your father is very heavy," he said. "He must eat less and take drugs for his blood pressure." There wasn't much else to do.

After the doctor left, my uncle sighed. "I don't want to have to worry about what I eat for the rest of my life," he said.

"Tough," I heard my cousin mutter.

I followed her out of the hospital room and suggested that maybe he could learn to cook. If he prepared his own food, he would know what he could and couldn't eat. She looked at me as though I were a lunatic. "There is no way my father will ever set foot in the kitchen," she said.

I called my aunt a few days later to see how things were going. He was starting his diet, she reported, and she had finally figured out the trick. "Portion size," she said. "We ate fat-free for years when we should have been cutting down on how much we eat."

Did I know that? Well, yes, actually, I did. I'd even given her an article I'd written on portion control. I realized my aunt had never read past the first few sentences. I put a smile in my voice, squelched my frustration, and said that I was looking forward to helping at Christmas, only three weeks away.

That Christmas was a momentous one. My parents were visiting— having given up hope of my sister and me ever making it out west—

and it was the first time the two families were to spend the holidays together. I'd heard my uncle had been losing weight, 15 pounds so far—but he still had 60 to go.

When we arrived at the house, my aunt immediately set us to   12
preparing food: my mother to cutting up vegetables, my father to mashing potatoes with whole milk and butter. I wandered in and out of the kitchen, amazed at the abundance of rich, fattening food. I was bullied into sprinkling cups of brown sugar and pouring pints of maple syrup over a small number of yams.

When we sat down to dinner, however, I noticed that my uncle ate   13
well: turkey, a plain potato, steamed green beans. I was impressed, even envious.

Earlier, during the food preparation, we'd had our first real con-   14
versation. He'd talked about his exercising, about the seven-minute stints he did on the treadmill, his determination to lose weight. For once I felt some hope that my prodding was justified, maybe welcome. Then he told me that his father—a sharp quiet man watching TV in the next room—didn't know he was waiting for a heart transplant. "Why worry him?" he said.

Why not: He's his *father,* after all. This sad secrecy, this willingness   15
to keep something as serious as a heart transplant from his own father, stunned me. So did the other things I heard a few weeks later: that my uncle had tried to cut up the Christmas turkey for us to take back to the city and was too weak to do it; that my aunt had thrown a tantrum before we arrived and stalked out of the house; that she was furious with my uncle for letting himself get so sick and with herself for not stopping him.

Now we all felt guilty—and angry—at how we'd watched my uncle's   16
health deteriorate. But was there really anything we could have done?

I called William Castelli, a cardiologist and former director of the   17
legendary Framingham Heart Study, who's responsible for much of what we know about the causes of heart disease, lung cancer, and stroke. Over 30 years he repeatedly interviewed 13,000 participants and gave them advice time and again about eating and smoking—advice that was mostly ignored.

"How did you keep from getting angry?" I asked him.   18

Castelli seemed surprised; anger hadn't occurred to him. "Well, you   19
don't want to be unpleasant. . . . It's a tough problem. You have to create a reality. Most people won't change unless some disaster strikes them.

"But once they see a benefit, even just a slight one, they begin to get   20
a feeling of what they can accomplish," he continued. "Otherwise, all families can do is show love and respect but also remind them what the evidence is, what the route is, and what's at the end of the tunnel."

It hit me just how vain my so-called help had been: Had I really   21
hoped to save my uncle? Had I felt obliged to? Or had I just wanted to
be right after seeing my advice ignored for so long? In the thick of it, I
couldn't tell. And gradually I pulled back. I'd go on giving feedback, but
I stopped expecting it to matter.

Then, to my surprise, my uncle made the transplant list. He danced   22
and glowed at his daughter's wedding and became, for less than a year,
a man full of hope and conversation and life. We talked more during
those few months than we had in previous decades.

But it all came too late. In December he died of a third heart attack   23
while waiting for his transplant. I realized then, perhaps for the first
time, how being right can be a false reward. Being wrong, sometimes,
is so much better.

Examining the Reading

Finding Meaning

1. Describe the lifestyle of Allison Bernard's uncle.
2. Why was Bernard's uncle unable to have bypass surgery?
3. What did the doctor say her uncle should do after he had the second
   heart attack?
4. How did the author try to help her uncle?
5. According to Dr. Castelli, a cardiologist, what can families do for
   patients like the author's uncle?
6. How did the author feel about her uncle keeping his heart transplant a secret from his own father?

Understanding Technique

1. Describe how this essay is organized.
2. Evaluate Bernard's conclusion. What additional information does it
   contribute to the essay?

Thinking Critically

1. Why was it so difficult for the author's uncle to change his lifestyle?
2. Why did Bernard say that she "felt like a bystander watching an accident in slow motion" when she visited her uncle?
3. What did the author mean by "I realized then, perhaps for the first
   time, how being right can be a false reward"?
4. Is the title "Our Wounded Hearts" appropriate for this essay? Why
   or why not?

Writing About the Reading

A Paragraph

1. Write a paragraph describing the attitudes of Bernard's aunt and cousin toward her uncle. Explain why you think they felt as they did.
2. Choose a friend or relative who is particularly close to you. Write a paragraph explaining why you admire that person.

An Essay

1. Write an essay describing a time you tried to help a friend or family member by offering advice. Did the person follow your advice? If not, explain what you think you should have done differently to help that person.
2. Imagine that you are Allison Bernard. Write a letter she might have written to her uncle after her Thanksgiving visit.
3. Write an essay describing a situation in which someone close to you (a relative or grandparent) suffered a serious illness. Describe how this illness affected you.

A Creative Activity

Imagine that Bernard's uncle had lived. How do you think he might have felt, thought, and lived his life? Rewrite the ending of this essay as if he had lived.

Gay Marriages Unite, and Divide, Families

▶ **Elizabeth Armstrong**

*In the following essay, Elizabeth Armstrong examines the impact
of the recent legalization of gay marriage in Massachusetts. A
staff writer of the* Christian Science Monitor, *Armstrong finds
that the subject of same-sex marriage is just as controversial
within the family as throughout the nation.*

Journal Writing

Brainstorm a list of pros and cons of same-sex marriage.

Reading Strategy

This article describes differing reactions to same-sex marriage.
As you read, highlight the alternative viewpoints revealed
about gay marriage.

Vocabulary Preview

plaintiff (2) the complaining party in a lawsuit
abstract (3) not practical, detailed, or concrete
cohabitation (3) living together without being married
rile (6) annoy
staunch (7) strong; loyal
vilify (7) make derogatory or abusive statements about
enunciate (9) put into words

*H*eidi Norton and Gina Smith stepped through the doors of North-   1
ampton's City Hall into what looked more like a Hawaiian luau than a
crowd of wedding guests. Throngs cheered. Supporters waved rainbow
banners that read "Love does not discriminate." Children in bright lei
necklaces passed out homemade chocolate-chip cookies.

Heidi and Gina Nortonsmith, as they will now be called, are one of   2
the seven plaintiff couples in the landmark case that legalized gay mar-

riage in Massachusetts. Now, they're celebrities, too. Among those cheering them on were their sons, Avery and Quinn, and Heidi's father and stepmother, all grinning from granite steps. Notably absent, however, were two other relatives, Heidi's brother and stepsister, who express unwavering support of their sister, but not of gay marriage. "I love Heidi just as much as I ever did, and I love Gina," says Steve Norton, a fifth-grade teacher in Greenland, N.H., who, like his stepsister, is a fundamentalist Christian. "Do I believe [gay marriage] is right? I don't. But I still love her and Gina. It's a tricky thing." The Nortons' respectful divide is indicative of the way same-sex marriage is causing tensions in many U.S. households.

While the issue has been debated endlessly in legislatures and   3
courts as a matter of often abstract policy, the official legalization of gay marriage in Massachusetts this week has brought the subject home to thousands of families across the country on an intensely personal level. Many families, to be sure, fully support the idea of same-sex marriage. Others agree with cohabitation or civil unions, but stop short of embracing state-sanctioned unions. Still others struggle with the idea of homosexuality altogether. All these and many more emotions were on display at ceremonies this week as more than 1,000 gay and lesbian couples from Massachusetts and other states exchanged vows. Mostly, the events were celebratory. But underneath, differences were evident, as some family members didn't show up.

Moreover, such complex reactions are likely to become more visi-   4
ble as Americans increasingly choose sides on the gay-marriage issue: Some states are moving to amend their constitutions to prevent gay couples from marrying, while others—such as Rhode Island and New York—have decided to recognize marriage licenses from Massachusetts as valid in their own states.

Back at city hall some couples—like Michael DiPasquali and David   5
McGrath—are opting for a more subdued union, conscious of the tension their marriage can provoke. The men have been together 13 years and have two children, Jason and Marguerite. Each of their families, they say, supports their relationship—but their parents don't even want to hear the word "marriage." "We're not dying to go out and rent a hall and have a huge party," Mr. DiPasquali says. "We have not talked to our parents at all about marriage." Mr. McGrath isn't sure they ever will. "My father's been heard to say he hopes he doesn't live to see the day when his son marries another man," he says. "Now that's a sad thing."

Beyond family units, communities have divided sharply—and   6
more visibly than ever—as legislatures debate same-sex marriage into the night and lines of gay couples stream off the steps of city halls. Jesse Molina says acceptance in her community—the small town of Northampton, Mass., nestled in the foothills of the Berkshires—has

been just as important as her family's support. That's given her courage to confront those who disagree, she says—and, sometimes, to rile the opposition even more. In Northampton on Monday, as a lone protester held a sign reading "No Al 'Gay'da," Jesse jumped in front of him with her own poster, demanding to know why she shouldn't marry her partner, Euphemia. The protester replied, "It's just wrong." And as rest of the crowd sang, "Going to the Chapel," Jesse launched into her own verse: "Going to the chapel and I'm going to get dentally insured."

Heidi's father, Perry, says his daughter leads by example. A staunch supporter of his daughter and her wife, he says change has "just got to come by compassionate example—not to vilify the people who don't agree, but to let them see that not only is the world not going to come to an end; it's going to be enriched by what these people have had the courage to do." That drive for awareness, say Heidi and Gina, is part of their crusade. And along with a fight for the legal and economic benefits of marriage, they ground themselves in a larger struggle to encourage Americans to be more open about sexuality—something they feel families have long shied away from discussing.   7

"I find human beings and our emotions endlessly fascinating," Heidi said on the eve of their wedding as she set the table for pizza in their Northampton home. "Our sexual identities, and how we see ourselves, and how we change as people and experience ourselves—I find those all very interesting." Heidi and Gina, an interracial couple, decided years ago to have two children by one African-American sperm donor so that their kids would be full siblings. Heidi carried both. No one in her family has taken issue with the interracial component of the family—something that would have been unthinkable, Perry says, just 50 years ago.   8

As they gathered around the table for dinner, "Mom" (Heidi) and "Mommy" (Gina), their two sons, Avery and Quinn, and Heidi's father, Perry, and stepmother, Bonnie, clasped hands in Quaker tradition, taking a moment to enunciate what they're thankful for. Avery is thankful for all the things he loves in this world, he says; his younger brother Quinn is thankful for the purple flowers by his placemat. Next up is the grandmother, Bonnie. "I am thankful for all the things I don't love," she says, "because they make me a stronger person." The next day, after hours of cameras and questions, hugs from supporters, and honks from passing cars, the Nortonsmiths head back home to have their marriage certificate signed in private.   9

Years of struggle, of adjusting to the limelight, have left the couple craving the moment of peace later that day in which, with the undying support of their parents and sons, they will exchange their wedding vows. When night falls, the mothers will give Avery and Quinn a bath, make sure the boys brush their teeth and check off the flossing box   10 on the chore list pegged to the bathroom door, and head to the privacy of their own room, recognized for the first time in their 13-year relationship as a married union—together, they commit, 'til death do them part.

Examining the Reading

Finding Meaning

1. Where do the events described in the article take place?
2. According to the article, how many gay and lesbian couples exchanged vows after the legalization of gay marriage?
3. Name two states that have decided to recognize gay marriage licenses from Massachusetts as valid in their own states.
4. How long have Michael and David been together?
5. Along with a "drive for awareness," what are Heidi and Gina's other goals in their fight for gay marriage?
6. What are Heidi and Gina's children thankful for? What is Heidi's stepmother thankful for?

Understanding Technique

1. Locate the writer's thesis and express it in your own words.
2. Evaluate the effectiveness of opening the article with a description of a wedding celebration.
3. How is the ending of the article tied to the beginning?
4. What type(s) of evidence does the author use to support her ideas?

Thinking Critically

1. Do you think the author is sympathetic toward gay marriage? Why or why not? Underline words or phrases that provide clues about the author's attitude.
2. What does the author mean by a "respectful divide" (paragraph 2)?
3. How does the story of Michael and David (paragraph 5) help to illustrate the author's thesis?
4. Why does the author use the word "crusade" (paragraph 7)? Discuss the connotations of the word.
5. Why does the author include the information that Heidi and Gina are an interracial couple?

Writing About the Reading

A Paragraph

1. Although Heidi's brother disapproves of gay marriage, he expresses his love for Heidi and Gina, describing it as "a tricky thing." Think about an experience you have had when your feelings were in conflict with your beliefs and write a paragraph describing it, including how you resolved the conflict.
2. Certain family members of the gay couple expressed disapproval. Write a paragraph describing a situation in which someone close to you expressed their disapproval of you. Describe how you handled the situation.

An Essay

1. What is your state's stance on gay marriage? Write an essay addressing the issue of gay marriage and explaining why you support or oppose your state's policy.
2. Have you ever taken an unpopular position on a controversial issue? Write an essay describing the situation and its outcome. Did you have the support of family, friends, or community? Did that support (or lack of support) make a difference to you?

Creative Activities

1. The families described in this article can be considered nontraditional in some ways. Think about what "family" means to you and how you would define the word. Interview your own family members and friends for their definitions of "family" and write about the different forms a family can take.
2. Brainstorm a list of questions that children of gay couples may ask of their gay parents.

Food from the 'Hood

▸ **Lester Sloan**

This essay describes a student project that eventually became a national enterprise, producing funds for college scholarships. The account originally appeared in Newsweek.

Journal Writing

Write a journal entry exploring your feelings toward getting involved in community projects. Have you done so? Why or why not?

Reading Strategy

As you read, highlight the key details that describe how Food from the 'Hood began and what it has accomplished.

Vocabulary Preview

reclaim (1) take back
mural (1) wall painting
oasis (1) fertile area
buoyed (2) lifted up; inspired
roster (2) list
diversify (2) create more variety; branch out
burgeoning (2) rapidly expanding; blossoming
catapulted (2) hurled; quickly raised up or over
franchise (3) sell rights to market a product in a different
               area
logo (3) identifying symbol
mentor (3) experienced person who advises and guides a
               novice
incarcerated (3) imprisoned

*I*t may not be history's biggest victory garden, but don't underestimate   1
the size of the victory. Shortly after the Los Angeles riots in 1992, a
group of 40 students at Crenshaw High School and their energetic biology teacher decided to reclaim the weedy quarter-acre plot that had
long been abandoned behind the school's football field. The goal was

simple: to create a community garden that would bring life back to one of the city's most battered neighborhoods while giving the students some hands-on science experience. They planted flowers, herbs, lettuce, collard greens, and other vegetables. A colorful mural soon appeared on the back wall, with a brown hand reaching toward a white one. In the middle of South-Central L.A., an oasis bloomed. The kids donated some of the produce to needy families in South-Central and sold the rest at local farmers markets. They called their project Food from the 'Hood.

And the ideas kept on sprouting. Buoyed by their success and aided by a growing roster of adult volunteers, the Crenshaw students decided to diversify. They had the herbs, they had the lettuce—what could be a better accompaniment than salad dressing? The Food from the 'Hood members created their own recipe and designed their own label for the brand, called Straight Out 'the Garden. Local business leaders helped with the marketing and manufacturing, and now the dressing is sold, for $2.59 a bottle, in more than 2,000 stores in 23 states. The burgeoning enterprise has catapulted the student farmers into student owners; they expect to earn $50,000 in profits this year, which will go toward funding college scholarships. Ten of the 15 seniors in Food from the 'Hood have been accepted at four-year colleges—a remarkable record for an inner-city public school. "When a kid gets an acceptance letter to college, that's our immediate payoff," says Melinda McMullen, a marketing consultant who worked with teacher Tammy Bird to steer the kids toward produce and profits.

2

Even more important than the money is the sense of accomplish- 3
ment that has grown out of Food from the 'Hood. "We showed that
a group of inner-city kids can and did make a difference," says freshman Terie Smith, 15. The students run all aspects of the business—
from weeding and harvesting to public relations and computer logs.
They've received inquiries from across the country about duplicating
their business plan, and they may franchise their logo to a group of
New York kids who hope to sell applesauce. Food from the 'Hood
members also have set up a mentor system and an SAT preparatory
program. "We all try to help each other in everything," says Jaynell
Grayson, 17, who will attend Babson College on scholarship next year.
Grayson doesn't know who her father is; her mother has been incarcerated most of her life. Food from the 'Hood has been a substitute
family for her. "What comes from that garden is inspiration," says Mc-
Mullen. "From anything—even the riots—amazing things can grow."

Examining the Reading

Finding Meaning

1. What was the goal of the students when they began the gardening
   project?
2. How did they continue the project after they grew vegetables?
3. How will they spend the $50,000 they expect to earn this year?
4. What activities have the students who began Food from the 'Hood
   designed to help one other?

Understanding Technique

1. Analyze Sloan's use of topic sentences.
2. What types of details does he use to support his main points?

Thinking Critically

1. Why do you think the biology teacher took a special interest in helping students coordinate Food from the 'Hood?
2. What do you think has been the most important result of Food from
   the 'Hood?
3. In what sense can the Food from the 'Hood members be considered heroes?
4. What did McMullen mean when she said, "What comes from that
   garden is inspiration"?

Writing About the Reading

A Paragraph

1. Both the name of the group and the name of the salad dressing use nonstandard English. Write a paragraph describing situations in which you feel nonstandard English should and should not be used.
2. Write a paragraph explaining what, if anything, you feel the scholarship recipients should give back to the project. (Should they be required to work on the project during the summer, for example?)

An Essay

1. Suppose you were given the opportunity to coordinate a fundraising activity for college scholarships. Write an essay describing what product you would try to sell and how you would market it.
2. Suppose you were required, as part of your graduation requirements, to work in a community or college service program designed to help others. Write an essay describing the kind of project you'd like to get involved with and what you'd hope to accomplish.

Creative Activities

1. Suppose Food from the 'Hood continues to expand. What types of foods do you think they might sell next? Write a paragraph describing their expansion. Include the names of the new products, and explain where they will get their ingredients and materials.
2. Propose alternative solutions to the inner-city problems. Choose one and explore its feasibility.

Bill Gates:
Computer Wizard

▸ **Michael Schaller, Virginia Scharff,
and Robert D. Schulzinger**

*This reading describes how Bill Gates, the world's richest man,
built his Microsoft computer company. Taken from a United
States history textbook,* Present Tense, *it traces his life from
age 12 to 1997. Gates has been troubled by legal battles, both in
the United States and in Europe, for violating antitrust laws.
The company has had to pay hefty fines and reevaluate its practice of bundling software. Meanwhile Gates has pumped hundreds of millions of dollars into his charitable foundation,
which provides much needed funds for world health, education,
and other social issues.*

Journal Writing

Bill Gates is first and foremost an inventor. Brainstorm a list
of inventions that have influenced your life.

Reading Strategy

A time line is a diagram that shows events in the order in
which they happened. Draw a time line showing the major
events in Gates's life.

Vocabulary Preview

envisioned (1) saw in the mind; imagined
revolutionize (1) change completely
mainstream (1) normal; average
entrepreneurial (1) pertaining to one who starts a business
insatiable (1) never satisfied; limitless
penchant (2) strong liking; tendency
municipalities (3) political units incorporated for local self-
                        government
dominated (5) controlled; took over
squelch (6) put down; crush
contested (6) called into question; challenged

*I*n the mid-1960s, few Americans envisioned the ways in which com-   1
puters would later revolutionize American life. Even those who were
most familiar with the machines could not foresee the time when millions of American families would assume the necessity of owning, and
using daily, a personal computer. Being interested in computers then,
recalled William H. Gates III, was "not a mainstream thing. I couldn't
imagine spending the rest of my life at it." But by the 1990s, Bill Gates
would become America's richest man, an inventor and entrepreneurial
genius who built his vast fortune on the world's insatiable appetite for
computer technology.

The son of a well-to-do Seattle family, Gates first became fascinated   2
with computers as a child of twelve, in 1967, when he and three friends
from the exclusive Lakeside School formed the Lakeside Programming
Group. One of his first programs was a class schedule for the school,
which he engineered so that he would share classes with all the pretti-
est girls. The school paid him $4,200 for a summer's work. Soon, the
Lakeside students were doing consulting work for the Computer Center Corporation, but Gates's penchant for pulling pranks got him into
trouble when he hacked into, and crashed, Control Data Corporation's
CYBERNET computer system.

By the time Gates was 14, he was president of his own company,   3
Traf-o-Data. The firm earned $20,000 selling traffic-counting systems
to municipalities before its customers even found out that the company was run by high school students. He interrupted a thriving career,
however, and enrolled at Harvard University in 1973, planning to become a lawyer.

At Harvard, Gates remained fascinated by the possibilities of com-   4
puter programs, operating systems, and software. In 1975, at the end of
his sophomore year, he dropped out, moved to Albuquerque, New Mex-
ico, and with his old Lakeside friend Paul Allen, founded Microsoft. Securing a contract with the Tandy Corporation to develop software for
Radio Shack computers, Microsoft grew quickly and moved to Seattle.
The company hit the big time when IBM contacted Gates about creating an operating system for a new product, the "personal computer."
The result, the MS-DOS operating system, was eventually licensed to
more than one hundred companies producing IBM-compatible computers, and by 1981 Microsoft was earning $16 million a year.

Like Thomas Edison, Gates was the rare inventor who mastered the   5
marketplace as well as the laboratory. In the late 1980s, Microsoft introduced its Windows operating system, which allowed users to run IBM-
compatible computers with a handheld "mouse" and on-screen symbols.
Windows was as simple to use and "user-friendly" as the operating system
pioneered by arch-rival Apple Computer, and IBM "clones" were much

less expensive than Apple's famous Macintosh model. Soon Windows dominated the market, and Gates, at the age of 32, became a billionaire.

An intensely competitive man, Gates has often been described as   6
aloof, sarcastic, and abrupt, but also as charming, funny, and able to inspire strong loyalty in his employees. The very model of a nineties corporate executive, he puts in long days and works weekends, and he expects employees who aspire to upward mobility to do the same. Microsoft has also earned a reputation as a cutthroat competitor: the Federal Trade Commission has investigated allegations that the company used its dominant position to squelch competition. But however contested his business practices, Gates undeniably had more to do with bringing the computer revolution into American homes and offices than any other individual.

Examining the Reading

Finding Meaning

1. What was Bill Gates's first professional computer experience?
2. How did Bill Gates get into trouble with a major computer corporation when he was young?
3. When Gates was the president of his first company, what did his company do?
4. Describe the development that made Gates a billionaire.
5. How has Gates influenced his employees?
6. How has Gates been described by others?

Understanding Technique

1. What is the essay's thesis? Which sentence in the conclusion refers to it again?
2. Although the essay is primarily factual, the writers' attitudes toward Gates are quite clear. Highlight those sections in which the authors' attitudes are revealed.
3. Highlight the transitions.
4. Evaluate the essay's introduction. How do the writers capture your interest?

Thinking Critically

1. How did Gates's contributions influence the computer world?
2. Why was the development of Windows perceived as a major contribution?
3. In the reading, Bill Gates is compared with Thomas Edison. Do you think this is a fair and reasonable comparison? Why or why not?

4. This reading was taken from a U.S. history textbook. Do you think Bill Gates has already become an important historical figure?
5. From the reading, what can you conclude about Gates's methods of doing business?

Writing About the Reading

A Paragraph

1. The frequent and extensive use of computers in this country has both a negative and a positive side. Write a paragraph explaining whether you believe the advent of the computer is more positive than negative or the other way around.
2. Since Gates works long days and weekends, he might be described as a workaholic. Are you a workaholic or do you know someone who is? Write a paragraph describing the traits and characteristics of a workaholic.

An Essay

1. Suppose someone was willing to loan you $20,000 to start your own business. Write an essay describing the product, service, or project you would focus on and how you would get started.
2. The introductory paragraph of this article states that computers have revolutionized American life. Write an essay presenting reasons why you think this statement is or is not true.

A Creative Activity

Select a point in this article at which Bill Gates's life could have gone in a different direction if he had made a particular decision differently. Rewrite the remainder of this article as if he had made a different choice at this point.

Do unto Others

▶ **David Polmer**
Student Essay

In this essay, Polmer explains how his beliefs about sportsman-
ship have changed since childhood. He wrote this while he was a
student at Washington University in St. Louis.

*R*emember life when you were ten years old? It was simple. Your   1
responsibilities were to obey the rules your mother repeatedly
preached—the foremost being, "Do unto others as you would have others do unto you"—and if you followed these rules, she would declare
you the best child in the world. The rules were basic, and while you
may not have grasped them all as quickly as your mother would have
liked, before too long you had managed to conquer not only the easy
rules, but even some of the tougher ones (including looking both ways
before crossing the street and keeping your elbows off the dinner
table). The one rule that seemed obvious from the second Mom explained it to me was "do unto others." It was catchy, concise and, most
of all, easy to accept. Yet at age ten I learned that not even professional
athletes always adhere to the rule I had considered the easiest of my
mother's to follow.

On one of my first days as a ball boy for the ATP tennis tournament   2
in Washington, D.C., I was assigned to work a doubles match involving
highly ranked Brad Gilbert. What I witnessed that day permanently
changed my perception of Gilbert. After a close line call went against
him, Gilbert turned to the linesman, unleashed a profanity-filled
tirade, then let loose a wad of spit meant only for him. The instant I
witnessed Gilbert's actions, I decided (as only a kid can) that this guy
was not only my least favorite tennis player in the world, but an undesirable person altogether.

Ten years later, a similar incident occurred. It involved the same   3
scenario—an official, umpire John Hirschbeck, making a close call
that does not go in the player's favor. The player, Roberto Alomar of the
Orioles, turns to the umpire and spits in his face. There was, however,
one significant difference for me in the Alomar incident—the athlete
played for a team I have passionately rooted for my entire life, a team
that has not reached postseason play since 1983. Furthermore, I knew

that for the Orioles to have a successful postseason, Alomar would be desperately needed. Because of these factors, I tried to rationalize why Alomar should be exempt from my mother's "do unto others" rule and thereby escape banishment from the playoffs because of his actions.

And I do have my reasons.   4

First, Hirschbeck clearly blew the call at a crucial time during a crit-   5
ical season-ending series. Second, he apparently egged on Alomar after the player had begun to walk back to the dugout. And third, Alomar is a fierce competitor whose job entails competing at the highest level possible every night. (Hirschbeck no doubt approaches his work in the same manner.) Not only did my mother refuse to accept any of my theories, she pointed out that most of them could have held true for Brad Gilbert.

So why was my reaction to the two events so different? Why, after ten years, did I find myself trying to excuse a ballplayer's actions that a decade ago I would have acknowledged instantly as disgraceful for any individual?

Clearly, as long as fans create emotional ties to specific players and   6
teams, there will be some people willing to excuse misconduct involving their favorite players or teams, no matter how offensive their actions may be. When Albert Belle played for the Indians, his insolence usually was tolerated by Cleveland fans; now, it's different. Also, society bombards us with the message that winning must be achieved because the pain of losing is too great to handle. Most ten-year-olds have yet to establish emotional ties to specific players on teams. When a kid sees his team win or lose, he is affected for maybe half an hour.

Yet, as a boy grows up and becomes better acquainted with the ex-   7
pectations of society and the impact of money in pro sports (particularly as it relates to that great end-all, winning), the games he loves lose their purity.

Consider the New York media and Yankees fans who treated twelve-   8
year-old Jeff Maier like a king after his interference altered the outcome of Game 1 of the 1996 AL Championship Series. The next day, Maier was given box seats behind the Yankees' dugout, courtesy of the *New York Post*, and he became the star of every New York early-morning and late-night talk show. All this for a kid who, instead of going to school that day, assisted the Yankees in winning a big game. To every die-hard Yankees fan, Maier's actions were heroic; it was the victory that mattered, not how it was achieved. Thus, the lesson from society is evident. Simply enjoying the game, as you did as a child, isn't enough.

I have become a victim of these twisted rules. As I watch my fa-   9
vorite pro teams, I realize the fun is not in seeing them compete, but in seeing them win. And when I participate in sports, I find little satisfaction in the competition, or the exercise, or the skills I acquire. Winning is the must.

When I reflect on the simple "do unto others" rule my mother in- 10
stilled, I think of how much easier it was to believe in it back then.
When you're ten, the rule, like sports itself, is simple. Now that I have
grown, society has taught me—for better or worse—that my mother's
rule doesn't mix very well with today's sports world.

Unfortunately for Brad Gilbert, I had yet to be brainwashed by 11
society's crazy rules when I was a boy. Now that I am older, and
feel somehow trapped into accepting much of society's winning-is-
everything mentality, I try as best I can to excuse Roberto Alomar.
However, what I have learned most from these two spitting incidents is
that regardless of what society plants in my brain, my mother will love
me no matter what I choose to believe—although she would surely prefer that her kindness credo be a priority.

Examining the Essay

1. Identify and evaluate Polmer's thesis.
2. In what ways do Polmer's references to his mother's golden rule
   strengthen his essay?
3. Evaluate Polmer's introduction and conclusion.
4. Polmer bases his essay on two incidents, that of Brad Gilbert and that
   of Roberto Alomar. What other types of evidence would strengthen
   his thesis?

Writing an Essay

1. Write an essay about a belief or opinion you held as a child and describe how it changed as you grew older. Explain why you think the
   change occurred.
2. Besides the sports world, can you think of other situations in which
   winning seems to be the most important thing? Write an essay describing the situation.
3. Write an essay describing what you think are the most important
   aspects of playing or watching sports.

Making Connections

1. Both "The Promised Land" and "Gay Marriages Unite, and
   Divide, Families" deal with family relationships that affect
   the writers' lives. Write an essay comparing the ways in
   which the different authors perceive family relationships
   and how they were affected by them.

2. Both "Bill Gates: Computer Wizard" and "Food from the 'Hood" discuss entrepreneurship. Write an essay comparing the two business ventures.

Internet Connections

1. Habitat For Humanity helps people who have difficulty affording housing by building them houses with donated materials and volunteer labor. Visit their web site at **http://www.habitat.org.** Identify the projects in progress where you live and write an essay describing three of them.

2. Many people do not realize the contributions that women have made to science throughout history. The web site 4000 Years of Women in Science, at **http://crux.astr.ua. edu/4000WS/4000WS.html,** contains information on over 100 of these individuals. Visit the site and read about some of these women. Are you surprised by any of the biographies on this site? For example, you might look at En Hedu' Anna, Hypatia, or Mary Whiton Calkins. Write a summary of the contributions of one of the women whose achievements most surprised you. Be sure you do not copy information directly from the article.

3. Weddings can be beautiful, but they are only the beginning of a marriage. Read these tips for getting a marriage off to a good start: **http://www.oznet.ksu.edu/News/sty/2001/ dating6.htm.** Write a paragraph explaining which of these you find most important and why.

(If any of these web sites are unavailable, use a search engine to locate another appropriate site.)

Chapter 6

Media That Shape Our Lives

Hardly a day goes by when we do not pick up a newspaper, look at a magazine, watch some television, listen to a radio, or spend some time with all four types of media. New forms of media are also developing: laser disks, CD-ROMs, videos, infomercials, closed-circuit and interactive television. Media include all means of communicating information, ideas, or attitudes to an anonymous public audience. And everywhere there are advertisements—on public transportation; in shopping carts, ball parks, hotel rooms, even public rest rooms; on cable shows that air in some high schools; and, increasingly, on nonprofit public broadcasting stations. In fact, we are bombarded by the media, whether we like it or not.

The media have a powerful impact on our beliefs and desires. Through advertising, the media influence what we buy. By choosing to follow certain stories and trends and ignoring others, the media focus our attention on particular topics. Talk shows, television series, and movies affect what we might talk about at the dinner table, dream about, or feel about ourselves and others. The readings in this chapter explore the impact of the media on the lives of others. Through them you will come to a fuller realization of how the media affect your life.

In this chapter, you will read about television, including the popularity of Oprah Winfrey and the issues she raises on her talk show ("Oprah Winfrey"). You will examine the new trend in television programming—reality TV ("Sporting the Fan(tasy) of Reality TV")—and consider whether television shows should be used as a means of advertising products ("Prime-Time TV's New Guest Stars: Products"). You will read about the responsibility of the media in determining coverage of the news ("After the War Coverage"). You'll read about the effects of advertising both products and events in "Advertising: Institutionalized Lying." You'll also hear from a journalist who discusses her first professional writing experience ("My First Story"). You will also read about how one form of media, music, affects our lives ("Music 'n Moods").

Brainstorming About the Media

Class Activities:

1. Working in pairs, brainstorm a list of all the types of media you have come in contact with in the past twenty-four hours.
2. Brainstorm a list of programs that have influenced or inspired you or led you to a decision or important change.

Oprah Winfrey

▸ **Deborah Tannen**

In this 1998 essay from Time *magazine, Deborah Tannen, a noted authority on human communication, examines Oprah Winfrey's rise to fame and her impact on talk shows and our society.*

Journal Writing

1. Write a journal entry about a book or article you have read or a movie you have seen that was so much like your own life that you saw yourself over and over in it.
2. Write a journal entry expressing your opinion about Oprah Winfrey. Why has she become a celebrity?

Reading Strategy

As you read, highlight factors that account for Winfrey's popularity.

Vocabulary Preview

poised (1) self-confident; composed
insouciant (1) carefree; unconcerned
beacon (2) source of guidance
discourse (2) conversation; talk
solace (4) comfort; relief
overt (6) open; obvious
paradox (8) contradiction; puzzle
legacy (8) gift; something left to future generations
permeate (8) spread throughout

*T*he Sudanese-born supermodel Alek Wek stands poised and insouciant   1
as the talk-show host, admiring her classic African features, cradles Wek's cheek and says, "What a difference it would have made to my childhood if I had seen someone who looks like you on television." The host is Oprah Winfrey, and she has been making that difference for millions of viewers, young and old, black and white, for nearly a dozen years.

Winfrey stands as a beacon, not only in the worlds of media and en-   2
tertainment but also in the larger realm of public discourse. At 44, she has a personal fortune estimated at more than half a billion dollars. She

owns her own production company, which creates feature films, prime-time TV specials, and home videos. An accomplished actress, she won an Academy Award nomination for her role in *The Color Purple*, and this fall will star in her own film production of Toni Morrison's *Beloved*.

But it is through her talk show that her influence has been greatest. 3 When Winfrey talks, her viewers—an estimated 14 million daily in the U.S. and millions more in 132 other countries—listen. Any book she chooses for her on-air book club becomes an instant best seller. When she established the "world's largest piggy bank," people all over the country contributed spare change to raise more than $1 million (matched by Oprah) to send disadvantaged kids to college. When she blurted that hearing about the threat of mad-cow disease "just stopped me cold from eating another burger," the perceived threat to the beef industry was enough to trigger a multimillion-dollar lawsuit (which she won).

Born in 1954 to unmarried parents, Winfrey was raised by her 4 grandmother on a farm with no indoor plumbing in Kosciusko, Miss. By age 3 she was reading the Bible and reciting in church. At 6 she moved to her mother's home in Milwaukee, Wis.; later, to her father's in Nashville, Tenn. A lonely child, she found solace in books. When a seventh-grade teacher noticed the young girl reading during lunch, he got her a scholarship to a better school. Winfrey's talent for public performance and spontaneity in answering questions helped her win beauty contests—and get her first taste of public attention.

Crowned Miss Fire Prevention in Nashville at 17, Winfrey visited a 5 local radio station, where she was invited to read copy for a lark—and was hired to read news on the air. Two years later, while a sophomore at Tennessee State University, she was hired as Nashville's first female and first black TV-news anchor. After graduation, she took an anchor position in Baltimore, Md., but lacked the detachment to be a reporter. She cried when a story was sad, laughed when she misread a word. Instead, she was given an early-morning talk show. She had found her medium. In 1984 she moved on to be the host of *A.M. Chicago*, which became *The Oprah Winfrey Show*. It was syndicated in 1986—when Winfrey was 32—and soon overtook *Donahue* as the nation's top-rated talk show.

Women, especially, listen to Winfrey because they feel as if she's a 6 friend. Although Phil Donahue pioneered the format she uses (mike-holding host moves among an audience whose members question guests), his show was mostly what I call "report-talk," which often typifies men's conversation. The overt focus is on information. Winfrey transformed the format into what I call "rapport-talk," the back-and-forth conversation that is the basis of female friendship, with its emphasis on self-revealing intimacies. She turned the focus from experts

Oprah Winfrey

to ordinary people talking about personal issues. Girls' and women's friendships are often built on trading secrets. Winfrey's power is that she tells her own, divulging that she once ate a package of hot-dog buns drenched in maple syrup, that she had smoked cocaine, even that she had been raped as a child. With Winfrey, the talk show became more immediate, more confessional, more personal. When a guest's story moves her, she cries and spreads her arms for a hug.

When my book *You Just Don't Understand: Women and Men in Conversation* was published, I was lucky enough to appear on both *Donahue* and *Oprah*—and to glimpse the difference between them. Winfrey related my book to her own life: she began by saying that she had read the book and "saw myself over and over" in it. She then told one of my examples, adding, "I've done that a thousand times"—and illustrated it by describing herself and Stedman. (Like close friends, viewers know her "steady beau" by his first name.)

Winfrey saw television's power to blend public and private; while it   8 links strangers and conveys information over public airwaves, TV is most often viewed in the privacy of our homes. Like a family member, it sits down to meals with us and talks to us in the lonely afternoons. Grasping this paradox, Oprah exhorts viewers to improve their lives and the world. She makes people care because she cares. That is Winfrey's genius, and will be her legacy, as the changes she has wrought in the talk show continue to permeate our culture and shape our lives.

Examining the Reading

Finding Meaning

1. What was Winfrey's childhood like?
2. How did Winfrey first become a public figure?
3. What was the purpose of the "world's largest piggy bank"?
4. According to Tannen, what is the difference between the interview styles of Winfrey and Phil Donahue?
5. What did Winfrey do when she interviewed the author on her television show?

Understanding Technique

1. Identify Tannen's thesis statement.
2. Describe the organization of the essay.
3. The title of the essay identifies its subject, but it does little to capture the readers' interest or suggest its thesis. Suggest several possible alternative titles that might be more effective.

Thinking Critically

1. What did Winfrey mean when she told model Alek Wek, "What a difference it would have made to my childhood if I had seen someone who looks like you on television"?
2. Why was Winfrey sued by the beef industry? Why do you think the author included this incident in the article?
3. Why does the author describe television as a "paradox"?
4. What do you think makes Winfrey so different from others in her business?
5. The author believes that talk shows "shape our lives." Do you agree or disagree with her? Why?

Writing About the Reading

A Paragraph

1. Write a paragraph explaining why Winfrey has become so popular.
2. Talk shows deal with various issues. Write a paragraph describing an issue that is of major importance to you that you think talk shows should address.

An Essay

1. Write an essay about a public figure (a television personality, musician, politician, author, etc.) who has made a difference in your life. Describe how this person has influenced you and why.
2. Do you agree with Tannen that men and women speak to each other differently? Explain why you agree or disagree and give some examples from your experience to support your opinion.

A Creative Activity

Imagine you have been chosen to be interviewed on Winfrey's show. What would you like to discuss with Winfrey?

My First Story

> ▶ Patrice Gaines

Patrice Gaines, a successful journalist and writer, describes how her career began with a page filled with corrections and criticisms. This essay is taken from Gaines's autobiography, Laughing in the Dark.

Journal Writing

Write a journal entry describing your attitude toward your writing. Include likes, dislikes, rewards, problems, and so forth.

Reading Strategy

As you read, highlight words, phrases, and sentences that reveal Gaines's attitude toward her job and toward writing. Write annotations of any personal experiences about jobs or writing that the essay brings to mind.

Vocabulary Preview

muster (2) call forth; gather
fate (2) a force beyond one's control that directs events
excel (2) be better than others
confidant (3) one with whom secrets are shared
fretting (5) worrying

*D*iscovering I was the only black secretary at the paper didn't make   1
me angry, as it would today; it boosted my self-esteem—at least as
much as I would allow. Even though I loved to write, I wasn't excited
about working for a newspaper; I didn't have any desire to become a
newspaper reporter. I wrote short stories and poetry, not journalism. I
had written enough poems now to fill a book, which I kept tucked in
my underwear drawer. I wrote short stories with a heavy moral message. One story was about three soldiers killed in Vietnam, their bodies
destroyed beyond recognition by a grenade. Their remains were
shipped in one casket, and the families—Jewish, Baptist, and atheist—

---

had to hold one funeral. One soldier was black. I wrote a poem about the attention paid to pregnant women and the lack of care given the environment. It ended: "Would things have been different if the fathers of this country had been mothers instead?"

I wrote about matters of the heart and I couldn't see yet that journalists did this, too, with more skill and sense of communication than I could yet muster. Still, if there is such a thing as fate, it had acted on my behalf, to put me in a place where when I woke up I would have before me what I had wanted all the time, where, even though I hadn't been in the upper half of my graduating class, I could still learn to be a writer and, perhaps, have a chance to excel.

My new boss, Peter, was a white guy barely a year older than I was. We immediately struck up a comfortable friendship. He was a member of the new, young, white South, those who tried to build the bridge between the Confederate tradition of Jim Crow and the more integrated future of Martin Luther King, Jr. I became Peter's close confidant and assistant, in many ways no different from the scores of secretaries who in the course of their office duties compose personal as well as business letters, serving as human calendars, remembering flights and meetings, birthdays and anniversaries, covering for bosses who sneak off to play golf. Secretaries can be like members of the family, and with most of them being female, they often become the nurturing mother-wife and sister-friend. It was a position that suited me well for many years, and Peter was as near-perfect a boss-mate as possible.

He arranged for me to have my first chance to write for others, a position on the monthly employee newsletter, which I helped write during my extra time. This was a big deal to me. It was as close as I could get to imagining myself as a writer. Becoming a reporter was too big a dream; just writing for the employee newsletter frightened me to near paralysis.

My first story was about pets—talking birds, big snakes, and show dogs. The editor returned my draft covered with red marks, noting misspelled words, slang, wordiness, and whole paragraphs that needed to be rearranged or dropped. Accompanying his critique was a note: "An ego is too big to fit into a typewriter." I understood immediately what he was saying and dropped my initial feelings of embarrassment and disappointment. I stayed awake that night fretting, but by day my normally oversensitive self, who hurt at any hint of not being accepted, wrote with the attitude that every red mark was an opportunity to learn.

I discovered I thought differently when I wrote; I was smarter on paper. I saw where the mistakes were made and I corrected them. It took a while—maybe six months—but eventually there were fewer red ink marks and among the lines of criticism were a few compliments. For me, it was nothing short of magic to string together words in a way that made people notice and care. This was the answer to my prayers, to be able to touch people in a way that I had not been able to with my actions or the words from my mouth.

Examining the Reading

Finding Meaning

1. Given that the author wanted to be a writer, why was she not excited about working on a newspaper?
2. How did Gaines's boss help launch her career as a writer?
3. Describe Gaines's relationship with her boss.
4. Describe the types of stories Gaines enjoyed writing for herself.
5. Describe how Gaines improved her writing skills.

Understanding Technique

1. Describe this essay's organization.
2. Evaluate Gaines's sentence structure. How does she make sentences lively and interesting?

Thinking Critically

1. How did Gaines use the criticisms of her first story as a positive experience?
2. In what sense is journalism about "matters of the heart"?
3. Explain the meaning of the editor's note: "An ego is too big to fit into a typewriter."
4. Why did Gaines keep her short stories and poems in her underwear drawer?

Writing About the Reading

A Paragraph

1. Did you ever write something that was seriously criticized? Write a paragraph describing whether this was helpful or harmful to you.
2. Gaines enjoyed writing stories with moral messages. She wrote about "matters of the heart." Write a paragraph describing the kinds of writing or topics that are easy for you or that you enjoy.

An Essay

1. Write an essay describing someone's criticism of something other than your writing and explaining why or why not it was justified.

2. Gaines feels that fate acted on her behalf. Has fate ever worked on your behalf or against you? Write an essay describing a situation in which luck or fate seemed to be involved.

A Creative Activity

Write a paragraph describing what you think happened in Gaines's story about the funeral of the three soldiers.

Music 'n Moods

▸ **Carolyn Gard**

Music not only stirs up your emotions, it also can be beneficial. This article from Current Health *examines the wide-ranging effects of music.*

Journal Writing

Write a journal entry about a favorite song or musical piece. Explain why you like it and how it makes you feel.

Reading Strategy

As you read, make a list of the beneficial effects of music and the evidence Gard offers to substantiate each effect.

Vocabulary Preview

evokes (5) brings out
instills (6) implants; introduces gradually
discordant (6) harsh; unpleasant
cardiovascular (9) of the heart and blood vessels
neurological (10) pertaining to the nervous system
cadence (10) beat; rhythm
synchronized (10) occurred or caused to occur at the same time
verbalize (13) express in words
autistic children (14) mentally disturbed children who have extreme difficulty learning language, playing normally, and interacting with others
Alzheimer's disease (14) a brain disorder that causes memory loss, confusion, and disturbance of speech and movements.
baroque music (15) a form of classical music created in seventeenth- and eighteenth-century Western Europe; composers include Bach, Handel, and Vivaldi
conducive (16) tending to bring about

*Y*ou've seen *Psycho* many times. You know exactly what's going to hap-   1
pen in the shower scene—but you're still on the edge of your seat.

You're watching *Jaws* again. You know exactly when the shark is   2
going to appear—and you're still anxious.

Now rewind the movies and turn off the sound. Janet Leigh steps   3
into the shower, but this time she's just another tired tourist getting
ready for bed. Now do the same when watching *Jaws,* and the people
on the boat are simply sightseers out for an afternoon sail.

It's hard to imagine any movies without music, but originally Al-   4
fred Hitchcock didn't want any music in the shower scene in *Psycho.*
After he saw what screeching violins could do, he raised the com-
poser's salary.

Movie music always evokes strong emotions in the audience—   5
from fear and panic to tenderness and love.

The power of music to set the mood in a movie depends on the fact   6
that most people react in the same way to the same music. Low-
pitched, repetitive sounds suggest fear. A single tone that gets louder
and louder instills anxiety. Kettle drums provoke anger, and a shrill
blast of high notes with a discordant blare of bass notes will drive you
to panic.

Why Does Music Affect Our Emotions?

Although researchers know that music can comfort, delight, convince,   7
frighten, or move us, they don't know how it does this.

One theory is that a fetus responds to sounds. Because of this   8
early association, hearing may evoke a more emotional response than
sight. Music also triggers memory, allowing you to remember a past
experience.

According to Don Campbell, the founder of the Institute for Music,   9
Health, and Education, music is linked to many measurable changes
in body function. Music can relax and energize, release anger and
mask pain, cause muscles to tense, change skin temperature, and improve circulation and cardiovascular function. Every thought, feeling,
and movement has its own musical qualities. Your pulse and heartbeat
have a rhythm and tempo, your breath has pattern and flow.

Moving to Music

Music may produce a neurological effect that improves motor control.   10
The brain is organized in a complete pattern—your stride length, step
cadence, and posture are all centrally located. When muscle activity is
synchronized to rhythm, it becomes more regular and efficient. When
one part improves, everything improves.

Music can help you get more out of exercise. If you do jumping   11
jacks you may get tired after 100. With music in the background, you
may do 200 jumps before you get tired. The continuous rhythmic patterns in music increase the body's endurance and strength.

Music chosen specifically for exercising uses the natural rhythms   12
of the body. One company offers tapes of computer-generated music
that encourage you to regulate your walking from a 30-minute walk at
110 steps per minute to a race walk of a 10-minute mile at a rate of 170
steps per minute.

Music Communicates

Music lets you express emotions that are difficult to verbalize. Think   13
about the difference between saying the pledge of allegiance and
singing the national anthem. Which one is more likely to give you a
thrill? For the same reason, high schools and colleges have fight songs
to excite the fans at sports events.

The idea of using music to heal goes back to the ideas of Aristotle   14
and Plato. In music therapy, music is the instrument of communication between the therapist and the patient; the patient doesn't need any
particular musical skills to benefit. Music helps people come to an understanding of the inner self. Music therapy is extremely valuable in
helping disturbed and autistic children, as well as people with Alzheimer's disease.

Making Music Work for You

You've got a final tomorrow—how can music help you study? Don   15
Campbell suggests that you start with 10 minutes of good, energetic
dancing to pop music to get your body oxygenized. When you sit down
to study, listen to slow baroque music, such as Bach, that has fewer
than 60 beats per minute. This speed allows you to focus and concentrate. The best music for study has no words; words distract you by encouraging your brain to sort them out and make sense of them.

New Age music with a slow pulse is conducive to sleep. And music   16
with a fast beat, above 90 beats per minute, will give you energy for
getting things done.

A recent study conducted at the University of California at Irvine   17
indicates that listening to the music of Mozart can raise a person's IQ.
It seems that Mozart's music speaks directly to the parts of the brain
that enhance learning.

On an even more personal level, music can help you become more   18
aware of your inner self and your feelings.

Suppose you're in a major slump—you flunked a test or you ended   19
a relationship. Campbell finds that there is a therapeutic strain in certain music that helps you get in touch with your emotions. He suggests

you find five tapes or CDs that make you feel "safe" and calm so you can feel your own emotions. Play the soundtrack from *Out of Africa* or a symphonic piece such as "A Little Night Music" by Mozart, and write or draw how you're feeling. The music helps you relax, allowing the emotion to come out. When you've worked through your sadness, you'll be ready to face the world again.

Examining the Reading

Finding Meaning

1. How do soundtracks affect audience reaction to films?
2. What kind of music evokes each of the following emotions: fear, anxiety, anger, and panic?
3. How can music help people exercise better?
4. What is music therapy?
5. According to this article, what type of music is best to listen to while you study? To help you fall asleep? To raise your IQ?

Understanding Technique

1. The thesis of this essay is suggested in the title, but it is not directly stated anywhere in the essay itself. Discuss whether you feel a thesis statement is needed. If so, write a possible thesis statement for this essay.
2. What types of evidence does Gard offer to support her claim that music affects us?

Thinking Critically

1. Why do you think music therapy might be helpful for autistic children or for Alzheimer's patients?
2. What did the author mean by "music can help you become more aware of your inner self and your feelings"?
3. Do you agree that classical music is the best music to listen to while studying? Why or why not?

Writing About the Reading

A Paragraph

1. Choose an activity you like to do while listening to music. Write a paragraph describing the type of music you prefer while doing this activity and how you think the music affects your performance.

2. You probably react differently when you hear a poem read and when you listen to a song. Write a paragraph explaining the difference.

An Essay

1. Write an essay about a movie you saw recently. Describe the sound-track and explain how the music added to, or detracted from, your enjoyment of the movie. Be sure to use specific examples.
2. Write a letter to your college president, proposing that students should be allowed to listen to music while taking exams. Use the information presented in this article to back your argument.

A Creative Activity

Imagine that you just had a fight with your best friend and you are very upset about it. Name five CDs or individual pieces of music you think would be helpful to listen to at this time. Explain why you chose this music.

Advertising: Institutionalized Lying

▶ **Donna Woolfolk Cross**

Are advertisements true? Can you believe their claims? This essay explores the issue of false and misleading advertising. It is an excerpt from a book titled Mediaspeak.

Journal Writing

Explore your reaction to advertising by freewriting or brainstorming about ads and about whether they can or should be believed, disbelieved, or ignored.

Reading Strategy

This reading contains several examples of misleading advertising. Highlight or annotate why each is misleading. Also, highlight or annotate what the mouthwash story is intended to demonstrate.

Vocabulary Preview

inferential (1) concluded from presented evidence
rebuked (2) reprimanded
undaunted (2) not discouraged
purport (2) to claim, often falsely
deterred (5) discouraged from acting
eliciting (6) bringing forth
halitosis (6) bad breath
smiting (7) afflicting
ensued (7) followed as a consequence or result
discourse (7) speak or write formally and at length

*T*he fact is that advertising is institutionalized lying. The lies are tol-   1
erated—even encouraged—because they serve the needs of the corporate establishment. . . . By now the falsity—either direct or inferential—of most television commercials is a matter of well-documented fact. Most

people accept that ads are not true and yet, because they do not understand the methods by which they are influenced, are still taken in. Can *you* detect the deception behind the following statements?

- *"All aspirin is not alike. In tests for quality, Bayer proved superior."*

Most people assume this means that Bayer aspirin has been shown to relieve pain better than other aspirin. In fact the "tests for quality," which were conducted by Bayer and not an independent testing agency, showed that Bayer was superior, in its own manufacturer's opinion, because the tablets were whiter and less breakable than the other aspirins tested. Nevertheless, this claim is so effective that a recent FTC [Federal Trade Commission] survey revealed that forty percent of consumers believe Bayer is the most effective aspirin.

- *"Sominex makes you drowsy so you can sleep."*

Time and again the advertising agencies peddling over-the-counter   2
remedies for insomnia have been rebuked for stating or implying that these products insure a good night's sleep. Undaunted, the nimble admen simply found a new way of making the same claim: The remedies still do not insure a good night's sleep, but they purport to make us drowsy so we *can* sleep. Reading a dull book or watching an uninteresting TV show would probably have the same effect. It is even possible that ads for insomnia cures can put you to sleep sooner than their product will.

- *"Gallo: because the wine remembers."*

If true, this should put a crimp in dinnertime conversations: "Hush, dear, not in front of the Hearty Burgundy."

The late August Sebastiani, who scorned selling techniques such as   3
this, would not allow his wines to be advertised on TV, saying, "If you spend enough on advertising, you can get people to drink sauerkraut juice, juice you couldn't get a thirsty hog to drink."

If there is absolutely no need for a particular product, the adman   4
must invent one. He must convince you that your health and happiness will be in jeopardy if you don't buy his product.

Believe it or not, In the Beginning there was no mouthwash.   5
Proper oral hygiene consisted of a thorough brushing with a good toothpaste. Then one day an enterprising stranger rode into town peddling a new product, a liquid made of water, alcohol, and assorted additives that would "freshen your breath." People weren't interested. "What can this stuff do for me that toothpaste can't?" they asked. Not to be deterred, the stranger hired himself an advertising agency.

Soon the television disease-control center was informing people   6
about a new and terrible disease. No one was immune from it: House-

wives and clerics, teenagers, cab drivers, lawyers, new mothers, were being struck down with a devastating malady. Far from eliciting sympathy, a person who contracted this disease was sure to lose his promotion, friends, loved ones, and paper boy. The sufferer himself was always the last to learn, usually from a hastily departing relative, that his affliction was . . . *halitosis.*

Bad breath was smiting the land, the righteous along with the sinners. A great panic might have ensued but for the miraculously timed appearance, at that very moment, of a cure: *mouthwash.* Soon Americans were buying bottles of it by the millions, and many could discourse knowledgeably about the virtues of various brands: "mediciney" versus "sweet," etc. Skeptical about claims for the product, the American Dental Association and the National Academy of Sciences, after several intensive studies, issued a report stating that mouthwash has no lasting effect on bad breath, and that rinsing one's mouth with salt water is just as beneficial as using mouthwash. But medical science delivered its verdict too late. People had been taught to *believe* in mouthwash. The stranger rode out of town a very rich man.

Examining the Reading

Finding Meaning

1. How does Cross define advertising?
2. According to this reading, do most people believe ads are true or false?
3. In the "tests for quality," give one reason why Bayer was considered superior to other aspirin.
4. If the public has no need for a specific product, how do the advertisers "sell" the product?
5. After many studies on mouthwash, what did the medical organizations conclude about it?

Understanding Technique

1. How does Cross make the transition from examples of misleading advertising to a discussion of how advertisers create a so-called need for a product?
2. Evaluate the essay's final paragraph. How does it summarize the essay?

Thinking Critically

1. If the public recognizes that television ads are false, why do they continue to buy the products advertised?

2. Is there such a thing as advertising that is true but misleading? Explain.
3. Discuss how ads for Sominex and other anti-insomnia products may affect our thinking.
4. How does false advertising shape our lives?
5. Identify an example of false advertising not given in the reading and explain why it is false or deceptive.

Writing About the Reading

A Paragraph

1. Mouthwash is an example of a product that was sold to the public by advertising agencies. What other products do you think are popular because of the advertising attention they receive? Write a paragraph identifying these products and explaining how advertising makes them popular.
2. Write a paragraph describing the worst commercial you have ever seen. Explain why it was the worst.

An Essay

1. If advertising is false and/or misleading, should our legal system allow it to appear? Write an essay answering this question. Justify your position.
2. Do you ever buy a certain product simply because you liked the commercial? Write an essay on whether commercials influence what you buy. Include examples in your essay.

A Creative Activity

Find an ad that you think is false or misleading and add it to the essay. Write a paragraph explaining what is wrong with the advertisement.

Prime-Time TV's New Guest Stars: Products

> **Brian Steinberg and Suzanne Vranica**

This article, which first appeared in the Wall Street Journal *(Eastern Edition) on January 12, 2004, explores the use of product placement in television shows as an alternative to traditional advertising.*

Journal Writing

Have you ever noticed specific brand name products used in television shows? Do you think this is an effective form of advertising?

Reading Strategy

As you read, look for evidence of the authors' opinion about product placement.

Vocabulary Preview

overt (1) open to view
resonate (1) be filled with sound; echo
sacrosanct (2) most sacred or holy
grappling (3) coming to grips with
cede (3) to surrender possession of; to hand over
lucrative (3) producing wealth
leery (3) suspicious
decried (6) expressed strong disapproval of
protégé (8) one who is promoted by an influential person

*I*f it were a made-for-TV movie, it might be called "Invasion of the Advertisers." With audiences for network television shrinking, and more viewers zapping through commercials on recorded TV, some of the industry's most powerful advertisers are securing roles for their products inside prime-time sitcoms and dramas, once considered off limits for such overt promotions. "Traditional commercials resonate better when they accompany products placed within a show," says Jeff Bell, vice president of marketing for Chrysler and Jeep at Chrysler Group, a unit of DaimlerChrysler AG.

Forms of product placement have been around almost as long as   2
TV advertising itself, but the practice has been limited largely to sports
telecasts, live entertainment and, more recently, reality shows and
soap operas—not the blue-chip scripted shows that are among the
most valuable real estate on TV. But even those shows are no longer
sacrosanct on some networks. In the current season, for example, Ford
Motor Co.'s vehicles have been featured on "24," the acclaimed action
drama on News Corp.'s Fox. And a shiny orange Beetle convertible
from Volkswagen AG had a big role in the teen superhero drama
"Smallville" on Time Warner Inc.'s WB network last year.

NBC, the No. 1 network among 18- to 49-year-old viewers, adver-   3
tisers' most sought-after group, is grappling with how much content
territory to cede to marketers. NBC rejected a lucrative deal involving
marketers including Ford's Lincoln Mercury and Sony Corp.'s Sony
Electronics for its glitzy new drama "Las Vegas" last year. According to
people familiar with the matter, the network was leery of offending traditional advertisers. NBC says it passed on the idea "for creative reasons."
"We continue to explore the value," of product-placement in scripted
comedies and dramas, says Marianne Gambelli, executive vice president
overseeing prime-time ad sales for the network. "How do you make it
work? Where does it fit in? Where doesn't it fit in? How do you make it
organic?" CBS and UPN also are charting their way. So far, they haven't
directly placed advertisers' brands or logos into prime-time fare. CBS
says it remains open to product placement on scripted shows.

The networks aren't the only ones that make such deals. Familiar   4
brands often pop up in prime time not as part of network-advertising
deals, but as the result of behind-the-scenes maneuverings of so-called
product-placement shops. These tiny, discreet outfits maintain close ties
with prop masters, set designers and executives at production studios
and use their connections to get advertisers' branded products—from
handbags to computers—in front of the camera on TV's hottest shows.

In June, AIM Productions Inc., a New York product-placement   5
concern, got Unilever PLC's Ragu Express, a packaged pasta-and-sauce
meal, an eye-catching role on "Everybody Loves Raymond" on Viacom
Inc.'s CBS; in the episode, Ray stalked his wife in a supermarket and
knocked over an entire display of the product. AIM also got Interbrew
SA's Rolling Rock beer a gig on "Ed," on General Electric Co.'s NBC in
October. Another placement firm, Norm Marshal & Associates Inc., got
Microsoft Corp.'s Xbox game machine onto CBS's "Two and a Half
Men" in September. It also helped arrange the ongoing appearances
of General Motors Corp.'s Hummer H2 in episodes of CBS's "CSI: Mi-
ami." Advertisers themselves—not their ad agencies—generally keep
product-placement companies on retainers ranging from $20,000 to
$100,000 a year, says Patricia Ganguzza, president of AIM Produc-
tions, which counts Unilever and Kraft Foods Inc. as clients.

Watchdog groups have long decried product placements for blur-   6
ring the line between content and advertising without adequately informing viewers. And the networks themselves appear to be divided on
how far they want to open the gate. "You've got to wonder when it
starts to destroy the entertainment value," asks Tom Wolzien, a former
television executive who is senior media analyst for investment research firm Sanford C. Bernstein & Co.

In some instances, placements are extremely subtle. For example,   7
Euro RSCG MVBMS Partners, an ad-agency owned by Havas SA and
working for client Polaroid, handed cameras to the band Outkast,
whose hit song "Hey Ya" includes the lyric, "Shake it like a Polaroid picture." According to Ron Berger, the ad firm's chief executive, the cameras have appeared with the band on NBC's "Saturday Night Live" and
the "Vibe Awards" on Viacom's UPN. "It's like advertising," says Mr.
Berger. "If it's done very well, it's great. If it's done badly, it's horrible."

When it comes to reality shows and soap operas, the networks have   8
welcomed product placement. Earlier this month, NBC agreed with
DaimlerChrysler to weave a Chrysler automobile into "The Apprentice,"
a reality show about a competition to become Donald Trump's protégé.
And Procter & Gamble Co. products are set to appear on the next round
of CBS's "Survivor," which will premiere after the Super Bowl. Last
year, Avon Products Inc.'s Mark cosmetics line, aimed at young women,
got a prominent role on the NBC soap opera "Passions." A young female
character became a Mark representative and talked up the brand. CBS,
meanwhile, approved a deal weaving Butterball turkeys into storylines
on "As The World Turns" and "Guiding Light" near Thanksgiving.

WB, Fox and Walt Disney Co.'s ABC say they examine product   9
placements on a case-by-case basis. "There are do's and don'ts, and
they are evolving," says Bill Morningstar, executive vice president of
media sales at the WB network.

Ms. Ganguzza, of AIM Productions, expects to see more placement   10
deals involving prime-time dramas and comedies. "The brands hold
the reins and the networks realize that marketers have started shifting
more dollars into nontraditional media, including product placement,
because of its sexy appeal," she says.

Examining the Reading

Finding Meaning

1. Why are advertisers trying to find new ways to promote their products on TV?
2. What is a product-placement shop?
3. Why are watchdog groups unhappy about product placements in
   television shows?

4. What are some of the ways that products are currently being placed in television shows?

Understanding Technique

1. Do the authors of this article reveal their opinion about product placements? How would the article be different if the authors' opinions were more obvious?
2. Reread the first line of the article. What does it accomplish?
3. What is the authors' thesis statement?
4. The authors give multiple examples of actual product placements. What effect does this have on the article?
5. Does the article have an effective conclusion? Why or why not?

Thinking Critically

1. Explain why traditional commercials might "resonate better when they accompany products placed within a show."
2. Why do you think product placement has typically been limited to sports telecasts, soap operas, and reality shows?
3. Why would networks be afraid to offend traditional advertisers?
4. What does Ms. Ganguzza mean when she says that nontraditional media, including product placement, have "sexy appeal"?

Writing About the Reading

A Paragraph

1. Imagine that you are an executive producer of a television show. Write a short statement describing the circumstances under which you would consider allowing placement of a product in your show.
2. Do you think it is appropriate to advertise products through product placements? Write a paragraph explaining your answer.
3. What makes an effective advertisement? Choose a product and explain what an effective advertisement should do to sell a product.

An Essay

1. Write an essay that explores the advantages and disadvantages of using product placements in television shows from several points of view. For example, you might consider the priorities and concerns of television producers, advertisers, product creators, or consumers.
2. Describe how product placement might affect a particular demographic group, such as children, senior citizens, or recent immi-

grants to the United States. Should special guidelines be enacted to protect these groups? Why or why not?

A Creative Activity

Pick a product that you use and enjoy. Write a letter to the producers of your favorite television show describing how the product could be placed in the show and why that product is appropriate.

After the War Coverage

> ▸ Barb Palser

This article describes the efforts of various news sites to provide ongoing coverage of the aftermath of the war in Iraq. The article first appeared in American Journalism Review *in 2004.*

Journal Writing

Write a journal entry about a web site or television news show you have visited or seen that presents information or news in a powerful or moving way.

Reading Strategy

As you read, pay attention to how the author's choice of words and phrases contributes to the tone of the article.

Vocabulary Preview

commemorate (1) to acknowledge and pay tribute to
lauded (4) praised
sustainability (8) the ability to be maintained or kept up
robust (8) full of health and strength
sporadically (8) on an irregular basis
voluminous (9) extensive; lengthy
montage (9) a combination of several different elements
vigilant (11) watchful

While some Iraq special sections froze at the time major combat operations ended, other news sites continue to commemorate the casualties. Scroll slowly down this Web page and see if it doesn't grip your heart: www.cnn.com/specials/2003/iraq/forces/casualties/.   1

There you'll find the names, ages, combat units, hometowns and   2
circumstances of death for each U.S. and coalition serviceperson killed in Iraq since fighting began more than a year ago, sorted alphabetically. Photographs are included for nearly all of them. The effect is powerful, personal and entirely different from what a reader gets with the steady trickle of newspaper headlines reporting one casualty one day, two more the next.

Source: Reprinted by permission of *American Journalism Review.*

　　For CNN.com Senior Vice President and Executive Producer Mitch　3
Gelman, the decision to maintain this page—as well as CNN.com's ex-
pansive special sections on the war and post-war Iraq—was a matter of
course. "It's our responsibility as a national and international news
organization to continue to report on the progress of the conflict and
the efforts to rebuild the nation," Gelman explains. "There are many
men and women who have been willing to make a great sacrifice in
this conflict, and we feel an obligation to honor the memory of those
who have been lost by recording the circumstances in which they gave
their lives."

　　CNN.com readers have lauded the site's efforts. Says Gelman:　4
"We've received many e-mails from people thanking us for honoring
the soldiers, including notes from family members who we know from
their letters appreciate the fact that we remember the sacrifices that their
loved ones have made." It's worthy journalistic work, clearly. The daily
effort to keep a record of casualties may not be large—but it's regular
and continuous. Someone needs to gather the information and photos
of each soldier killed and publish them day after day, month after
month. CNN.com's staff also maintains charts that categorize the fatalities by nationality, race, age, gender and hostile versus non-hostile
circumstances of death.

　　Several other news sites update casualty trackers at varying levels　5
of detail; washingtonpost.com's "Faces of the Fallen" is another out-
standing example. It's a more highly produced Flash presentation,
arranged chronologically, but with much of the same information as
CNN.com's page. (When I visited in mid-March, however, it appeared
to be updated less frequently.)

　　In these cases and in every newsroom every day, the toughest task　6
for a news manager is not deciding which stories and projects are important, but which are most important.

　　Part of that calculation should be whether the organization is—　7
like CNN.com—uniquely able to cover the material, or to present it in
ways that other media can't.

　　Another factor is sustainability. When the war in Iraq began virtu-　8
ally all news organizations—local and national—threw all of their
resources into that story. More than a year later, the Web is strewn
with robust special sections either frozen at the time major combat
ended—or updated sporadically, as when Saddam Hussein was captured.
Sites that have curtailed their coverage haven't done so because they
believe the story ended last spring, but because they simply couldn't
maintain that level of depth as other national and international stories
rose to the fore.

　　Some sites, such as washingtonpost.com, have retired their spe-　9
cial war sections more gracefully than others. "Retired" isn't entirely

accurate, as some of the content—news headlines and "Faces of the Fallen"—continues to be updated. The bulk of the "War in Iraq" page (www.washingtonpost.com/wp-srv/iraq/front.htm) is a well-organized retrospective of the site's voluminous war coverage—including a video montage of the most striking sights and sounds of Operation Iraqi Freedom, highlights of online discussion forums, and archived reports and commentary. This is an exemplary way to keep special, in-depth coverage valuable and accessible long after it has ceased to be current news. (The Post's site does, of course, continue to comprehensively cover the rebuilding efforts, just not as a full-blown section.)

The way news sites have handled coverage after the war is, in some   10
ways, more instructive than the way they covered the war itself. In the midst of the story everybody knew what to do. In the aftermath, when the story is no longer front-and-center every day, the choices regarding how and where to continue coverage are much less clear.

In these situations, online news managers need to be bold at   11
choosing the projects they should do from among the many they could do. They should select those that matter to the site's journalistic mission, even if—especially if—they lead off the beaten path. And they must always be vigilant for projects, like a virtual memorial or coverage archive, that the Web can present in formats that are better—or different—than traditional media. Exploring new ways to convey the depth of a story and preserve history is more than an advantage of this medium; it's the Web's responsibility.

Examining the Reading

Finding Meaning

1. In addition to a photograph, list at least four pieces of information provided on CNN.com about each serviceperson killed in Iraq.
2. CNN.com's staff also maintains charts that categorize the fatalities in Iraq. What five categories do they use?
3. According to the author, what is the most difficult task for a news manager every day?
4. Explain why coverage of the war in Iraq has become more limited on some news sites.
5. Describe three aspects of the *Washington Post*'s online coverage included on its "War in Iraq" page.
6. According to the author, what is the Web's responsibility regarding news stories?

Understanding Technique

1. Highlight the author's thesis.
2. Describe the author's tone.
3. What is the purpose of the reference in the first paragraph to a particular web site on the Internet?

Thinking Critically

1. Does the author reveal her personal feelings about the war in Iraq? Why or why not?
2. How do the comments of CNN.com's Mitch Gelman (paragraphs 3–4) support the author's thesis?
3. Explain what the author means when she says CNN.com is "uniquely able" (paragraph 7) to provide coverage of the war. How do online news organizations present material "in ways that other media can't?"
4. The author believes that online news managers must be "bold" and "vigilant" in choosing news projects that matter. What does she mean by this? Do you agree?

Writing About the Reading

A Paragraph

1. Write a paragraph describing another way or ways those killed in the Iraq War could be recognized or commemorated.
2. How can the Web preserve history differently than print sources (newspapers, history books, etc.) can? Write a paragraph responding to the author's assertion that the Web is responsible for exploring new ways to preserve history.

An Essay

1. Visit each of the web sites mentioned in the article* and write an essay describing your response to them and what you learned from them. Do you agree with the author that CNN.com's site "grips your heart" (paragraph 1)?
2. How do you typically take in the day's news? Write an essay describing the different options available to you (such as radio, local

---

* If any of these sites are no longer available, do a Web search and visit other news sites.

television channels, cable television, newspaper, news magazine, online news site) and explain which method(s) you prefer and why.

3. The author states that news managers must decide which stories are most important. Write an essay suggesting what standards should be used to determine which stories and events deserve the most attention and coverage.

A Creative Activity

Imagine that you have been asked to design an online news page featuring coverage of local or campus current events. How will you decide what the focus of your page will be? What elements will you include on your page to make it interesting and informative? What is your responsibility to your readers?

Sporting the Fan(tasy) of Reality TV

▶ **Colleen Diez**
  Student Essay

Colleen Diez, a college student, explains the popularity of so-called reality TV shows.

"*A*aaagh!" my friend Mary screams at the television. "I can't believe   1
the tribal council kicked him off! He was my favorite!" She is referring,
of course, to *Survivor,* one of a slew of reality shows on current prime-
time TV. Everywhere, these "reality" shows appear to capture the
imagination of viewers. The media pretends this concept is a new idea,
but many MTV watchers recall the popular first seasons of *The Real
World* and *Road Rules.* We are fascinated by shows that cast "real" people, or nonactors, in the main roles. These shows have created a new
kind of entertainment, a new type of sport, and the reasons for the
popularity of this new form of entertainment are easy to identify.

Reality TV feeds our desire to know about and control other people.   2
We want to know the details about other people's lives because we are
curious, and because we have a need to identify with others. We buy
tabloid newpapers about movie stars in order to read about intimate
details that make the star seem closer to earth and to us. These personal,
sometimes flawed, characteristics make an actor seem more human.
Such details are plentiful in a reality show. We learn about someone's
children, spouse, or even sex life. By seeking similarities in another's situation, we feel closely tied to a person we've never met. A reality show
also gives us a sense of power over the people on the show. For example, in *Big Brother,* the viewer at home may see into people's lives without being seen. This watching while unseen can be called voyeurism.
The *Big Brother* voyeuristic audience also claims the right to determine
the outcome of the show. Each week, viewers may call in or vote online
to decide which group member will be removed. Reality TV makes us
feel powerful and superior to the cast, one of its big attractions.

The primary attraction of television is escapism, that is, escape   3
from reality. While television may be educational, most of us watch TV

to relax and to be entertained after a hard day at work or school. Escaping from the negative, repetitive aspects of our everyday lives appeals to us. Television stimulates us with exciting, new experiences. Reality TV specifically helps us to escape, but makes us unaware that we are escaping. This is part of the appeal. Shows like *Survivor* and *Temptation Island* bring us to exotic, fantasy locations, but because the people are not actors, we accept the situation as more realistic. We feel that we are watching something real, not artificial. These shows make fantasy, like being lost on a desert island, into reality. We escape into this fantasy, while thinking that we actually confront reality in the cast of "real" people. We willingly allow ourselves to be fooled by TV into thinking that we are not escaping. That in itself is escapism.

Finally, this new generation of reality TV appeals to us as a new kind of sport. All of the new shows feature competition, either against oneself or others, to win a highly valued prize. *Survivor* displays competition first between teams, and then among individuals, while on *Fear Factor*, contestants subject themselves to their greatest fears (like being locked in a coffin with rats) in order to win money. As an audience to this kind of entertainment, we side with certain contestants, and root them on, just as one would during a football game or any other sport. My friend Mary, who I mentioned earlier, was one of numerous TV viewers who threw a *Survivor* final-episode party in her dorm room. The number of guests could only be compared to a Super Bowl party.

These shows make us feel as if we are participating or even interacting with the cast on the reality TV show. This participation also gives us both power and identity connected with the show. Reality television shows appeal to us because they feed our desire to know about other people, and they provide us the ability to escape into an exotic world where we participate in a new sport. Whether it's surviving in the Australian outback, testing one's greatest fears, or simply learning to live with other people, the possibilities of reality television are endless. Networks constantly attempt to create new shows that sport the fantasy of reality TV shows. As prime-time shows become more interactive, what we watch helps to define a new genre of TV dinner theater.

Examining the Essay

1. Highlight and evaluate Diez's thesis statement.
2. Highlight and evaluate Diez's topic sentences.
3. Explain and evaluate the essay's title.
4. Examine Diez's use of examples. What do they contribute to the essay?
5. Diez begins her first paragraph with dialogue. Evaluate the effectiveness of her introduction.

Writing an Essay

1. Write an essay about reality TV shows that you have watched. Did you find them appealing in the ways Diez describes? Why or why not?
2. Write an essay describing the differences and similarities between watching real people on TV and reading about them in biographies and memoirs.
3. Write an essay comparing reality TV to other types of sports. Discuss their similarities and differences.
4. Suppose some readers of Diez's essay had never watched a reality TV show. Evaluate whether Diez provides sufficient background information to make the essay understandable to these readers.

Making Connections

1. Drawing upon the information presented in the readings by Tannen, "Oprah Winfrey," and Cross, "Advertising: Institutionalized Lying," as well as your own knowledge about talk shows and advertising, answer the following question: In what sense do both television talk shows and advertising influence the public?

2. "Advertising: Institutionalized Lying," and "Oprah Winfrey" discuss aspects of television viewing. Write an essay describing what attitudes or viewpoints the authors (Cross and Tannen) hold in common.

3. Compare the different issues and perspectives on television as a media form as described in "Prime-Time TV's New Guest Stars: Products" and "Sporting the Fan(tasy) of Reality TV."

Internet Connections

1. Many news web sites are available online. Browse the following web sites:

   http:// www.courier-journal.com/
   http://abcnews.go.com/
   http://www.ocweekly.com
   http://news.npr.org/

   Write an essay comparing these web sites to the news sources you rely on. Do you prefer news web sites or newspapers? Why?

2. The government provides tips to the media about fraudulent advertising at **http://www.ftc.gov/bcp/conline/pubs/buspubs/adscreen.htm.** Write a paragraph explaining the purpose of this web site and how it applies to the average consumer.

3. Visit the web site for Fairness and Accuracy in Reporting at **http://www.fair.org/.** Write a paragraph explaining the purpose of this site. Do you agree with this organization's mission? Why or why not?

(If any of these web sites are unavailable, use a search engine to locate another appropriate site.)

Chapter 7

Technology That Shapes Our Lives

How many tools, machines, or appliances have you used already today? Your list might include a clock radio, Walkman, coffeemaker, hair dryer, toaster, lock and key, computer, and car or bus. Most of us are so used to these inventions that we don't give them a second thought, but in fact all of these items are the result of study and research. Research has also produced daily conveniences such as no-iron clothing, Post-it notes, and orange juice from concentrate. The use of scientific research to create products or services is called *technology*.

In many cases, technology directly controls our lives. For instance, if your car does not start or the bus breaks down, you may miss classes. If your brakes malfunction, your life could be in danger. If a storm causes an electrical failure, your home may be without heat, light, or cooking facilities. People's hearts have been restarted by a machine.

In other situations, technology influences or shapes the quality of our lives. Without technology, we would not have many conveniences we take for granted: elevators, automatic teller machines, microwave ovens, and so forth. Technology affects our communication through radio and telephones; our diet with convenience and low-fat foods; our comfort with furnaces, air conditioners, and plumbing systems; our health with vaccines, genetic engineering, and drugs; and our jobs with computers, copiers, and fax machines. In fact, it is difficult to think of any aspect of daily life that remains untouched by technology.

In this chapter, the reading selections explore the effects of technology and examine specific instances in which technology has made an impact. The first reading presents one author's listing of the seven most valuable inventions ("The Seven Sustainable Wonders of the World"). Three readings discuss the contributions that technology has made or will make through the use of online dating services, cell phones, and RFID tags ("New Trends Help Seekers Find Love Online," "Thoughts, Interrupted: Cell Phone's Convenience Also Comes with a Price—Constant Distraction," and "RFID Tags: Big Brother in Small Packages"). Technological research suggests that swimming with dolphins may improve human health ("Dr. Dolphin"). You'll read further about the influence of computer technology, both positive, such as computers that can simulate reality for disabled persons ("Stepping Through a Computer Screen, Disabled Veterans Savor Freedom"), and negative, as reflected in "Human Interaction."

Brainstorming About Technology

Class Activities:

1. Working in groups, brainstorm a list of inventions that were developed or that came into widespread use during your lifetime.
2. Working in groups, list inventions that you would eliminate to improve the quality of life.

The Seven Sustainable Wonders of the World

▶ **Alan Thein Durning**

Simple little things can make a big difference in one's life. In this reading, the writer casts his vote for the seven key inventions— most of them quite simple—that make the biggest difference in our lives. This reading first appeared in the Utne Reader *in 1994.*

Journal Writing

Brainstorm about the author's choice of "wonders." What do you consider to be the seven wonders of the world?

Reading Strategy

Read the heading that introduces each invention. Before you read the section that follows it, predict why the writer feels the invention is important.

Vocabulary Preview

sustainable (title) capable of being kept in existence, maintained
thermodynamically (2) having to do with the use of heat energy
climes (4) climates
flotsam and jetsam (8) debris or wreckage and discards
scourge (12) source or means of inflicting suffering

I've never seen any of the Seven Wonders of the World, and to tell you the truth I wouldn't really want to. To me, the real wonders are all the little things—little things that work, especially when they do it without hurting the earth. Here's my list of simple things that, though we take them for granted, are absolute wonders. These implements solve every-day problems so elegantly that everyone in the world today—and everyone who is likely to live in it in the next century—could make use of them without Mother Nature's being any the worse for wear.

1. The Bicycle

The most thermodynamically efficient transportation device ever cre ated and the most widely used private vehicle in the world, the bicycle lets you travel three times as far on a plateful of calories as you could walking. And they're 53 times more energy efficient—comparing food calories with gasoline calories—than the typical car. Not to mention the fact that they don't pollute the air, lead to oil spills (and oil wars), change the climate, send cities sprawling over the countryside, lock up half of urban space in roads and parking lots, or kill a quarter million people in traffic accidents each year.

The world doesn't yet have enough bikes for everybody to ride, but 3 it's getting there quickly: Best estimates put the world's expanding fleet of two-wheelers at 850 million—double the number of autos. We Americans have no excuses on this count: We have more bikes per person than China, where they are the principal vehicle. We just don't ride them much.

2. *The Ceiling Fan*

Appropriate technology's answer to air conditioning, ceiling fans cool 4 tens of millions of people in Asia and Africa. A fan over your bed brings relief in sweltering climes, as I've had plenty of time to reflect on during episodes of digestive turmoil in cheap tropical hotels.

Air conditioning, found in two-thirds of U.S. homes, is a juice hog 5 and the bane of the stratospheric ozone layer because of its CFC coolants. Ceiling fans, on the other hand, are simple, durable, and repairable and take little energy to run.

3. *The Clothesline*

A few years ago, I read about an engineering laboratory that claimed it 6 had all but perfected a microwave clothes dryer. The dryer, the story went, would get the moisture out of the wash with one-third the energy of a conventional unit and cause less wear and tear on the fabric.

I don't know if they ever got it on the market, but it struck me at the 7 time that if simple wonders had a PR agent, there might have been a news story instead about the perfection of a solar clothes dryer. It takes few materials to manufacture, is safe for kids, requires absolutely no electricity or fuel, and even gets people outdoors where they can talk to their neighbors.

4. *The Telephone*

The greatest innovation in human communications since Gutenberg's 8 printing press, telephone systems are the only entry on my wonders list invented in this century, and—hype of the information age notwithstanding—I'll wager that they never lose ground to other communications technologies. Unlike fax machines, personal computers and computer networks, televisions, VCRs and camcorders, CD-ROMs, and all the other flotsam and jetsam of the information age, telephones are a simple extension of the most time-tested means of human communication: speech.

5. The Public Library

Public libraries are the most democratic institutions yet invented. 9 Think of it! Equal access to information for any citizen who comes inside. A lifetime of learning, all free. Libraries foster community, too, by bringing people of different classes, races, and ages together in that endangered form of human habitat: noncommercial public space.

Although conceived without any ecological intention whatsoever, 10 libraries are waste reduction at its best. Each library saves a forestful of trees by making thousands of personal copies of books and periodicals unnecessary. All that paper savings means huge reductions in energy use and water and air pollution, too. In principle, the library concept could be applied to other things—cameras and camcorders, tapes and CDs, cleaning equipment and extra dining chairs—further reducing the number of things our society needs without reducing people's access to them. The town of Takoma Park, Maryland, for example, has a tool library where people can check out a lawn mower, a ratchet set, or a sledgehammer.

6. The Interdepartmental Envelope

I don't know what they're really called: those old-fashioned slotted 11 manila envelopes bound with a string and covered with lines for routing papers to one person after another. Whatever they're called, they put modern recycling to shame.

7. The Condom

It's a remarkable little device: highly effective, inexpensive, and portable. 12 A few purist Greens might complain about disposability and excess packaging, but these objections are trivial considering the work the condom has to do—battling the scourge of AIDS and stabilizing the human population at a level the earth can comfortably support.

Examining the Reading

Finding Meaning

1. Why is the bicycle more efficient than the automobile?
2. In what ways are ceiling fans better than air conditioners?
3. Explain the statement, "Public libraries are the most democratic institutions yet invented."
4. In what ways do libraries "foster community"?

Understanding Technique

1. Evaluate the effectiveness of using a numbered list to organize the essay. Consider both the advantages and the disadvantages.
2. This essay lacks a conclusion. Suggest possible ways the writer could have concluded this essay.

Thinking Critically

1. Do you agree with the author that each library "saves a forestful of trees"?
2. What other kinds of libraries can you think of that the author didn't mention?
3. Do you agree with the author that the telephone is a better invention than, for example, a computer or a fax machine? Why or why not?

Writing About the Reading

A Paragraph

1. Write a paragraph explaining which of the wonders identified by the author you would rank as most important. Justify your choice.
2. Write a paragraph identifying what you believe is the best invention, old or new, other than those listed by the author. Justify your choice.

An Essay

1. Write an essay titled "Three *More* Sustainable Wonders of the World." Use Durning's organization as a model for your own essay.
2. Write an essay comparing your choices for the above assignment with Durning's choices. How did your choices differ? Would you substitute any of Durning's "wonders" for your own? Would you replace any of his with yours? Which ones, and why?

A Creative Activity

This reading identifies the most important inventions of the world. Suppose it had been titled "The Seven *Least* Sustainable Wonders of the World" and had discussed the most useless, silliest, or most wasteful inventions or gadgets ever invented. What do you think it might have included? Write an essay explaining your choices.

Stepping Through a Computer Screen, Disabled Veterans Savor Freedom

▸ **N. R. Kleinfield**

Virtual reality, a new computer technology, will probably affect all of our lives in the future. Journalist N. R. Kleinfield wrote this New York Times *article about what virtual reality is and how it is being used to help disabled veterans.*

Journal Writing

List the virtual reality events—real or imagined—that you would like to participate in.

Reading Strategy

As you read, highlight or annotate specific uses of virtual reality for those with physical disabilities.

Vocabulary Preview

savor (title) taste; enjoy
paraplegic (1) one who is paralyzed from the waist down
quadriplegic (2) one who is paralyzed from the neck down
full-fledged (5) fully developed; complete
provocative (6) exciting; stimulating
tantalizing (9) arousing desire; tempting
muscular dystrophy (11) a disease in which some muscles
lose the ability to function
troves (13) hoards
buoyant (17) cheerful
mobility (18) ability to move

The other day, Angelo Degree single-handedly lifted a couch and effort-   1
lessly hauled it into another room. He moved around a lamp, a crate. He
snatched hold of a man and ran outside with him. Ever since he was shot
in the head and spine while being robbed in 1981, Mr. Degree has been

a paraplegic. His legs are a wheelchair. One day he is hoping to play football. Tackle.

The man who plans to suit him up is William Meredith, who is not a doctor with a miracle cure but a recording engineer with a black bag flush with interactive computer technology. His subjects are the paraplegics and quadriplegics in the spinal cord injury ward at the Bronx Veterans Affairs Medical Center.

For some 10 years Mr. Meredith has done volunteer work for the Veterans Bedside Network, a 46-year-old organization made up largely of show-business people who try to rally the spirits of sick veterans, engaging them in plays and song-and-dance routines.

"But I always felt there was one group who we weren't able to reach that well, and those were the quadriplegics and paraplegics," Mr. Meredith explained. "And so I thought about virtual reality."

Virtual reality, for those unfamiliar with the outer envelope of technology, enables people to feel, through interactive computers, as though they are inside a three-dimensional electronic image. In full-fledged systems, they can actually sense that they are moving and feel virtual reality objects. To participate, all that is required is a working mind.

The more Mr. Meredith, 52, chewed over the notion, the more provocative it became. "These visions ran through my mind," he said. "These people could fly, which they can't. They could walk, which they can't. They could play sports, which they can't."

After winning over officials at the Bronx Veterans Medical Center and getting a $5,000 equipment budget from the Veterans Bedside Network, Mr. Meredith was in business. In mid-October he got his idea off the ground.

Every Tuesday and Thursday afternoon, he lugs three laptop computers to the Bronx hospital. He is an Air Force man himself, and teaches virtual reality at various schools as well as uses it in his recording work for films. He usually travels to the hospital with Michael Storch, who recently joined Veterans Bedside Network and is studying to enter the virtual reality field. They report to the first-floor spinal cord injury unit, where there are about 50 patients, and set up their equipment in the physical rehabilitation room.

From 2 P.M. to 4:30 P.M., wheelchairs roll up to their corner and patients enter the tantalizing world of virtual reality.

The patients use goggles in which they see a three-dimensional image and a glove that is wired to the computer in a way that, when they move their hand, they seem to grasp and move things on the computer screen. Mr. Meredith has yet to incorporate equipment that enables patients to feel and smell the virtual world they enter, though he hopes to do so soon.

It seemed only a matter of time for this to happen. Virtual reality is being used by therapists to help treat children who have suffered child abuse. It is being used to teach sufferers of muscular dystrophy how to

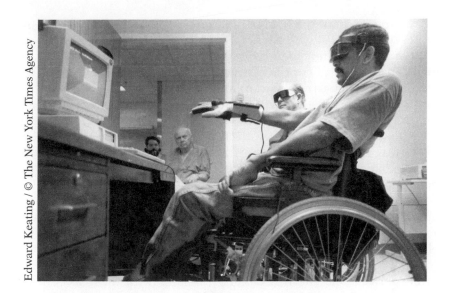

Edward Keating / © The New York Times Agency

operate a wheelchair. It is being used to help people overcome a fear of heights. They are ushered onto a virtual reality ledge, many stories in the sky. Go on, they are told. Look down.

At this early stage in the program, Mr. Meredith is able to offer only   12
limited options to the patients. There are several virtual reality games, including Heretic, which involves wandering through creepy dungeons and staving off demons and menacing creatures. There is a program that allows patients to redecorate a house by moving furniture around through the use of a Power Glove. There is a chess game, which has proved especially popular. And Mr. Meredith has designed his own virtual reality baseball game, where patients see the field from whichever position they assume.

In addition, Mr. Meredith brings along various computer programs   13
that are not virtual reality but enable patients to look up vast troves of information on the computers. One man has been researching the places where he made bomber runs during World War II.

The other day, Mr. Degree, 39, finished rearranging the virtual re-   14
ality house and moved on to Heretic. He was reasonably accomplished. He destroyed quite a few knights and flying beasts before mistakenly grabbing a gas bomb.

"You better work on your recognition," Mr. Meredith chided him.   15

"Next time, I'll give it to them real good," he promised.   16

Mr. Degree was buoyant about the program. "You know why a lot   17
of veterans are in and out of hospitals?" he asked. "Stress. If they want to have any dreams, they have to get them from a bottle. Here, you can

have dreams without the bottle. All I can do is look here and see a lot of potential. An angel with a lot of wings."

Mike Abelson, the chief of recreation services for the hospital, is   18
equally enthusiastic. "For these guys, it opens up a whole new world," he said. "Physical barriers don't matter. Mobility barriers don't exist."

Mr. Meredith has elaborate ambitions. Many veterans relish their   19
trips to the Intrepid Sea-Air-Space Museum aboard the aircraft carrier permanently moored on West 46th Street. Spinal cord patients usually don't go. Mr. Meredith is having a virtual reality tour of the Intrepid designed so patients can experience it from their beds. He hopes it will be ready by July.

"Ultimately, I want to have interactive sports," Mr. Meredith said.   20
"I'd like to link up several hospitals and have leagues and everything. They'll play baseball, football, whatever they want. They'll be able to feel every hit."

Some patients have employed the computers to assist them in pro-   21
saic concerns. "One guy was having problems with the grass on his lawn on Staten Island," Mr. Meredith said, "and so he looked up in one of the data bases in the computer ways of dealing with Bluegrass diseases. I believe he found his answer."

Whatever use they make of the technology, the patients find their   22
bedimmed lives galvanized.

Wilfred Garcia, 55, was keen to gain knowledge. "I've been looking   23
up where I was stationed in Berlin in 1958," he said. "Brings back the memories. I'm into biography. I looked up Christopher Columbus. I looked up Marco Polo. He was born in the same city as Columbus. I looked up Clark Gable. Man, what an actor."

In 1986, Mr. Garcia had an allergic reaction to a tuna sandwich   24
while he was driving on the New York Thruway. He blacked out and his car crashed down an embankment. He was left an "incomplete paraplegic," meaning he can stand up and walk short distances on crutches, but has no balance.

Now he immersed himself in chess. He was a novice. The com-   25
puter demolished him. "I might look into boxing on this," he said. "I used to box. At the age of 16, I was going to join the Golden Gloves but my mother wouldn't let me."

With limited resources and equipment, Mr. Meredith has been con-   26
fined to offering his program to those able to come to the rehabilitation room. His goal is to take systems to patient bedsides, which, after all, is what Veterans Bedside Network is supposed to be about.

There are patients itchy to see that happen. Osvaldo Arias, 35, par-   27
alyzed from the neck down since being shot in the back by unseen assailants in the Bronx in 1978, was lying in his room at the Veterans hospital. Recovering from surgery, he could not get to the rehabilitation room.

"When you spend a lot of time in bed, you can go crazy," he said.   28
"Right now, I can't get out of bed. I'm bored. You watch TV for a while, then you get tired of it. I try to write letters. An idle mind is the devil's workshop. I want to see that system in here. It's meant for those who can't get out of bed to keep them from going stir crazy."

Examining the Reading

Finding Meaning

1. What is the specific purpose of the Veterans Bedside Network?
2. Describe the equipment used with virtual reality.
3. Name two activities in the world of virtual reality that Meredith has not yet incorporated.
4. Identify two ways in which therapists have used virtual reality.
5. How and why is virtual reality especially useful to patients with spinal cord injuries?
6. What did Degree mean when he said, "Here, you can have dreams without the bottle"?

Understanding Technique

1. How does Kleinfield make the essay lively and interesting?
2. Evaluate the introduction and conclusion. Why are they effective?

Thinking Critically

1. Other than the examples cited in the article, name one way in which virtual reality can help people.
2. If you had a complete virtual reality system, how would you use it?
3. What do you think the single most important use of virtual reality will be in the future?
4. Design and describe a virtual reality game that would be interesting and challenging to college students.

Writing About the Reading

A Paragraph

1. Suppose you became a paraplegic. Write a paragraph describing in detail three virtual reality activities you would enjoy.
2. Write a paragraph defining virtual reality for someone who has never heard of it.

An Essay

1. Write an essay explaining the process by which a virtual reality system could be used to lessen or eliminate a particular fear.

2. Many tasks are difficult to learn without hands-on experience (driving a car, using a computer, and so forth). In the future, virtual reality may take the place of hands-on training in many fields. Assume it is the year 2025. Write an essay predicting how training for a particular job, occupation, or profession might be different than it is now.

A Creative Activity

Assume that interactive sports using virtual reality became possible. Add a paragraph to the reading explaining the benefits and describing the veterans' reactions to playing interactive sports.

New Trends Help Seekers Find Love Online

▶ **Michael Jones**

This article describes several technological advances that are changing the ways people use the Internet to find potential mates. This article first appeared on LoveCompass Online Dating Weblog *in February of 2004.*

Journal Writing

Why are online dating sites popular? What are their advantages over traditional ways of finding a date?

Reading Strategy

As you read, highlight each new use of technology that has changed online dating.

Vocabulary Preview

infusion (2) continuous, slow, gradual introduction
disclosure (3) the act of making information public
compile (4) collect
spurring (5) stimulating to action
evolution (5) gradual change and development
burgeoning (8) growing and expanding rapidly
nuances (9) subtle distinctions
proliferation (10) rapid growth

*L*ove may be all around, but right now, online dating is booming like   1
never before.

- Some 44 percent of Americans believe that individuals have a better chance of meeting a partner online than in a singles bar, according to Ipsos-Reid, an international market and social research company.
- The Personals/Dating category surpassed Business/Investing and Entertainment/Lifestyles content to become the leading paid content category in Q3 2002 with $87 million in revenues, a 387

percent gain over the same quarter the previous year, according to the Online Publishers Association.

But just like with dating itself, the numbers don't tell the whole story. The question is, "Is there anything interesting behind the pretty face?"

Thanks to new trends involving technological advancements along   2
with genuine creativity, there is. In fact, so-called "social networking" Websites—dating sites in particular—are on the rise not only in the area of consumer usage. Of late, the segment has witnessed a significant infusion of capital, as the industry progresses toward providing both real interaction online and the business models to support on-going online communities.

Nowhere is this more evident than in the online dating scene. The   3
evolution of Internet dating is not unlike that of its offline counter-part. From arranged marriages, to chaperoned courtship, to slightly more freedom to almost anything goes—traditional offline dating pro-gressed from a system that involved knowing hardly more than name and rank on the wedding day, to the point at which parties now ask from complete financial and medical disclosure and can purchase full-scale background checks over the Internet.

Online dating is following a similar evolutionary process. Many   4
matchmaking sites compile lists of potential mates using photos and only the most basic information—age, gender and location. With this bare-bones "profile," people are directed to a list of potential mates—almost like looking for love in the phone book. In the end, decisions are made almost exclusively based on a photo.

But over the past few years new trends have emerged, spurring the   5
evolution of online dating and shifting the matchmaking process from the "arranged marriage" end of the spectrum toward informed choices based on relevant information. Recent technological advancements have created an online dating scene in which participants can meet people from the comforts of their own homes, talk face-to-face in real time using audio and video, and access online journals that reveal thoughts and opinions.

Friendster, MySpace, Say Hello to Blogs

One of the more recent evolutionary steps came with Web sites like   6
Friendster.com and MySpace.com, services that connect people through online networks of mutual friends. Members join, then invite their friends to join, creating a coast-to-coast online social network. This new social-networking trend connects friends-of-friends, helping peo-ple find possible mates or simply new friends. It goes beyond the age, gender, location formula to match individuals based on mutual friends and similar interests.

This approach offers a more personal experience than the list-cruising of the past, and allows for more custom searching based on relevant information. The industry is gaining attention of late through a series of announcements about new venture capital funding for Friendster and some of its rivals—LinkedIn, ZeroDegrees, Tribe.Net and others. Even standbys like eVite.com are rethinking their strategies in favor of joining the broader social networking bandwagon.

At the same time, the burgeoning practice of blogging is pushing online dating even further toward "informed choice." Blogs, short for weblogs, are a kind of online diary. Through a blogging service, anyone can maintain a running commentary online—accessible to anyone with Internet access. While dating sites typically restrict the creation of individual personal home pages, blogs offer a forum for sharing anything from deeply held convictions to random musings. Bloggers can create and post content immediately, and often update their blogs daily—even multiple times per day. Blogs provide a formula of creating online identities—or at least sharing one's offline identity with anyone who cares to notice—giving potential suitors a much deeper, more relevant personal profile.

Expanding Instant Messaging

Much like the offline dating world's phone call, instant messaging (IM) capabilities transform static data on a page into actual online, real-time conversations. But while providing a handy form of communication, text-based messaging systems are limited to the keyboard. There's no visual or audio, making it difficult to create a true personal connection. Emotions are expressed through a common language of key strokes :), rather than through more meaningful nuances of voice fluctuation and other verbal clues. Progress has been made; while previous systems only displayed the conversations, today's IM users may have access to some personal information to help provide an initial spark. But it's still a one-dimensional conversation.

Growth in online audio and video capabilities—and the proliferation of higher bandwidth to support them—is bumping online communication up a notch into the two-dimensional world. Integrating audio and video into a live online dating experience gives the entire process more validity and increased security.

- People will not be able to pass themselves off as something they're not—at least in the obvious ways.
- Video profiles offer more depth and expression than do lists of likes and dislikes.
- Real-time, online dates that use audio and video provide real interaction while allowing each participant location anonymity and

security—there's no immediate need to give out phone numbers, addresses or to meet in person.

Users have the opportunity to date online "virtually"—allowing for a much more personal experience than before—without leaving the comfort and security of home. According to Tim Sullivan, president of Match.com: "Online dating is going to evolve with the convergence of various technologies. We believe video and voice are going to be a big part of our business."

The Future of Online Dating

The future of online dating will include all of these trends: Friendster's   11
relevant searching method, instant messaging capabilities and the use of audio and video—which all combine to create personal meaningful interactions. And the integration of blogging tools will give users the ability to truly create an online identity, and give the website that houses that profile a lifelong customer.

But beyond the technological advancements that give users better   12
tools for getting to know each other, online dating will explode as new business models take shape:

- Profiles will become commodities that are shared outside the "walls" of the individual dating sites.
- Systems soon will allow profiles to be searched through standard file-sharing mechanisms. Imagine a video profile along with an abbreviated data file that can be placed into Kazaa and searched through a peer-to-peer file-sharing network. After selecting profiles of interest, users register with the particular dating Web site to gain access to the complete file—including contact information. This enables a dating Web site to circulate its dating inventory externally on computers around the world.
- A system to standardize user profiles will take shape, to allow universal access to "networks" of dating Web sites.
- And in perhaps the biggest endorsement yet of the online dating sector, AOL recently unveiled Love.com, a personals site that incorporates AOL's popular Instant Messenger (AIM) service—with audio and video capabilities. Leveraging AOL's current user base of paid AOL subscribers and free AOL IM subscribers, AOL has essentially invited all AOL users to join Love.com.

As consumer magazines weekly attest, there's no shortage of dating   13
pitfalls and mishaps—whether online or off. But as more and more people look for love on the Internet, the evolution of online dating will continue to make it just a little bit easier than before.

Examining the Reading

Finding Meaning

1. How has online dating changed over the past few years?
2. What is a blog? How are blogs used by dating sites?
3. What are the limitations of using instant messaging to talk with a potential date?
4. What are some of the advantages of integrating audio and video into a live online dating experience?
5. Describe some of the technologies available.

Understanding Technique

1. Highlight the author's thesis statement and evaluate the effectiveness of its placement.
2. Evaluate the evidence Jones provides to support his thesis. Is it adequate and convincing?
3. Why does the author include statistics at the beginning of the article?
4. Jones includes one quotation from a person working for an Internet dating site. Would the inclusion of additional quotations have been useful?
5. Is the conclusion of the article effective? Explain your answer.

Thinking Critically

1. What is the author's attitude toward online dating? Give specific examples.
2. What are the advantages of using "social networking" web sites to find dates?
3. What may account for the popularity of online dating services?
4. What are the advantages of using blogs instead of traditional e-mail communication?
5. Which of the futuristic applications of online dating seem most practical and useful?

Writing About the Reading

A Paragraph

1. If you were going to join a social networking web site or an online dating site, what information about yourself would you include in your profile? What information would you not include? Why?

2. Describe some precautions people should take when dating online to protect their security and privacy.

An Essay

1. Identify the ways or places that people meet to find potential dates. In an essay, discuss the advantages and disadvantages of each.
2. Visit several blogs. Assume you have decided to establish your own blog. Write an essay to post on your blog today.
3. Visit the web sites of several online dating services. Write an essay comparing the sites. Which sites would you use or recommend to a friend? What additional information would you like to have before using one?

Creative Activities

1. Invent a short story describing a couple who meet through an on-line dating service.
2. Make a poster or flier identifying ways that people in your community can meet other people. For example, you may want to include information on local volunteer organizations, churches, recreational clubs, and educational classes.

Thoughts, Interrupted: Cell Phone's Convenience Also Comes with a Price— Constant Distraction

▶ Amy Joyce

The advantages of widespread cell phone use—including increased convenience and safety—are well known. This article explores the ways in which our cell phones have affected us. The article first appeared in the Washington Post *on January 18, 2004.*

Journal Writing

Write a list of advantages and disadvantages of cell phone use.

Reading Strategy

As you read, take note of each disadvantage of cell phone use that the author mentions.

Vocabulary Preview

barrage (2) overwhelming outpouring
solitude (2) state of being alone
conundrum (5) intricate and difficult problem
consensus (11) general agreement

As I drove to work the other day, cell phone perched on the passenger seat just in case, I tried to remember what it felt like to work when cell phones weren't the norm. We actually had alone time in the car. There was no way anyone could reach us. Whatever it was, it could simply wait. We hear about this issue of being connected to work all the time, but the reality hit me that day while I was driving, just how nice it would be to be completely alone with my thoughts. Of course, those of us who use a cell phone—154 million people in the United States by industry count—appreciate the convenience and safety a cell phone brings us. But it also means we have lost something.

It may be that the nature of my job has changed, but when I first   2
started to work I read a lot more on the days I used public transportation. By reading, I mean Gabriel Garcia Marquez, not just newspapers
and magazines. Because that's just how much extra time I felt I had.
Now when I drive to work, interviews or meetings, even if there is an
interesting NPR show on the radio, my cell phone sits there. Haunting
me. And I don't fully concentrate on NPR. Or the road. Or the changing leaves. So what if it's not ringing? It could ring. And so what if
I don't need to call anyone? I find someone to call. Even if I'm walking to work, I'll leave a message for myself at work if I have an idea
that I'm afraid might slip away in the time it takes me to get to the office. Oh, how I miss Gabriel Garcia Marquez. After the constant barrage of calls or almost calls, don't we all sometimes wish for 100 years
of solitude?

Before he had a cell phone, Derrick Span, president of the Com-   3
munity Action Partnership, a poverty-fighting nonprofit based in the
District, used driving time to enjoy the scenery a bit or, better yet, he
was able to "focus on the road"—a big topic in Washington, now that
the D.C. Council passed legislation that would fine those who drive
while using a phone. That cell-free time also gave Span a moment to
"get my mind away from the job for a while." If he was in a restaurant,
he actually enjoyed a meal. Or took time out to have a focused conversation. Although so many of us think our quality of life is better now
that we have cell phones—and in many ways it is—we have also lost
something. "The quality of meetings was a lot better. The quality of
travel was a lot better," he said.

Julie Morgenstern, professional organizer and author of "Time Man-   4
agement From the Inside Out: The Foolproof System for Taking Control
of Your Schedule and Your Life," agrees. "When you were driving in a
car, sitting on a train, waiting for a bus, there was nothing else you were
supposed to be doing," she said. "It was free, choice time." Those private
moments gave us perspective, a chance to recharge, and time to think
about something in a completely new way, she said.

"The main thing is, [the cell phone] takes us out of our present and   5
makes us far less attentive," said Cindy Morgan-Jaffe, founder of the
Career Studio in Bethesda, a career-counseling service for young people. If the phone rings when she is with a client or at lunch, she wonders whether to grab it or to concentrate on what is in front of her. And
if she doesn't answer it, or she decides it is time to turn it off, she is
anxious that it could be her children calling with an emergency. What
a conundrum we have created for ourselves.

Now that this is a cell phone society, life for Lura Pittman, a Denver-   6
based recruiter, means a lot less waiting around. When she started re-

cruiting about 15 years ago, workdays were slower and steadier. She would call a client who was looking for a job, leave a message if the client was not home, then sit by her phone to wait for a return call. That was a lot of time spent waiting, but there was a lot that could be accomplished in that time that she might not get to now. Like organizing files, creating new contacts, listening more intently to clients.

Today, Pittman's job seekers are reachable 24/7, as they say, thanks to the "cell." If they are in a meeting at work and someone else wants to interview them? No problem. They grab their ringing cell phone, say excuse me, and take the call in the hallway. Interview is set up for next Wednesday at 5. "Job candidates use this as their primary number now," Pittman said. "They're reachable now. It makes it easier on those of us in the search business." Sure, work is busier for her now, which can be a great thing for revenue and job seekers both. But what naturally follows is that work is more stressful. "We keep so many balls in the air because we can," she said. 7

But even without cell phones and the Internet, and all those "time-saving" devices we now are tied to, how much free, relaxing time would we really have? Probably not much, by way of our nature, Morgenstern said. Think about the introduction of TV dinners in the 1950s. They were created to cut cooking time. But those extra minutes were probably just spent at the office. "We're really driven to work," she said. "Any time that is actually saved is invested back into work. People feel guilty taking time for themselves." 8

But today is different from the 1950s. Pre–cell phones, people were more organized and conscious of setting up conversations, Morgan-Jaffe says. Now, it is simple for us to tell friends, business associates, clients, "Oh, I'll call you at some point tomorrow afternoon, between meetings." That's because we don't need to be in front of our desk phone to make that call. We can be anywhere. The problem is, a lot of times, we can't coordinate, because we're somehow less scheduled. More reachable, less attentive. Heck, we can call anytime. 9

Snowshoeing up a mountainside in Colorado is an example. That is where Kim Kuo, spokeswoman for the Cellular Telecommunications & Internet Association, was caught by cell the Monday after Christmas. But, she said, that's what the phones are for. Without them, she explained to her parents who tease her about it, she probably could not do things like visit Mom and Dad for an extended Christmas vacation. 10

Sure, once we have the comfort of the cell phone, it's nearly impossible to give up. Many of us use it as our main business line now, our home phone and our connection to our little worlds. But before this? What did we do with that time on the Metro? Read the newspaper? Talk to a stranger? Think? More than anything, the consensus 11 seems to be, we lived more in the moment. Well, when we weren't look-ing at our watches.

Remember the old office slang? "Phone tag" or "Rolodex roulette"   12
come to mind. Times have changed. Most of us don't do phone tag be-cause we can use our cells. Rolodex now means Palms or BlackBerrys. What office terms have come up with the new office culture? E-mail nominations to lifeatwork@washpost.com.

Examining the Reading

Finding Meaning

1. According to Joyce, what are the advantages and disadvantages of cell phones?
2. What does it mean to be "completely alone" with one's thoughts?
3. What are the advantages of "free, choice time"?
4. How is use of a cell phone an advantage for job seekers?
5. What does the author mean when she writes, "What a conundrum we have created for ourselves"?

Understanding Technique

1. The author begins the article with a description of her own cell phone use. Is this an effective introduction?
2. Why does the author use examples and quotations from other cell phone users? What effect do these quotations have on the article?
3. In paragraphs 2 and 11, the author poses questions. Why do you think the author does this? Are they intended to be answered? Is this technique effective?
4. Evaluate the title. Is it effective? Is it too detailed? How does it dif-fer from a thesis statement?

Thinking Critically

1. What are the advantages and disadvantages of being completely alone?
2. Why did the Washington, D.C., Council pass legislation that would fine those who drive while using a phone?
3. What does the author mean when she writes that before cell phones, we lived more "in the moment"?
4. Why do people feel "guilty taking time for themselves"?
5. The article focuses on cell phones and the workplace. How relevant is this article to college students?

Writing About the Reading

A Paragraph

1. How would your life improve if cell phone use were suddenly forbidden or eliminated? In what ways would your life be more difficult?
2. Do you believe that people should be allowed to drive while using a cell phone? Why or why not? Write a paragraph in which you present a point of view and support it with examples and details.

An Essay

1. What other modern inventions have caused us to lose some quality in our lives? Despite this fact, which inventions would be very difficult to give up? Choose one invention and discuss its effects.
2. Do you believe that "time-saving" devices really save you time? Think of another modern invention designed to save us time and explain if modern use of the invention has increased the amount of time you have for other pursuits.
3. The author of the article states that people need time to "be completely alone" with their thoughts in order to "recharge" and "think about something in a completely new way." What are some ways that you can find time for these private moments? How do you feel when you don't get enough of this type of time?

A Creative Activity

Have you ever been in a situation where someone using a cell phone disturbed you at an inappropriate time? Write a script of what you could say to someone to discourage him or her from using a cell phone at inconvenient times and places, such as on a mountain peak, at a memorial service, or during a movie.

Dr. Dolphin

▶ Richard Blow

Scientific research often leads to life-saving discoveries. This reading explores the fascinating use of dolphins as therapy for humans. Blow's essay appeared in Mother Jones *magazine.*

Journal Writing

1. Generate a list of questions you would like to ask an expert about dolphins and their behavior.
2. If you could communicate with a dolphin, what would you say?

Reading Strategy

When you have finished reading, list the potential benefits of swimming with dolphins. Then write a brief explanation of how these benefits occur.

Vocabulary Preview

cadre (2) tightly knit group
proponents (3) supporters
black holes (5) regions of space-time from which nothing
    can escape
visionaries (5) people who have foresight
simulate (6) imitate
obviating (6) doing away with
prototype (7) original model; first of its kind
ambient (7) surrounding; encircling
sonar (20) method of locating objects using sound waves
echolocate (20) use sounds that are reflected back to
    determine the direction and location of objects
resonates (21) echoes; fills with sound
bolster (24) support; make stronger

David Cole knows that people consider him a little odd. Cole spends   1
much of his free time swimming with dolphins, and he has enough perspective to realize that this makes him, by most people's standards, eccentric. He doesn't mind.

Cole, a 28-year-old computer scientist, lives about half an hour 2
south of Los Angeles. With excitable gray eyes and long brown hair in
ringlets, he looks a little like a youthful Michael Bolton. Cole works for
a computer hardware manufacturer, but in his spare time he heads the
AquaThought Foundation, a cadre of computer wizards, doctors, and
naturalists researching "dolphin-assisted therapy."

For about two decades, physical therapists and psychologists have 3
argued that swimming with dolphins can help the sick and handi-
capped. Dolphin-assisted therapy seems to accelerate the vocal and
physical development of autistic and mentally retarded children, for example. Some researchers claim that dolphin swims also boost the
human immune system. Most proponents of the therapy say it helps
patients' psychological well-being; the dolphins distract them from their
suffering.

But Cole doesn't buy this conventional wisdom. He rejects the idea 4
that dolphins make humans feel better simply by making them happy.
That's what clowns are for. Cole believes that swimming with dolphins
can have a profound *physiological* effect on humans. The health of
your immune system, the state of your brain, the makeup of your
cells—these things, Cole believes, can be radically altered by dolphins.

To the layperson, all this might sound a little nutty. (Acquaintances 5
who knew I was working on this article kept making "Flipper" jokes.)
But then, black holes and cloning and artificial intelligence seemed
nutty, too—except to the people who believed in them, and who turned
one day from daydreamers into visionaries.

Cole asks me to try Cyberfin, a "virtual reality interaction" he in- 6
vented to simulate swimming with dolphins. Eventually he hopes to
make Cyberfin realistic enough to substitute for the real thing, helping
humans who can't afford a dolphin swim and obviating the need for
captive dolphins.

Cole has fashioned his prototype from a converted flotation tank in 7
his garage. Three-D goggles strapped around my head, I lie down on a
water mattress inside the tank. Directly overhead is a television monitor; ambient, surreal music pulses from speakers. I feel a little silly, like
I'm about to fight the Red Baron, but I try to keep an open mind.

The screen lights up, and suddenly I'm floating in a pool. Two dol- 8
phins cavort in the water, zipping by one side of me, a stream of bubbles
in their wake. Their whirs and clicks surround me. As I watch, my skep-
ticism fades into curiosity and wonder. One of them swims directly up
to my face, and instinctively I shake my head, thinking I'm about to be
bumped. Then, with a flip of its tail, the dolphin disappears.

Ordinarily, I would never admit this. But I find myself hoping that 9
it will come back soon.

* * *

Cole grew up in Winter Park, Fla., not far from NASA. After graduating   10
from the University of Central Florida in 1988, he founded a software
company called Studiotronics. A year later, Cole hooked up with a
group that was conducting dolphin-assisted therapy with cancer patients. They told Cole that the dolphins seemed to have a profound effect on the mental states of their patients; Cole offered to perform
neurological tests to see what was going on.

"At first I thought our equipment was not working," Cole remem-   11
bers. "We were using a fairly conventional statistical evaluation of
EEG—'This is your brain, this is your brain on dolphins.' The level of
change was like nothing I'd ever seen."

Essentially, Cole found a far greater harmony between the left   12
and right sides of the brain after a subject swam with dolphins—a crude
suggestion that the brain is functioning more efficiently than normal.

When Cole studied the medical literature to try to explain this phe-   13
nomenon, he couldn't find anything. So in 1991 Cole sold Studiotronics to a Japanese company called Chinon, moved to California, and
founded AquaThought with a colleague. Though he now works for Chinon, the company gives him all the time he needs to pursue his dolphin
research. To facilitate that research, he and a colleague invented a device called MindSet. Looking like a bathing cap with electrodes attached to it, MindSet translates brain waves into real-time images; the
fluctuating brain waves are projected onto a computer screen, and the
resulting picture bears some resemblance to a lava lamp. The pair created the device because they couldn't afford a $75,000 EEG.

Three years after founding AquaThought, Cole thinks he has fig-   14
ured out why dolphins have beneficial effects on humans. He warns,
however, that a lot of people aren't going to believe what he has to say.

Cole isn't the first freethinker to be obsessed with dolphins. He's a dis-   15
ciple of futurist writer and scientist John Lilly, who in 1975 founded
the Human/Dolphin Foundation to explore the possibility of inter-
species communication. (Lilly himself believed he was following in the
footsteps of Aristotle, who had an interest in dolphins.) The dolphins
he was studying, Lilly wrote in his 1978 work "Communication between Man and Dolphin," "would do anything to convince the humans
that they were sentient and capable."

The field of dolphin-assisted therapy was probably started by Dr.   16
Betsy Smith, an educational anthropologist at Florida International
University. In 1971 Smith, who was researching dolphin-human interaction, let her mentally retarded brother wade into the water with two
adolescent dolphins. "They were pretty rough dolphins," Smith remembers. But not with her brother. "The dolphins were around him,
still, gentle, rubbing on him." Somehow, they knew he was different.

There are now 150 dolphin-assisted therapy researchers world- 17
wide, and there seems little doubt that dolphin swims can help humans
with disabilities such as Down's syndrome, autism, depression, attention deficit disorder, muscular dystrophy, and spinal cord injuries.
Mentally retarded children who swam with dolphins, for example,
"learned their lessons two to 10 times faster than in a normal classroom setting," says Chris Harre of the Dolphin Research Center in
Grassy Key, Fla.

Other researchers have found that swimming with dolphins boosts 18
the production of infection-fighting T cells. The generally accepted theory is that swimming with dolphins increases relaxation, which helps
stimulate the immune system.

Such vague psychological explanations drive Cole crazy; he calls 19
them "horseshit," though he's not a very good swearer. Cole doesn't deny
that relaxation helps T cell production. ("I could send you to Tahiti for
a week, and your T cell count would probably go up," he says.) But
Cole believes that relaxation can't explain the changes in brain waves
and blood chemistry in humans who've swum with dolphins.

Cole thinks these changes are caused by dolphins' sonar, which 20
they use to scan the water around them. The sonar is incredibly precise; dolphins can "echolocate" a shark half a mile away in the ocean
and determine whether its stomach is full or empty—and, consequently, whether it might be feeding.

"The dolphins produce an intense amount of echolocation energy," 21
Cole says. "It resonates in your bones. You can feel it pass through you
and travel up your spine."

Cole's theory is too complicated to do justice here, but it goes basi- 22
cally like this: A dolphin's sonar can cause a phenomenon called cavitation, a ripping apart of molecules. (You see it in everyday life when, for
example, you throw the throttle of a speedboat all the way down, but the
boat doesn't move; for that second, the propeller is cavitating the water.)

"It's very possible that dolphins are causing cavitation inside soft tis- 23
sue in the body," Cole says. "And if they did that with cellular membranes
which are the boundaries between cells, they could completely change
biomolecules." That could mean stimulating the production of T cells
or the release of endorphins, hormones that prompt deep relaxation.

Someday, Cole says, scientists may be able to replicate dolphin 24
sonar and use it in a precise, targeted way to bolster the immune system. But for now, he says, "the dolphin is a part of the experience."

In the cloudy water, I hear the dolphins before I see them: whirs, clicks, 25
and buzzes fill the water.

To find out what it's really like to swim with dolphins, I have 26
come to Dolphins Plus in Key Largo. It's a family-run place, surprisingly

small, a suburban house that borders a canal with several large hold-ing pens fenced off. (The dolphins can swim in the canal, but they al-ways return to the pens.) Half an hour in the water costs $75, but before we can take the plunge we are given some guidelines. We are asked not to touch the dolphins; if they want to, they will touch us. We should swim with our hands at our sides, and avoid swimming directly at or behind the dolphins, which they might interpret as hostile. Dol-phins generally like children best, women after that, and men last.

Equipped with flippers, mask, and snorkel, I slide off the dock. I   27
can see only a few yards in the murky water. I am so nervous that I worry I won't be able to breathe through the snorkel, but my breath eventually settles into a steady rattle.

Quickly come the dolphin noises, seeming to feel me out. Still, I   28
see nothing. Suddenly, there is a flash of white and gray to my side; a few moments later, a dolphin passes below me. It looks even larger in the water than it does on the surface.

The next time one passes, I dive down. As instructed, I try to make   29
eye contact; for a few seconds the dolphin and I are swimming eye to eye, looking at and—I would swear to it—thinking about each other. These are not just cute, lovable puppy eyes; there's an intelligence here.

More dolphins swim by me, moving too fast for me to keep up. As   30
they swim, huge yet graceful in the water, I am acutely aware of my human clumsiness, and grateful that these animals are letting me swim with them. I can't resist the temptation to wave slowly, hoping that they'll understand the gesture. (This is not so bad: One woman sang "Happy birthday, dear dolphin" through her snorkel for her entire half hour.)

The dolphins swim so close that I'm convinced I'll bump into   31
them, but somehow they always keep an inch, two, three, between us. The temptation to touch them is great, yet resistable. Corny as it sounds, I want them to like me. To touch them would be like coughing at the opera.

At one point I am swimming with a mother and calf; the mother   32
makes eye contact with me, and suddenly I feel it: the zap of the dolphin echolocating me, almost like an electric shock. This, I decide later, is what telepathy must feel like: You hear a sound in your head, but it didn't get there through your ears. It startles me, and I stop swimming. The dolphin opens her mouth, seeming to smile, and she and her calf dart away.

When I get out of the water after 30 fleeting minutes, I feel an in-   33
credible calm. I wonder if there is a purely psychological explana-tion—the magic of the experience affecting me. But it feels deeper than that. Somehow, my body feels different. At this moment, I think David Cole is right.

A woman who was swimming with me sits down. She puts her face 34
in her hands and begins sobbing quietly. "I thought I would be all
right," she says to a companion. I never do find out what she means.

Not everyone likes the idea that swimming with dolphins helps hu- 35
mans. Animal rights groups are concerned that such a theory could
lead to an explosion in the number of captured dolphins. "We don't feel
it's right," says Jenny Woods of People for the Ethical Treatment of Animals. "The animal has to be caged for the program to work."

Cole and other dolphin researchers share this concern. Betsy Smith, 36
for example, has given up swimming with captive dolphins and now
only swims with dolphins in the wild. (One concern of Smith's is that
echolocation is less common among captive dolphins. When I tell her
that I was echolocated, she says the dolphin must have found something about me interesting. "That's flattering," I remark. "Not necessarily," she says. "It may have been a tumor.")

For his part, Cole is trying hard to perfect Cyberfin, so people can 37
virtually swim with dolphins.

Smith and Cole may be racing against time. As more and more 38
people hear of dolphins' therapeutic effects, the desire to exploit the
animals for a quick buck will spread.

But to Cole, this is not a reason to stop working with dolphins. He 39
wants to establish a permanent dolphin research facility, something
that doesn't exist right now. "We're not looking for a magic bullet," Cole
says. "We're looking for ways of interfering with the progression of disease. It's virgin territory."

And if it means that people think he's a little odd—well, David Cole 40
can live with that.

Examining the Reading

Finding Meaning

1. What does the term "dolphin-assisted therapy" mean?
2. To what do most professionals attribute the positive effects of
   dolphin-assisted therapy?
3. According to Cole, how do dolphins make people feel better?
4. According to researcher Dr. Betsy Smith, dolphins may be able to
   help people with what disabilities?
5. Cole believes that swimming with dolphins has physiological effects
   on humans. After the author swims with dolphins, what does he
   conclude about the effect? What effects have occurred in others?
6. What is Cyberfin?

Understanding Technique

1. Evaluate Blow's sentence structure. How does he use it to add variety and interest to the essay?
2. The middle portion of the essay is written in the first person (I, me), while the first and last sections are written in the third person (he, Cole, etc.). Usually a writer uses one point of view consistently throughout the essay. What is the effect of not doing so?

Thinking Critically

1. Discuss why animal rights groups don't like the idea of people swimming with dolphins (or don't like Cole's research).
2. What is Cole's real (or long-range) goal in conducting his research?
3. What does the author mean when he says this about swimming with dolphins: "To touch [dolphins] would be like coughing at the opera."
4. What does the article imply about the effect of relaxation on the immune system? Explain your answer.
5. What does this article imply about our attitudes toward animals?

Writing About the Reading

A Paragraph

1. Imagine that you get paid to invent products and services that would help people who have physical or mental disabilities. Write a paragraph describing what you would like to invent and how it would be beneficial to people.
2. Write a paragraph explaining how you think Cole would react to a proposed federal law that would ban all animal research.

An Essay

1. The author makes a point of reminding the reader that certain scientific theories that originally seemed "nutty" ended up being factual. He cites black holes, cloning, and artificial intelligence as examples. Did you or a family member ever have an idea that other people thought was "nutty" but that turned out to be reasonable? Write a story that explains your idea and the reaction it received.
2. Assume that further research discovers that swimming with dolphins can cure certain types of cancers. What types of problems do you see? What types of rules and regulations would be needed? Write an essay exploring potential problems.

A Creative Activity

Assume that you are an animal rights activist who is opposed to the use of dolphins for research and therapy. Write a letter to David Cole outlining your objections.

RFID Tags: Big Brother in Small Packages

▸ Declan McCullagh

In the introduction to this chapter, we state, "In many cases, technology directly controls our lives." This essay describes a new technology, radio frequency identification (RFID) tags, that could be used to track our movements, purchases, and preferences through our personal possessions. This article appeared on News.com January 13, 2003.

Journal Writing

How important to you is personal privacy? Write a journal entry brainstorming the ways in which technology might violate your privacy.

Reading Strategy

In this article, the author presents reasons why people should be uneasy about the unlimited use of RFID tags by retailers. As you read, note the words Mr. McCullagh uses that express this unease.

Vocabulary Preview

generic (2) general, or having a nonproprietary, common-use name
miniscule (2) very small
unnervingly (4) causing loss of courage or power to act
disquieting (4) disturbing; alarming
eroded (5) diminished or destroyed by degrees
fret (8) worry
microns (11) very small measures
nascent (11) having recently come into existence

*C*ould we be constantly tracked through our clothes, shoes or   1
even our cash in the future? I'm not talking about having a micro-

---

chip surgically implanted beneath your skin, which is what Applied Digital Systems of Palm Beach, Fla., would like to do. Nor am I talking about John Poindexter's creepy Total Information Awareness spy-veillance system, which I wrote about last week. Instead, in the future, we could be tracked because we'll be wearing, eating and carrying objects that are carefully designed to do so.

The generic name for this technology is RFID, which stands for radio frequency identification. RFID tags are minuscule microchips, which already have shrunk to half the size of a grain of sand. They listen for a radio query and respond by transmitting their unique ID code. Most RFID tags have no batteries: They use the power from the initial radio signal to transmit their response. 2

You should become familiar with RFID technology because you'll be hearing much more about it soon. Retailers adore the concept, and CNET News.com's own Alorie Gilbert wrote last week about how Wal-Mart and the U.K.-based grocery chain Tesco are starting to install "smart shelves" with networked RFID readers. In what will become the largest test of the technology, consumer goods giant Gillette recently said it would purchase 500 million RFID tags from Alien Technology of Morgan Hills, Calif. Alien Technology won't reveal how it charges for each tag, but industry estimates hover around 25 cents. The company does predict that in quantities of 1 billion, RFID tags will approach 10 cents each, and in lots of 10 billion, the industry's holy grail of 5 cents a tag. 3

It becomes unnervingly easy to imagine a scenario where every-thing you buy that's more expensive than a Snickers will sport RFID tags, which typically include a 64-bit unique identifier yielding about 18 thousand trillion possible values. KSW-Microtec, a German company, has invented washable RFID tags designed to be sewn into clothing. And according to EE Times, the European central bank is considering embedding RFID tags into banknotes by 2005. That raises the disquiet-ing possibility of being tracked through our personal possessions. Imagine: The Gap links your sweater's RFID tags with the credit card you used to buy it and recognizes you by name when you return. Grocery stores flash ads on wall-sized screens based on your spending patterns, just like in "Minority Report." Police gain a trendy method of constant, cradle-to-grave surveillance. 4

You can imagine nightmare legal scenarios that don't involve the cops. Future divorce cases could involve one party seeking a subpoena for RFID logs—to prove that a spouse was in a certain location at a certain time. Future burglars could canvass alleys with RFID detectors, looking for RFID tags on discarded packaging that indicates expensive electronic gear is nearby. In all of these scenarios, the ability to remain anonymous is eroded. 5

Don't get me wrong, RFID tags are, on the whole, a useful devel- 6
opment and a compelling technology. They permit retailers to slim
inventory levels and reduce theft, which one industry group estimates
at $50 billion a year. With RFID tags providing economic efficiencies
for businesses, consumers likely will end up with more choices and
lower prices. Besides, wouldn't it be handy to grab a few items from
store shelves and simply walk out, with the purchase automatically
debited from your (hopefully secure) RFID'd credit card?

The privacy threat comes when RFID tags remain active once you 7
leave a store. That's the scenario that should raise alarms—and currently RFID industry seems to be giving mixed signals about whether
the tags will be disabled or left enabled by default. In an interview with
News.com's Gilbert last week, Gillette Vice President Dick Cantwell
said that its RFID tags would be disabled at the cash register only if the
consumer chooses to "opt out" and asks for the tags to be turned off.
"The protocol for the tag is that it has built in opt-out function for the
retailer, manufacturer, consumer," Cantwell said. Wal-Mart, on the
other hand, says that's not the case. When asked if Wal-Mart will dis-
able the RFID tags at checkout, company spokesman Bill Wertz told
Gilbert: "My understanding is that we will."

Cantwell asserts that there's no reason to fret. "At this stage of the 8
game, the tag is no good outside the store," he said. "At this point in
time, the tag is useless beyond the store shelf. There is no value and no
harm in the tag outside the distribution channel. There is no way it can
be read or that (the) data would be at all meaningful to anyone." That's
true as far as it goes, but it doesn't address what might happen if RFID
tags and readers become widespread.

If the tags stay active after they leave the store, the biggest privacy 9
worries depend on the range of the RFID readers. There's a big difference between tags that can be read from an inch away compared to
dozens or hundreds of feet away. For its part, Allen Technology says
RFID tags can be read up to 15 feet away. "When we talk about the
range of these tags being 3 to 5 meters, that's a range in free space,"
said Tom Pounds, a company vice president. "That's optimally oriented
in front of a reader in free space. In fact if you put a tag up against your
body or on a metal Rolex watch in free space, the read range drops
to zero."

But what about a more powerful RFID reader, created by criminals 10
or police who don't mind violating FCC regulations? Eric Blossom, a
veteran radio engineer, said it would not be difficult to build a beefier
transmitter and a more sensitive receiver that would make the range
far greater. "I don't see any problem building a sensitive receiver," Blossom said. "It's well-known technology, particularly if it's a specialty
item where you're willing to spend five times as much."

Privacy worries also depend on the size of the tags. Matrics of   11
Columbia, Md., said it has claimed the record for the smallest RFID
tag, a flat square measuring 550 microns a side with an antenna that
varies between half an inch long to four inches by four inches, depending on the application. Without an antenna, the RFID tag is about
the size of a flake of pepper. Matrics CEO Piyush Sodha said the RFID
industry is still in a state of experimentation. "All of the customers are
participating in a phase of extensive field trials," Sodha said. "Then
adoption and use in true business practices will happen. . . . Those pi-
lots are only going to start early this year." To the credit of the people
in the nascent RFID industry, these trials are allowing them to think
through the privacy concerns. An MIT-affiliated standards group called
the Auto-ID Center said in an e-mailed statement to News.com that they
have "designed a kill feature to be built into every (RFID) tag. If consumers are concerned, the tags can be easily destroyed with an inexpensive reader. How this will be executed i.e. in the home or at point of
sale is still being defined, and will be tested in the third phase of the
field test."

If you care about privacy, now's your chance to let the industry   12
know how you feel. (And, no, I'm not calling for new laws or regulations.) Tell them that RFID tags are perfectly acceptable inside stores to
track pallets and crates, but that if retailers wish to use them on consumer goods, they should follow four voluntary guidelines. First, consumers should be notified—a notice on a checkout receipt would
work—when RFID tags are present in what they're buying. Second,
RFID tags should be disabled by default at the checkout counter. Third,
RFID tags should be placed on the product's packaging instead of the
product when possible. Fourth, RFID tags should be readily visible and
easily removable.

Given RFID's potential for tracking your every move, is that too   13
much to ask?

Examining the Reading

Finding Meaning

1. How does an RFID tag work?
2. Why do retailers want to use RFID tags?
3. How can RFID tags be used to commit crimes or invade a person's
   privacy?
4. Why does a powerful RFID reader or a very small RFID tag worry
   the author?
5. What voluntary guidelines does the author recommend retailers
   should follow if they want to use RFID tags on consumer goods?

6. How could RFID tags help retailers to slim inventory levels and reduce theft?

Understanding Technique

1. What is the tone of the article? How does the author walk the fine line between expressing his concerns and sounding paranoid?
2. How does the author suggest that the RFID industry is giving mixed signals about whether the tags will be disabled or will be left enabled by default?
3. Evaluate the author's introduction. Why was it effective?
4. Look for transitions between paragraphs. Is the author's use of transitions effective?

Thinking Critically

1. In paragraph 3, McCullagh describes the cost of RFID tags. Why is the cost an important detail?
2. The author describes a future scenario in which a person could choose items from a store shelf and just walk out with them, letting the RFID tags allow debit of the price of the items from the person's RFID-tagged credit card. What are the advantages of such a scenario? What would be the disadvantages?
3. After the author asks you to let the RFID industry know how you feel about the tags, he states, "And, no, I'm not calling for new laws or regulations." Why does the author make this statement?
4. Discuss how you would react if you learned an RFID tag was attached to an item you purchased.

Writing About the Reading

A Paragraph

1. The author describes scenarios in which RFID tags could be used in divorce cases and by burglars. He states, "In all these scenarios, the ability to remain anonymous is eroded." In what aspects of your life is anonymity important? Write a paragraph explaining your answer.
2. RFID tags seem to have benefits for society if law-abiding people use them appropriately. Write a paragraph describing several ways that RFID tags could make life easier for you at your school, your library, or your job or in one of your extracurricular activities.

An Essay

1. Write a letter to a congressman or a retailer arguing for or against the use of RFID readers. Be sure to support your position with examples.
2. Compare the use of RFID tags with another use of technology that has threatened your privacy, such as the use of cookies on the Internet or the placement of a coded form of your fingerprint on your driver's license. What lessons have been learned from the application of that technology that could apply to the use of RFID tags?
3. Do you think RFID tag use should be controlled by laws and regulations or by voluntary guidelines? What are the advantages and disadvantages of each type of oversight?

A Creative Activity

Create a scenario describing what life might be like if the use of RFID tags becomes widespread. Without explicitly stating your position, include descriptive details that allow a reader to know your stand on RFID tag use.

Human Interaction

▶ **Christine Choi**
Student Essay

*A college student explains how people are interacting directly
with their computers more than with other people.*

Commercials and catalogs everywhere advertising faster Internet con-   1
nections, wrist pads, screen covers, and contoured "therapeutic" mice
indicate that we are being drawn into an age of computer efficiency,
spending longer hours at glowing screens extracting more information
while expending less effort. Services like America Online's Instant Messenger allow us to communicate virtually and instantly with friends all
over the world. At the same time, we sit in our swivel chairs, buy CDs
online, complete assignments online, self-diagnose our illnesses online,
and even date online. But while computers today have the ability to ful-
fill virtually every human need, actual social interaction is still important and necessary during the course of a day's computing.

AOL Instant Messenger (AIM) is easily one of the leading causes of   2
the decrease in human interaction. Particularly on college campuses, it
is easier to click on one's "Buddy List" and check if "Webwombat"
wants to meet for dinner than it would be to look up his number, pick
up the phone, punch in each of the digits, and actually talk to him.
Phone usage also deprives us of such luxuries as posting an "away message" that says "brb" (be right back)—stunningly efficient communication in just three convenient letters. But AIM can be addictive, causing
the user to forget that direct, face-to-face conversation still remains an
option. I once "IM'ed" my friend Amy to ask if a friend of ours was in
his room. She replied that his screen name was idle, that his away
message wasn't up, and that I should therefore wait until his name
changed color from light gray to black again, indicating that he was
back online. Despite her advice, I followed a hunch and called him. He
was there. This demonstrates how the convenient little world of chim-
ing pop-up windows may not accurately reflect the real world. There
are people out there whose names don't appear on our buddy lists, and
there are alternative, more gratifying ways of interacting with them
outside AIM.

Computer technology offers ways to substitute not only real con-   3
versations, but also basic activities such as shopping for clothing or

food. Popular web sites like Peapod.com allow their users to fill their virtual grocery carts with everything from Turkish apricots to eyelash curlers with mere clicks of a mouse. Customers are even granted the freedom to personally select between green or ripe bananas, rolled or loose mints. Why sift through piles of fruit at the market, sniffing, squeezing, checking for brown spots, when one can simply click on "ripe"? Also through the Internet, crowded malls and shops can be avoided completely, and shoppers can instead double-click on a 1" × 2" photo of an anonymous pair of legs wearing cotton-blend cropped pants, available in lavender, shale, or moss. The advantages of shopping from the still-warm swivel chair are apparent, especially to the busy and tired. But with the number of big-name online shopping services growing rapidly, it is easy to forget that shopping for things we need, despite our busy and important lives, has its own value. Do we really want to trade in the pleasure of trying on clothing and feeling textures of fabrics, for those few extra hours of typing? Leaving the house once in a while to smell a peach or try on leather sandals is refreshing and provides an excellent opportunity to be with friends or family, to exchange smiles, gestures, and dialogue—to interact with real people.

The world of real human interaction also offers opportunities for 4
learning that could not be achieved as effectively through interaction with a small glowing screen. Increasingly, professors are posting their syllabi, grades, announcements, and lectures on the Web, and encouraging inter-class "chat" among students through e-mail, inviting them to log in more hours of their day blinking at computers. The fact that some courses are taught completely online excites some and frightens others. While these online courses enable a student to roll out of bed and "attend class" in a shamelessly rugged, pajama-clad state, they restrict opportunities for actual hands-on learning and helpful student discussions. Furthermore, while the routine greetings we exchange on the walk to class may seem trivial, losing them is a small step toward the extinction of social interaction. Even outside the classroom, the Internet is full of "do-it-yourself" web sites where one could learn to do everything from self-diagnose medical symptoms, to build his or her own aquarium—all without having to budge from the swivel chair.

While new computer technology does not necessarily force people to 5
become moles, it does allow people to turn away from good old interpersonal interaction and head toward a world in which speaking and gesturing is replaced by soft clicking. When technological opportunities are new and exciting, it is easy to be lured by the pressure to take advantage of what is available. At the same time, it is important to stop and ask ourselves if the long hours we spend sending Instant Messages to a friend two doors down or purchasing produce from a laptop is really necessary.

Examining the Essay

1. What is Choi's thesis? What types of evidence does she use to support it?
2. Highlight and evaluate Choi's topic sentences.
3. Examine the descriptive language used by the author. How does it strengthen her essay? Highlight several particularly effective examples.
4. Evaluate Choi's introduction and conclusion.

Writing an Essay

1. Write an essay evaluating your degree of dependency on computers and whether it limits your social interaction.
2. Technology has changed American life drastically in the past 100 years. Write an essay explaining the pros and cons of one form of technology.
3. Write an essay that examines how today's children may be affected by growing up with computers. How are their lives different from those of their parents because of computer accessibility?
4. Choi considers shopping in real stores as a worthwhile experience. Explain whether shopping is important or unimportant to you and how you approach it. Do you prefer online or real store shopping?

Making Connections

1. "Stepping Through a Computer Screen, Disabled Veterans Savor Freedom," "New Trends Help Seekers Find Love Online," and "Human Interaction" are all concerned with the use of computers. Compare the ways in which computers are used in each of these readings.

2. Reconsider the following articles: "Dr. Dolphin," "New Trends Help Seekers Find Love Online," and "RFID Tags: Big Brother in Small Packages." In each article, the author discusses new or future directions for the application of technology. Write an essay explaining how feasible you feel each new use of technology is. Make projections about which applications will be in widespread use in twenty-five years and which will not.

3. Can there be too much technology? Consider the messages of "The Seven Sustainable Wonders of the World,"

"Thoughts Interrupted: Cell Phone's Convenience Also Comes with a Price—Constant Distractions," and "Human Interaction."

Internet Connections

1. How much do you know about the Internet? Find out by trying some of the quizzes at **http://www.netsurfquiz.com/.** Summarize what you learned about the Internet, one of our newest and most influential technologies.

2. Read the information about some of the inventors on this site: **http://www.invent.org/hall_of_fame/1_1_search.asp.** Write a paragraph about the individual who made a technological contribution that you found to be the most interesting.

3. Visit the web site for Community Voice Mail at **http://www.cvm.org/index.html.** Write an essay evaluating this program and suggesting other ways in which we can use technology to help the less fortunate members of our world.

(If any of these web sites are unavailable, use a search engine to locate another appropriate site.)

Glossary

analyze to separate into parts to study

annotate to write notes or comments in response or reaction to what you read

argument a set of ideas that states a position (or claim) and offers reasons and evidence in support of that position

biased one-sided; prejudiced

brainstorming a method of developing ideas by writing a list of everything that comes to mind about the topic

chronological sequence an organization of ideas according to the order in which they happen

compare to discover how two or more persons or things are alike and how they differ

conclusion the ending of an essay that draws it to a close and often re-emphasizes the thesis statement; a decision, judgment, or opinion reached by reasoning

connotative meaning the implied meanings, or shades of meaning, that are attached to a word

describe to provide an account of something in words

details specific information that explains a topic sentence; particulars

develop to make bigger, fuller, or more complete by providing greater detail

dialogue conversation between two or more people

discuss to examine in speech or writing; to talk over

evaluate to consider the worth, value, or importance of something

evidence facts that show why something is true or not true; proof

highlight to mark important information using a fluorescent marker

illustrate to make clear or to explain using stories, examples, comparisons, and so forth

implied thesis a thesis that is suggested but not directly stated in the essay

imply (implied) to suggest, but not to state directly

introduction the opening of an essay that identifies the topic and often presents the thesis statement

justify to demonstrate that something is correct or right

opinion a belief; what one thinks about something

organization the arrangement or sequence of ideas

point of view the perspective from which a story is told; the attitude of a narrator

sentence structure the arrangement or order of the parts of a sentence

structure arrangement or order

subject a general or broad topic

summarize to express only the main points

technique the method, skill, or system a writer uses to compose and express ideas

theme an implicit or recurrent idea

thesis statement a sentence that identifies and explains what an essay will be about and what its point will be

tone the attitude of the author toward the subject matter (examples: serious, apologetic, humorous, angry)

topic sentence a sentence that states the main idea of a paragraph

transitions words, phrases, sentences, or series of sentences that connect ideas within a discourse

Acknowledgments

Insert   PABLO NERUDA   From *Neruda and Vallejo: Selected Poems*, edited by Robert Bly, Beacon Press, Boston, 1971, 1993. Copyright © 1971, 1993 by Robert Bly. Reprinted with his permission.

Chapter 1   LAURA CUNNINGHAM   "The Chosen One" by Laura Shaine Cunningham. Copyright © 1994 by Laura Shaine Cunningham. Reprinted by permission of Brandt and Hochman Literary Agents, Inc.; DIRK JOHNSON ET AL.   Dirk Johnson et al., "A Heroic Life," from *Newsweek*, May 3, 2004. © 2004 Newsweek, Inc. All rights reserved. Reprinted by permission; JENNIFER S. DICKMAN   "Saying Good-bye to Eric" by Jennifer S. Dickman, *Nursing* 95 25 (2): 26. Reprinted by permission of Jennifer Dickman Hermann; BARBARA TUNICK   Barbara Tunick, "Why Go Veg?" *Vegetarian Times*, July 2002, Issue 299, p. 33. Reprinted by permission of the author. Barbara Tunick is a nationally syndicated writer. Her work has appeared in numerous books, magazines, and newspapers. A former magazine editor, she specializes in women's issues, health, and nutrition; MARIAN BURROS   Marian Burros, "Hold the Fries. Hey, Not All of Them!" *New York Times*, March 10, 2004. Copyright © 2004 by The New York Times Co. Reprinted with permission.

Chapter 2   MARTA SALINAS   Marta Salinas, "The Scholarship Jacket," from *Nosotras: Latina Literature Today* (1986), edited by Maria del Carmen Boza, Beverly Silva, and Carmen Valle. Copyright © 1986 by Bilingual Press/Editorial Belingue, Arizona State University, Tempe, AZ. Reprinted by permission; ALTON FITZGERALD WHITE   "Ragtime, My Time," by Alton Fitzgerald White, is reprinted with permission from the October 11, 1999 issue of *The Nation*. For subscription information call 1-800-333-8536. Portions of each week's *Nation* magazine can be accessed at **http://www.thenation.com;** SIU WAI ANDERSON   Siu Wai Anderson, "A Letter to My Daughter" © 1990 by Siu Wai Anderson. From *Making Face, Making Soul/Haciendo Caras* © 1990 edited by Gloria Anzaldua. Reprinted by permission of Aunt Lute Books; JEFFREY ROSEN   Jeffrey Rosen, "Naked Terror," *New York Times Magazine*, January 4, 2004, p. 10. © 2004, Jeffrey Rosen. Reprinted by permission of the *New York Times;* JONATHAN ROSEN   "Breaking Glass" by Jonathan Rosen, *New York Times Magazine*, November 18, 1996. Reprinted by permission of the author; KARL TARO GREENFELD   Karl Taro Greenfeld, "Blind to Faith," *TIME Magazine*, June 18, 2000.

Chapter 3   DEBORAH TANNEN   Excerpt from *You Just Don't Understand* by Deborah Tannen. Copyright © 1990 by Deborah Tannen. Reprinted by permission of HarperCollins Publishers Inc.; MARY ELLEN SLAYTER   "Seven Easy Ways to Become an Unhappy Job Seeker," *The*

Washington Post, September 14, 2003, p K. 01; JILL RACHLIN MARBAIX Jill Rachlin Marbaix, "Job Search 2.OH!" *U.S. News & World Report*, March 8, 2004, Vol. 136, Issue 8, p. 60. Copyright 2004 U.S. News & World Report, L.P. Reprinted with permission.

Chapter 4   KIM McLARIN   "Primary Colors" by Kim McLarin, *New York Times Magazine*, May 24, 1998. Copyright © 1998 by Kim McLarin. Reprinted by permission of Inkwell Management; ROBERTO SANTIAGO "Black *and* Latino" by Roberto Santiago, *Essence Magazine*. Roberto Santiago is the editor of *Boricuas: Influential Puerto Rican Writings—An Anthology* (Ballantine/One World Books, 1995). Reprinted by permission of the author; LARS EIGHNER   Lars Eighner, "Dumpster Diving." Copyright © 1993 by Lars Eighner. From *Travels with Lizbeth* by Lars Eighner. Reprinted by permission of St. Martin's Press, LLC; RICHARD APPEL-BAUM and WILLIAM J. CHAMBLISS   *Sociology*, by Richard P. Appelbaum and William J. Chambliss, ScottForesman/Addison Wesley, 1995, p. 369.

Chapter 5   CAROL FLEISCHMAN   "Shopping Can Be a Challenge with Curious Onlookers, Puzzled Clerks and a Guide Dog" by Carol Fleischman, *Buffalo News*, February 24, 1998. Reprinted by permission of the author; ALLISON BERNARD   "Our Wounded Hearts" by Alison Bernard. Reprinted with permission from *Health*, © 1998; LESTER SLOAN   Lester Sloan, "Planting Seeds, Harvesting Scholarships: Food from the 'Hood," from *Newsweek*, May 29, 1995, © 1995 Newsweek, Inc. All rights reserved. Reprinted by permission; MICHAEL SCHALLER, VIRGINIA SCHARFF, and ROBERT D. SCHULZINGER   From Michael Schaller, Virginia Scharff, and Robert Schulzinger, *Present Tense: The United States Since 1945*, 2/e. Copyright © 1996 by Houghton Mifflin Company. Used with permission.

Chapter 6   DEBORAH TANNEN   "Oprah Winfrey" by Deborah Tannen, *TIME*, June 8, 1998, copyright Deborah Tannen. Reprinted by permission; CAROLYN GARD   "Music 'n Moods" by Carolyn Gard. Special permission granted, *Current Health 2®*, copyright © 1997, published by Weekly Reader Corporation. All rights reserved; BRIAN STEINBERG and SUZANNE VRANICA   *Wall Street Journal* Eastern Edition [Staff Produced Copy Only] by Brian Steinberg and Suzanne Vranica. Copyright 2004 by Dow Jones & Co. Inc. Reproduced with permission of Dow Jones & Co. Inc. in the format Textbook via Copyright Clearance Center; BARB PALSER   "After the War Coverage," *American Journalism Review*, Apr/May 2004, Vol. 26, Issue 2.

Chapter 7   ALAN THEIN DURNING   "The Seven Sustainable Wonders of the World" by Alan Thein Durning, director of Northwest Environment Watch in Seattle and author of *This Place on Earth* (Sasquatch Books,

1996). Reprinted from *Utne Reader*; N. R. KLEINFIELD   "Stepping Through a Computer Screen, Disabled Veterans Savor Freedom" by N. R. Kleinfield, *New York Times*, Sunday, March 12, 1995; MICHAEL JONES Michael Jones, "New Trends Help Seekers Find Love Online," *LoveCompass*. Reprinted by permission of the author; AMY JOYCE   "Thoughts, Interrupted: Cell Phone's Convenience Also Comes With a Price—Constant Distraction," *Washington Post*, January 18, 2004; RICHARD BLOW Richard Blow, "Dr. Dolphin," *Mother Jones* Magazine, January/February 1995, pp. 28–31. Reprinted with permission from *Mother Jones* Magazine, © 1995, Foundation for National Progress.

Index of Authors and Titles

REVISION CHECKLIST FOR ESSAYS

	Yes	No
1. Have you narrowed your topic so that it is covered thoroughly in your essay?	☐	☐
2. Does your introduction identify your topic, present your thesis statement, and interest your reader?	☐	☐
3. Is your main point clearly expressed in your thesis statement?	☐	☐
4. Does each paragraph support and explain your thesis statement?	☐	☐
5. Does each paragraph have a topic sentence that supports your main point?	☐	☐
6. Is each paragraph's topic sentence supported with details?	☐	☐
7. Are transitional words and phrases used to lead the reader from idea to idea?	☐	☐
8. Does your conclusion reemphasize your thesis statement and draw your essay to a close?	☐	☐
9. Have you proofread your paper and corrected errors in grammar, punctuation, and spelling?	☐	☐